THE

"DANGEROUS CLASSES OF NEW YORK,"

AND

TWENTY YEARS' WORK AMONG THEM.

BY

CHARLES LORING BRACE,

AUTHOR OF

"HUNGARY IN 1851," "HOME LIFE IN GERMANY," "THE RACES
OF THE OLD WORLD," ETC., ETC.

"Améliorer l'homme par la terre et la terre par l'homme."—*Demetz.*

NEW YORK.
WYNKOOP & HALLENBECK, PUBLISHERS,
113 FULTON STREET.
1872.

THE

DANGEROUS CLASSES OF NEW YORK,

AND

TWENTY YEARS' WORK AMONG THEM.

BY

CHARLES LORING BRACE,

AUTHOR OF

"HUNGARY IN 1851," "HOME LIFE IN GERMANY," "THE RACES
OF THE OLD WORLD," ETC., ETC.

"Améliorer l'homme par la terre et la terre par l'homme."—Demetz.

NEW YORK.
WYNKOOP & HALLENBECK, PUBLISHERS,
113 FULTON STREET.

1872.

LODGING-HOUSES FOR HOMELESS BOYS—AS THEY WERE.

No. 1.

ENTERED, according to Act of Congress, in the year 1872, by

CHARLES LORING BRACE,

in the Office of the Librarian of Congress at Washington.

WYNKOOP & HALLENBECK,
FINE BOOK PRINTERS.

DEDICATION.

To the many co-laborers, men and women, who have not held their comfort or even their lives dear unto themselves, but have striven, through many years, to teach the ignorant, to raise up the depressed, to cheer the despairing, to impart a higher life and a Christian hope to the outcast and neglected youth of this city, and thus save society from their excesses, this simple record of common labors, and this sketch of the terrible evils sought to be cured, is respectfully dedicated.

INTRODUCTION.

THE great pioneer in the United States, in the labors of penal Reform and the prevention of crime,—EDWARD LIVINGSTON,—said as long ago as 1833, in his famous "Introductory Report to the Code of Reform and Prison Discipline": "As prevention in the diseases of the body is less painful, less expensive, and more efficacious than the most skillful cure, so in the moral maladies of society, to arrest the vicious before the profligacy assumes the shape of crime; to take away from the poor the cause or pretence of relieving themselves by fraud or theft; to reform them by education and make their own industry contribute to their support, although difficult and expensive, will be found more effectual in the suppression of offences and more economical than the best organized system of punishment."—(p. 322.)

My great object in the present work is to prove to society the practical truth of Mr. Livingston's theoretical statement: that the cheapest and most efficacious way of dealing with the "Dangerous Classes" of large cities, is not to punish them, but to prevent their growth; to so throw the influences of education and discipline and religion about the abandoned and destitute youth of our large towns; to so change their material circumstances, and draw them under the influence of the moral and fortunate classes, that they shall grow up as useful producers and members of society, able and inclined to aid it in its progress.

In the view of this book, the class of a large city most dangerous to its property, its morals and its political life, are the ignorant, destitute, untrained, and abandoned youth: the outcast street-children grown up to be voters, to be the implements of demagogues, the "feeders" of the criminals, and the sources of domestic outbreaks and violations of law.

The various chapters of this work contain a detailed account of the constituents of this class in New York, and of the twenty years' labors of the writer, and many men and women, to purify and elevate it; what the principles were of the work, what its fruits, what its success.

So much interest at home and abroad has been manifested in these extended charities, and so many inquiries are received continually about them, that it seemed at length time to give a simple record of them, and of the evils they have sought to cure.

If the narrative shall lead the citizens of other large towns to inaugurate comprehensive and organized movements for the improvement of their "Dangerous Classes," my object will be fully attained.

I have the hope, too, that these little stories of the lot of the poor in cities, and the incidents related of their trials and temptations, may bring the two ends of society nearer together in human sympathy.

The discussion of the Causes of Juvenile Crime contained in this work must aid others who would found similar reformatory and preventive movements, to base them on principles and motives which should reach similar profound and threatening evils.

CHARLES LORING BRACE.
19 EAST 4TH STREET, NEW YORK.

June 1, 1872.

CONTENTS OF CHAPTERS.

CHAPTER I.

CHRIST IN CHARITY AND REFORM, AND CONDITION OF NEGLECTED CHILDREN BEFORE CHRISTIANITY.

CHAPTER II.

THE PROLÉTAIRES OF NEW YORK.

CHAPTER III.

CAUSES OF CRIME.

1

CHAPTER XVII.

THE LITTLE ITALIAN ORGAN-GRINDERS.

CHAPTER XVIII.

THE "LAMBS" OF COTTAGE PLACE.

CHAPTER XIX.

THE BEST REMEDY FOR JUVENILE PAUPERISM.

THE DANGEROUS CLASSES

OF NEW YORK;

AND TWENTY YEARS' WORK AMONG THEM.

CHAPTER I.

CHRIST IN CHARITY AND REFORM.

THE CONDITION OF NEGLECTED CHILDREN BEFORE CHRISTIANITY.

THE central figure in the world's charity is CHRIST.

An eloquent rationalistic writer—Mr. Lecky—speaking of the Christian efforts in early ages in behalf of exposed children and against infanticide, says:

"Whatever mistakes may have been made, the entire movement I have traced displays an anxiety not only for the life, but for the moral well-being, of the castaways of society, such as the most humane nations of antiquity had never reached. This minute and scrupulous care for human life and human virtue in the humblest forms, in the slave, the

gladiator, the savage, or the infant, was indeed
wholly foreign to the genius of Paganism.   It was
produced by the Christian doctrine of the inestima-
ble value of each immortal soul.

"It is the distinguishing and transcendent characteristic of every society into which the spirit of
Christianity has passed."

Christ has indeed given a new value to the
poorest and most despised human being.

When one thinks what was the fate before He
lived, throughout the civilized world, of for instance
one large and pitiable class of human beings—unfortunate children, destitute orphans, foundlings, the
deformed and sickly, and female children of the
poor; how almost universal, even under the highest
pagan civilization—the Greek and Roman—infanticide was; how Plato and Aristotle both approved
of it; how even more common was the dreadful
exposure of children who were physically imperfect
or for any cause disagreeable to their parents, so
that crowds of these little unfortunates were to be
seen exposed around a column near the Velabrum
at Rome—some being taken to be raised as slaves,
others as prostitutes, others carried off by beggars
and maimed for exhibition, or captured by witches
to be murdered, and their bodies used in their
magical preparations; when one remembers for
how many centuries, even after the nominal intro-

duction of Christianity, the sale of free children
was permitted by law, and then recalls how utterly
the spirit of the Founder of Christianity has exter-
minated these barbarous practices from the civilized
world; what vast and ingenious charities exist in
every Christian country for this unfortunate class;
what time and wealth and thought are bestowed to
heal the diseases, purify the morals, raise the character, and make happy the life of foundlings, outcast
girls and boys and orphans, we can easily understand that the source of the charities of civilized
nations has been especially in CHRIST; and knowing
how vital the moral care of unfortunate children is
to civilization itself, the most skeptical among us
may still put Him at the head of even modern social
reform.

EXPOSURE OF CHILDREN.

The "exposure of children" is spoken of casually
and with indifference by numerous Latin authors.
The comedians include the custom in their pictures
of the daily Roman life, usually without even a
passing condemnation. Thus, in Terence's play
(Heauton: Act iii., sc. v.), the very character who
uttered the apothegm which has become a proverb
of humanity for all ages—"I am a man, and nothing
belonging to man is alien to me"—is represented, on
the eve of his departure on a long journey, as urging
his wife to destroy the infant soon to be born, if it

should prove to be a girl, rather than expose it. She, however, exposes it, and it was taken, as was usual, and brought up as a prostitute. This play turns in its plot, as is true of many popular comedies, on this exposition of the abandoned child.

It is frequently commented on by Roman dramatists, and subsequently by the early Christian preachers, that, owing to this terrible custom, brothers might marry sisters, or fathers share in the ruin of their unknown daughters in houses of crime.

Seneca, who certainly always writes with propriety and aims to be governed by reason, in his treatise on Anger (De Irâ: i., 15), comments thus calmly on the practice: "Portentos fœtus extinguimus; liberos quoque si debiles, monstrosique editi sunt, mergimus. Non ira, sed *ratio* est, a sanis, inutilia secernere." (Monstrous offspring we destroy; children too, if weak and unnaturally formed from birth, we drown. It is not anger, but reason, thus to separate the useless from the sound.)

In another work (Controversi, lib. v., 33), he denounces the horrible practice, common in Rome, of maiming these unfortunate children and then offering them to the gaze of the compassionate. He describes the miserable little creatures with shortened limbs, broken joints, and curved backs, exhibited by the villainous beggars who had gathered them at the *Lactaria*, and then deformed them: "Volo nosse,"

"I should like to know," says the moralist, with a burst of human indignation, "illam calamitatum humanarum officinam—illud infantum spoliarium!" —"that workshop of human misfortunes—those shambles of infants!"

On the day that Germanicus died, says Suetonius (in Calig., n. 5), "Subversae Deûm arae, partus conjugum expositi," parents exposed their new-born babes.

The early Christian preachers and writers were unceasing in their denunciations of the practice.

Quintilian (Decl. 306, vol vi., p. 236) draws a most moving picture of the fate of these unhappy children left in the Forum: "Rarum est ut expositi vivant! Vos ponite ante oculos puerum statim neglectum * * * inter feras et volucres."

"It is rare that the exposed survive!" he says.

Tertullian, in an eloquent passage (Apol., c. 9), asks: "Quot vultis ex his circumstantibus et in christianum sanguinem hiantibus * * * apud conscientias pulsem, qui natos sibi liberos enecent?"

"How many, do you suppose, of those standing about and panting for the blood of Christians, if I should put it to them before their very conscience, would deny that they killed their own children?"

Lactantius, who was the tutor of the son of Constantine, in a book dedicated to Constantine, protests: "It is impossible to grant that one has the right to strangle one's new-born children"; and speaks of exposition as exposing one's own blood—"ad servitutem vel ad lupanar"—"for slavery or the brothel." "It is a crime as execrable to expose a child as to kill him."

So fearfully did the numbers increase, under the Roman Empire, of these unfortunate children, that the spark of charity, which is never utterly extinguished in the human breast, began to kindle. Pliny the Younger is said to have appropriated a sum equivalent to $52,000 (see Epist., v., 7), to found an asylum for fathers unable to support their children.

THE FIRST CHILDREN'S ASYLUM.

Probably the first society or asylum in history for poor children was the foundation established by the Emperor Trajan (about A. D. 110) for destitute and abandoned children. The property thus established in perpetuity, with real estate and money at interest (at five per cent.), was equivalent in value to $920,000, and supported some five thousand children of both sexes. Singularly enough, there seems to have been only one illegitimate child to one hundred and fifty legitimate in these institutions.

The Antonines, as might be expected, did not neglect this charity; but both Antoninus Pius and Marcus Aurelius founded associations for destitute girls. Alexander Severus established one also for poor children. These form the only organized efforts made for this object, during many centuries, by the most civilized and refined state of antiquity.

The number, however, of these wretched creatures increased beyond all cure from scattered exceptional efforts like these. Everywhere the poor got rid of their children by exposure, or sold them as slaves. The rich, if indifferent to their offspring, or unwilling to take the trouble of rearing them, sent them out to the public square, where pimps, beggars, witches, and slave-dealers gleaned their horrible harvest. At length, under the influence of Christianity, legislation began to take cognizance of the practice.

The Emperor Constantine, the Emperor Valentian, Valens, and Gratian, sixty years later, continued this humane legislation.

They ordered, under strict penalties, that every one should nourish his own children, and forbade exposition; declaring also that no one had the right to reclaim the children he had abandoned; the motive to this law being the desire to make it for the interest of those "taking up" exposed children to keep them, even if necessary, as slaves, against any outside claims.

Unfortunately, at that period, slavery was held a less evil than the ordinary fate to which the poor left their children.

The punishment of death was also decreed against infanticide,

It is an interesting fact that a portion, and probably the whole, of our ancestral tribes looked with
the greatest horror on abortion and infanticide. The
laws of the Visigoths punished these offenses with
death or blindness. Their influence, of course, should
always be considered, as well as that of Christianity,
in estimating the modern position of woman and the
outcast child, as compared with their status under
Greek and Roman civilization.

At a later period (412 A. D.) the imperial legislation again endeavored to prevent the reclaiming of
exposed children from compassionate persons who
had taken them. "Were they right to say that those
children belonged to them when they had despised
them even to the point of abandoning them to
death?"

It was provided also, that in future no one should
"take from the ground" exposed children except in
the presence of witnesses, and that the archbishop
should put his signature on the document of guard-
ianship which was prepared. (Cod. Theod., lib. 5, tit.
7, De Expositis.)

Hitherto, exposed children had generally been
taken and reared as slaves; but in A. D. 529, Justin-
ian decreed that not only the father lost all legitimate
authority over the child if he exposed it, but also that
the child itself preserved its liberty.

This law applied only to the Eastern Empire; in

the Western the slavery of exposed children continued for centuries. (Lecky: Hist. of Europ. Morals, vol. ii., p. 32.) The Christian churches throughout the early centuries took especial care of orphans, in parish orphan nurseries, or *orphanotrophiœ*.

The first asylums for deserted and foundling children which are recorded in the Christian era are one in Trêves in the sixth century, one at Angiers in the seventh, and a more famous one in Milan, A. D. 787.

Societies for the protection of children were also formed in Milan in the middle of the twelfth century.

At the end of that century a monk of Montpelier, Brother GUY, formed what may be called the first " Children's Aid Society," for the protection, shelter, and education of destitute children, a fraternity which subsequently spread over Europe.

One great cause of the final extreme corruption and extinction of ancient pagan society was the existence of large classes of unfortunate beings, whom no social moral movement of renovation ever reached —the slaves, the gladiators, the barbarian strangers, and the outcast children.

To all these deep strata of misery and crime Christianity gradually penetrated, and brought life and light, and finally an almost entire metamorphosis. As criminal and unfortunate classes, they have—with the exception only of the children—ceased to exist

under modern civilization.   We have no longer at
the basis of modern society the dangers of a multitude of ignorant slaves, or of disaffected barbarous
foreigners, or of a profession of gladiators—brutal,
brutalizing; but we do still have masses of unfortunate youth, whose condition, though immensely improved and lightened by the influences of Christianity,
is still one of the most threatening and painful
phenomena of modern society in nearly all civilized
countries.

Still, unlike the experience of Paganism under the
Roman Empire and before it, rays of light, of intelligence, and of moral and spiritual influence pene-
trate to the depths of these masses.   The spirit of
Christ is slowly and irresistibly permeating even
this lowest class of miserable, unfortunate, or criminal
beings; inspiring those who perseveringly labor for
them, drawing from wealth its dole and from intelligence its service of love, educating the fortunate in
the habit of duty to the unfortunate, giving a dignity
to the most degraded, and offering hope to the
despairing.

CHRIST leads the Reform of the world, as well as
its Charity.

Those who have much to do with alms-giving and
plans of human improvement soon see how superficial
and comparatively useless all assistance or organiza-

tion is, which does not touch habits of life and the inner forces which form character. The poor helped each year become poorer in force and independence. Education is a better preventive of pauperism than charity. The best police and the most complete form of government are nothing if the individual morality be not there. But Christianity is the highest educa- tion of character. Give the poor that, and only seldom will either alms or punishment be necessary.

When one comes to know the peculiar overpower- ing temptations which beset the class of unfortunate children and similar classes; the inducements to sharpness, deception, roguery, lying, fraud, coarse- ness, vice in many forms, besides toward open offenses against the law; the few restraining influences in social opinion, good example, or inherited self-control; the forces without and the organization within im- pelling to crime, and then sees how immensely power- ful the belief in and love for a supernatural and noble character and Friend is upon such wild natures; how it inspires to nobleness, restrains low passions, changes bad habits, and transforms base hearts; how the thoughts of this supernatural Friend can accom- pany a child of the street, and make his daily hard life an offering of loving service; how the unseen sympathy can dry the orphan's tears, and throw a light of cheerfulness around the wan, pale face of the little vagrant, and bring down something of the splendor of heaven to the dark cellars and dreary dens of a great city: whoever has had this experience—not once, but many times—will begin to understand that Christ must lead Reform as well as Charity, and that without Him the worst diseases of modern society can never be cured.

THE FORTUNES OF A STREET WAIF.

(First Stage.)

CHAPTER II.

THE PROLETAIRES OF NEW YORK.

NEW YORK is a much younger city than its European rivals; and with perhaps one-third the population of London, yet it presents varieties of life among the "masses" quite as picturesque, and elements of population even more dangerous. The throng of different nationalities in the American city gives a peculiarly variegated air to the life beneath the surface, and the enormous over-crowding in portions of the poor quarters intensifies the evils, peculiar to large towns, to a degree seen only in a few districts in such cities as London and Liverpool.

The *mass* of poverty and wretchedness is, of course, far greater in the English capital. There are classes with inherited pauperism and crime more deeply stamped in them, in London or Glasgow, than we ever behold in New York; but certain small districts can be found in our metropolis with the unhappy fame of containing more human beings packed to the square yard, and stained with more acts of blood and riot, within a given period, than is true of any other equal space of earth in the civilized world.

There are houses, well known to sanitary boards and the police, where Fever has taken a perennial lease, and will obey no legal summons to quit; where Cholera—if a single germ-seed of it float.anywhere in American atmosphere—at once ripens a black har-vest; where Murder has stained every floor of its gloomy stories, and Vice skulks or riots from one year's end to the other. Such houses are never reformed. The only hope for them is in the march of street improvements, which will utterly sweep them away.

It is often urged that the breaking-up of these " dens" and "fever-nests" only scatters the pesti-lence and moral disease, but does not put an end to them.

The objection is more apparent than real. The abolishing of one of these centres of crime and pov-erty is somewhat like withdrawing the virus from one diseased limb and diffusing it through an otherwise healthy body. It seems to lose its intensity. The diffusion weakens. Above all, it is less likely to become hereditary.

One of the remarkable and hopeful things about New York, to a close observer of its "dangerous classes," is, as I shall show in a future chapter, that they do not tend to become fixed and inherited, as in European cities.

But, though the crime and pauperism of New York

are not so deeply stamped in the blood of the population, they are even more dangerous. The intensity of the American temperament is felt in every fibre of these children of poverty and vice. Their crimes have the unrestrained and sanguinary character of a race accustomed to overcome all obstacles. They rifle a bank, where English thieves pick a pocket; they murder, where European *prolétaires* cudgel or fight with fists; in a riot, they begin what seems about to be the sacking of a city, where English rioters would merely batter policemen, or smash lamps. The "dangerous classes" of New York are mainly American-born, but the children of Irish and German immigrants. They are as ignorant as London flash-men or costermongers. They are far more brutal than the peasantry from whom they descend, and they are much banded together, in associations, such as "Dead Rabbit," "Plug-ugly," and various target companies. They are our *enfants perdus*, grown up to young manhood. The murder of an unoffending old man, like Mr. Rogers, is nothing to them. They are ready for any offense or crime, however degraded or bloody. New York has never experienced the full effect of the nurture of these youthful ruffians as she will one day. They showed their hand only slightly in the riots during the war. At present, they are like the athletes and gladiators of the Roman demagogues. They are the "roughs" who sustain the ward politicians, and frighten honest voters. They can "repeat" to an unlimited extent, and serve their employers. They live on "*panem et circenses*," or City-Hall places and pot-houses, where they have full credit.

We shall speak more particularly of the causes of crime in future chapters, but we may say in brief, that the young ruffians of New York are the products of accident, ignorance, and vice. Among a million people, such as compose the population of this city and its suburbs, there will always be a great number of misfortunes; fathers die, and leave their children unprovided for; parents drink, and abuse their little ones, and they float away on the currents of the street; step-mothers or step-fathers drive out, by neglect and ill-treatment, their sons from home. Thousands are the children of poor foreigners, who have permitted them to grow up without school, education, or religion. All the neglect and bad education and evil example of a poor class tend to form others, who, as they mature, swell the ranks of ruffians and criminals. So, at length, a great multitude of ignorant, untrained, passionate, irreligious boys and young men are formed, who become the "dangerous class" of our city. They form the "Nineteenth-street Gangs," the young burglars and murderers, the garroters and rioters, the thieves and flash-men, the "repeaters" and ruffians, so well known to all who know this metropolis.

THE DANGERS.

It has been common, since the recent terrible Communistic outbreak in Paris, to assume that France alone is exposed to such horrors; but, in the judgment of one who has been familiar with our "dangerous classes" for twenty years, there are just the same explosive social elements beneath the surface of New York as of Paris.

There are thousands on thousands in New York who have no assignable home, and "flit" from attic to attic, and cellar to cellar; there are other thousands more or less connected with criminal enterprises; and still other tens of thousands, poor, hard-pressed, and depending for daily bread on the day's earnings, swarming in tenement-houses, who behold the gilded rewards of toil all about them, but are never permitted to touch them.

All these great masses of destitute, miserable, and criminal persons believe that for ages the rich have had all the good things of life, while to them have been left the evil things. Capital to them is the tyrant.

Let but Law lift its hand from them for a season, or let the civilizing influences of American life fail to reach them, and, if the opportunity offered, we should see an explosion from this class which might leave this city in ashes and blood.

To those incredulous of this, we would recall the

scenes in our streets during the riots in 1863, when, for a short period, the guardians of good order—the local militia—had been withdrawn for national purposes, and when the ignorant masses were excited by dread of the draft.

Who will ever forget the marvelous rapidity with which the better streets were filled with a ruffianly and desperate multitude, such as in ordinary times we seldom see—creatures who seemed to have crept from their burrows and dens to join in the plunder of the city—how quickly certain houses were marked out for sacking and ruin, and what wild and brutal crimes were committed on the unoffending negroes? It will be recalled, too, how much *women* figured in these horrible scenes, as they did in the Communistic outbreak in Paris. It was evident to all careful observers then, that had another day of license been given the crowd, the attack would have been directed at the apparent wealth of the city—the banks, jewelers' shops, and rich private houses.

No one doubted then, or during the Orange riot of 1871, the existence of "dangerous classes" in New York. And yet the separate members of these riotous and ruffianly masses are simply neglected and street-wandering children who have come to early manhood. The true preventive of social catastrophes like these, are just such Christian reformatory and educational movements as we are about to describe.

Of the number of the distinctively homeless and
vagrant youth in New York, it is difficult to speak
with precision. We should be inclined to estimate it,
after long observation, as fluctuating each year between 20,000 and 30,000.* But to these, as they
mature, must be added, in the composition of the
dangerous classes, all those who are professionally
criminal, and who have homes and lodging-places.
And again to these, portions of that vast and ignor-
ant† multitude, who, in prosperous times, just keep
their heads above water, who are pressed down by
poverty or misfortune, and who look with envy and
greed at the signs of wealth and luxury all around
them, while they themselves have nothing but hardship, penury, and unceasing drudgery.

* The homeless children who come each year under the
charitable efforts afterwards to be described amount to some
12,000.

† It should be remembered that there are in this city over
60,000 persons above ten years of age who cannot write their
names.

CHAPTER III.

THE CAUSES OF CRIME.

THE great practical division of causes of crime may be made into preventible and non-preventible. Among the preventible, or those which can be in good part removed, may be placed ignorance, intemperance, over-crowding of population, want of work, idleness, vagrancy, the weakness of the marriage-tie, and bad legislation.

Among those which cannot be entirely removed are inheritance, the effects of emigration, orphanage, accident or misfortune, the strength of the sexual and other passions, and a natural weakness of moral or mental powers.

IGNORANCE.

There needs hardly a word to be said in this country on the intimate connection between ignorance and crime.

The precise statistical relation between them in the State of New York would seem to be this: about thirty-one per cent. of the adult criminals cannot read or write, while of the adult population at large about six (6.08) per cent. are illiterate; or nearly one-

THE FORTUNES OF A STREET WAIF.

(Second Stage.)

third of the crime is committed by six-hundredths of the population. In the city prisons for 1870, out of 49,423 criminals, 18,442 could not write and could barely read, or more than thirty-three per cent.

In the Reformatories of the country, according to the statement of Dr. Bittinger before the National Congress on prison-discipline at Cincinnati, out of the average number of the inmates for 1868, of 7,963 twenty-seven per cent. were wholly illiterate.

Very great criminality is, of course, possible with high education; but in the immense majority of cases a very small degree of mental training or intellectual tastes is a preventive of idleness and consequent crime and of extreme poverty. The difference between knowing how to read and not knowing will often be the line between utter poverty and a capacity for various occupations.

Among the inmates of the city prisons a large percentage are without a trade, and no doubt this idle condition is largely due to their ignorance and is one of the great stimulants to their criminal course. Who can say how much the knowledge of Geography alone may stimulate a child or a youth to emigrate, and thus leave his immediate temptations and escape pressing poverty?

ORPHANAGE.

Out of 452 criminal children received into the House of Refuge in New York during 1870, only 187 had both parents living, so that nearly sixty per cent. had lost one or both of their parents, or were otherwise separated from them.

According to Dr. Bittinger,[*] of the 7,963 inmates of the reformatories in the United States in 1870, fifty-five per cent. were orphans or half orphans.

The following figures strikingly show the extent to which orphanage and inheritance influence the moral condition of children.

Mettrai, the celebrated French reformatory, has received since its foundation 3,580 youthful inmates. Of these, there are 707 whose parents are convicts; 308 whose parents live in concubinage; 534 "natural" children; 221 foundlings; 504 children of a second marriage; and 1,542 without either father or mother.[†]

An intelligent French writer, M. de Marsangy,[‡] in writing of the causes of juvenile crime in France, says that "a fifth of those who have been the objects of judicial pursuit are composed of orphans; the half have no father, a quarter no mother, and as for those who have a family, nearly all are dragged by it into evil."

EMIGRATION.

There is no question that the breaking of the ties with one's country has a bad moral effect,

[*] Transactions of the National Congress, p. 279.
[†] Une visite à Mettray. Paris, 1868.
[‡] Moralisation de l'enfance coupable, p. 18.

especially on a laboring class. The Emigrant is released from the social inspection and judgment to which he has been subjected at home, and the tie of church and priesthood is weakened. If a Roman Catholic, he is often a worse Catholic, without being a better Protestant. If a Protestant, he often becomes indifferent. Moral ties are loosened with the religious. The intervening process which occurs here, between his abandoning the old state of things and fitting himself to the new, is not favorable to morals or character.

The consequence is, that ⌐an immense proportion⌐ of our ignorant and criminal class are foreign-born; and of the dangerous classes here, a very large part, though native-born, are of foreign parentage. Thus, out of the whole number of foreigners in New York State, in 1860, 16.69 per cent. could not read or write; while of the native-born only 1.83 per cent. were illiterate.

Of the 49,423 prisoners in our city prisons, in prison for one year before January, 1870, 32,225 were of foreign birth, and, no doubt, a large proportion of the remainder of foreign parentage. Of the foreign-born, 21,887 were from Ireland; and yet at home the Irish are one of the most law-abiding and virtuous of populations—the proportion of criminals being smaller than in England or Scotland.

In the Eastern Penitentiary of Pennsylvania, ac-

cording to Dr. Bittinger, from one-fourth to one-third
of the inmates are foreigners; in Auburn, from a third
to a half; in Clinton, one-half; in Sing Sing, between
one-half and six-sevenths.   In the Albany Penitentiary, the aggregate number of prisoners during the
last twenty years was 18,390, of whom 10,770 were
foreign-born.*

It is another marked instance of the demoralizing
influence of emigration, that so large a proportion of
the female criminal class should be Irish-born, though
the Irish female laboring class are well known to be
at home one of the most virtuous in the world.

A hopeful fact, however, begins to appear in regard to this matter; the worst effects of emigration in this country seem over.   The machinery for protecting and forwarding the newly-arrived immigrants,
so that they may escape the dangers and temptations
of the city, has been much improved.   Very few, comparatively, now remain in our sea-ports to swell the
current of poverty and crime.   The majority find
their way at once to the country districts.   The
quality, too, of the immigration has improved.   More
well-to-do farmers and peasantry, with small savings,
arrive than formerly, and the preponderance, as to
nationality, is inclining to the Germans.   It comparatively seldom happens now that paupers or persons absolutely without means, land in New York.

* Transact. of Nat. Cong., p. 262.

As one of the great causes of crime, Emigration will undoubtedly have a much feebler influence in the future in New York than it has had in the past.

WANT OF A TRADE.

It is remarkable how often, in questioning the youthful convicts in our prisons as to the causes of their downfall, they will reply that "if they had had a trade, they would not have been there." They disliked drudgery, they found places in offices and shops crowded; they would have enjoyed the companionship and the inventiveness of a trade, but they could not obtain one, and therefore they were led into stealing or gambling, as a quick mode of earning a living.

There is no doubt that a lad with a trade feels a peculiar independence of the world, and is much less likely to take up dishonest means of living than one depending on manual labor, or chance means of living.

There is nearly always a demand for his work; the lad feels himself a member of a craft and supported by the consciousness of this membership; the means of the "Unions" often sustain him when out of employment; his associates are more honest and respectable than those of boys depending on chance-labor, and so he is preserved from falling into crime.

Of course, if such a lad would walk forth to the nearest country village, he would find plenty of healthy and remunerative employment in the ground, as gardener or farmer. And to a country-lad, the farm offers a better chance than a trade. But many city boys and young men will not consent to leave the excitements of the city, so that the want of a mechanical occupation does expose them to many temptations.

The persons most responsible for this state of things are the members of such "Unions" as refuse to employ boys, or to encourage the training of apprentices. It is well-known that in many trades of New York, hardly any young laborers or apprentices are being trained. The result of this selfish policy will be to reduce the amount of skilled labor in this city, and thus compel the importation of foreign labor, and to increase juvenile crime and the burdens on the poor.

Another cause of this increasing separation from trades among the young is, no doubt, the increasing aversion of American children, whether poor or rich, to learn anything thoroughly; the boys of the street, like those of our merchants, preferring to make fortunes by lucky and sudden "turns," rather than by patient and steady industry.

Our hope in this matter is in the steady demand for juvenile labor in the country districts, and the substantial rewards which await industry there.

CHAPTER IV.

THE CAUSES OF CRIME.

WEAKNESS OF THE MARRIAGE-TIE.

IT is extraordinary, among the lowest classes, in how large a number of cases a second marriage, or the breaking of marriage, is the immediate cause of crime or vagrancy among the children. When questioning a homeless boy or street-wandering girl as to the former home, it is extremely common to hear "I couldn't get on with my step-mother," or "My step-father treated me badly," or "My father left, and we just took care of ourselves." These apparently exceptional events are so common in these classes as to fairly constitute them an important cause of juvenile crime. When one remembers the number of happy second marriages within one's acquaintance, and how many children have never felt the difference between their step-mother and their own mother, and what love and patience and self-sacrifice are shown by parents to their step-children, we may be surprised at the contrast in another class of the community. But the virtues of the poor spring very much from their affections and instincts; they

have comparatively little self-control; the high lessons of duty and consideration for others are seldom
stamped on them, and Religion does not much influence their more delicate relations with those associated with them.   They might shelter a strange orphan
for years with the greatest kindness; but the bearing·
and forbearing with the faults of another person's
child year after year, merely from motives of duty or
affection to its parent, belong to a higher range of
Christian virtues, to which they seldom attain.   Their
own want of self-control and their tendency to jealousy, and little understanding of true self-sacrifice,
combine to weaken and embitter these relations with
step-children.   The children themselves have plenty
of faults, and have doubtless been little governed, so
that soon both parties jar and rub against one another; and as neither have instincts or affections to
fall back upon, mere principle or sense of duty is
not enough to restrain them.   What would be simply
slights or jars in more controlled persons, become col-
lisions in this class.

Bitter quarrels spring up between step-son and
mother, or step-daughter and father; the other parent sometimes sides with the child, sometimes with
the father; but the result is similar.   The house becomes a kind of pandemonium, and the girls rush
desperately forth to the wild life of the streets, or the
boys gradually prefer the roaming existence of the

little city-Arab to such a quarrelsome home. Thus it happens that step-children among the poor are so often criminals or outcasts.

It needs a number of years among the lower working-classes to understand what a force public opinion is in all classes in keeping the marriage-bond sacred, and what sweeping misfortunes follow its violation. Many of the Irish peasants who have landed here have married from pure affection. Their marriage has been consecrated by the most solemn ceremonies of their church. They come of a people peculiarly faithful to the marriage-tie, and whose religion has especially guarded female purity and the fidelity of husband and wife. At home, in their native villages, they would have died sooner than break the bond or leave their wives. The social atmosphere about them and the influence of the priests make such an act almost impossible. And yet in this distant country, away from their neighbors and their religious instructors, they are continually making a practical test of "Free-Love" doctrines. As the wife grows old or ugly—as children increase and weigh the parents down—as the home becomes more noisy and less pleasant,—the man begins to forget the vows made at the altar, and the blooming girl he then took; and, perhaps meeting some prettier woman, or hearing of some chance for work at a distance, he slips quietly away, and the deserted wife, who seems to love him the more the more false he is, is left alone. For a time she has faith in him and seeks him far and near; but at length she abandons hope, and begins the heavy struggle of maintaining her little family herself. The boys gradually get beyond her control; they are kept in the street to earn something for their support; they become wild and vagrant, and soon end with being street-rovers, or petty thieves, or young criminals. The girls are trained in begging or peddling, and, meeting with bold company, they gradually learn the manners and morals of the streets, and after a while abandon the wretched home, and break what was left of the poor mother's hope and courage, by beginning a life of shame.

This sad history is lived out every day in New York. If any theorists desire to see what fruits "Free Love" or a weak marriage-bond can bear among the lowest working-classes, they have only to trace the histories of great numbers of the young thieves and outcasts and prostitutes in this city. With the dangerous classes, "elective affinities" are most honestly followed. The results are suffering, crime, want, and degradation to those who are innocent.

INHERITANCE.

A most powerful and continual source of crime with the young is Inheritance—the transmitted tendencies and qualities of their parents, or of several generations of ancestors.

It is well-known to those familiar with the criminal classes, that certain appetites or habits, if indulged abnormally and excessively through two or more generations, come to have an almost irresistible force, and, no doubt, modify the brain so as to constitute almost an insane condition. This is especially true of the appetite for liquor and of the sexual passion, and sometimes of the peculiar weakness, dependence and laziness which make confirmed paupers.

The writer knows of an instance in an almshouse in Western New York, where four generations of females were paupers and prostitutes. Almost every reader who is familiar with village life will recall poor families which have had dissolute or criminal members beyond the memory of the oldest inhabitant, and who still continue to breed such characters. I have known a child of nine or ten years, given up, apparently beyond control, to licentious habits and desires, and who in all different circumstances seemed to show the same tendencies; her mother had been of similar character, and quite likely her grandmother. The "gemmules," or latent tendencies, or forces, or cells of her immediate ancestors were in her system, and working in her blood, producing irresistible effects on her brain, nerves, and mental emotions, and finally, not being met early enough by other moral, mental, and physical influences, they have modified her organization, until her will is scarcely able to control them and she gives herself up to them. All those who instruct or govern "Houses of Refuge," or "Reform Schools," or Asylums for criminal children and youths, will recall many such instances.

They are much better known in the Old World than this; they are far more common here in the country than in the city.

My own experience during twenty years has been in this regard singularly hopeful. I have watched great numbers of degraded families in New York, and exceedingly few of them have transmitted new generations of paupers, criminals, or vagrants.

The causes of this encouraging state of things are not obscure. The action of the great law of "Natural Selection," in regard to the human race, is always towards temperance and virtue. That is, vice and extreme indulgence weaken the physical powers and undermine the constitution; they impair the faculties by which man struggles with adverse conditions and gets beyond the reach of poverty and want. The vicious and sensual and drunken die earlier, or they have fewer children, or their children are carried off by diseases more frequently, or they themselves are unable to resist or prevent poverty and suffering. As a consequence, in the lowest class, the more self- controlled and virtuous tend constantly to survive, and

to prevail in "the struggle for existence," over the
the vicious and ungoverned, and to transmit their
progeny. The natural drift among the poor is towards
virtue. Probably no vicious organization with very
extreme and abnormal tendencies is transmitted
beyond the fourth generation; it ends in insanity or
crètinism or the wildest crime.

The result is then, with the worst-endowed families,
that the "gemmules," or latent forces of hundreds of
virtuous, or at least, not vicious, generations, lie hid
in their constitutions. The immediate influences of
parents or grandparents are, of course, the strongest
in inheritance; but these may be overcome, and the
latent tendencies to good, coming down from remote
ancestors, be aroused and developed.

Thus is explained the extraordinary improvement
of the children of crime and poverty in our Industrial
Schools; and the reforms and happy changes seen in
the boys and girls of our dangerous classes when placed
in kind Western homes. The change of circumstances,
the improved food, the daily moral and mental influences, the effect of regular labor and discipline, and,
above all, the power of Religion, awaken these hidden
tendencies to good, both those coming from many
generations of comparative virtue and those inherent
in the soul, while they control and weaken and cause
to be forgotten those diseased appetites or extreme
passions which these unfortunate creatures inherit

directly, and substitute a higher moral sense for the low moral instincts which they obtained from their parents. So it happens, also, that American life, as compared with European, and city life, as compared with country, produces similar results. In the United States, a boundless hope pervades all classes; it reaches down to the outcast and vagrant. There is no fixity, as is so often the fact in Europe, from the sense of despair. Every individual, at least till he is old, hopes and expects to rise out of his condition.

The daughter of the rag-picker or vagrant sees the children she knows, continually dressing better or associating with more decent people; she beholds them attending the public schools and improving in education and manners; she comes in contact with the greatest force the poor know—public opinion, which requires a certain decency and respectability among themselves. She becomes ashamed of her squalid, ragged, or drunken mother. She enters an Industrial School, or creeps into a Ward School, or "goes out" as a servant. In every place, she feels the profound forces of American life; the desire of equality, ambition to rise, the sense of self-respect and the passion for education.

These new desires overcome the low appetites in her blood, and she continually rises and improves. If Religion in any form reach her, she attains a still greater height over the sensual and filthy ways of her parents. She is in no danger of sexual degradation, or of any extreme vice. The poison in her blood has found an antidote. When she marries, it will inevitably be with a class above her own. This process goes on continually throughout the country, and breaks up criminal inheritance.

Moreover, the incessant change of our people, especially in cities, the separation of children from parents, of brothers from sisters, and of all from their former localities, destroy that continuity of influence which bad parents and grandparents exert, and do away with those neighborhoods of crime and pauperism where vice concentrates and transmits itself with ever-increasing power. The fact that tenants must forever be "moving" in New York, is a preventive of some of the worst evils among the lower poor. The mill of American life, which grinds up so many delicate and fragile things, has its uses, when it is turned on the vicious fragments of the lower strata of society.

Villages, which are more stable and conservative, and tend to keep families together more and in the same neighborhoods, show more instances of inherited and concentrated wickedness and idleness. In New York the families are constantly broken up; some members improve, some die out, but they do not transmit a progeny of crime. There is little inherited criminality and pauperism.

A QUESTION.

Among these public influences on the young, it has been often a question with some, whether the Public Schools did not educate the daughters of the poor too much, and thus make them discontented with their condition, and exposed to temptation.

It is said that these working-girls, seeing such fine dresses about them, and learning many useless accomplishments, have become indifferent to steady hand-labor, and have sought in vice for the luxuries which they have first learned to know in the public schools. My own observation, however, leads me to doubt whether this occurs, unless as an exceptional fact. The influence of discipline and regular instruction is against the style of character which makes the prostitute. Where there is a habit of work, there are seldom the laziness and shiftlessness which especially cause or stimulate sexual vice. Some working-girls do, no doubt, become discontented with their former condition, and some rise to a much higher, while some fall; but this happens everywhere in the United States, and is not to be traced especially to the influence of our Free Schools.

We have spoken of the greater tendency of large cities, as compared with villages, in breaking up vicious families. There is another advantage of cities in this matter. The especial virtue of a village community is the self-respect and personal independence of its members. No benefits of charity or benevolent assistance and dependence could ever outweigh this. But this very virtue tends to keep a wicked or idle family in its present condition. The neighbors are not in the habit of interfering with it; no one advises or warns it. The children grow up as other people's children do, in the way the parents prefer; there is no machinery of charity to lift them out of the slime; and if any of their wealthier neighbors, from motives of benevolence, visited the house, and attempted to improve or educate the family, the effort would be resented or misconstrued. The whole family become a kind of *pariahs*; they are morally tabooed, and grow up in a vicious atmosphere of their own, and really come out much worse than a similar family in the city. This phenomenon is only a natural effect of the best virtues of the rural community.

In a large town, on the other hand, there exist machinery and organization through which benevolent and religious persons can approach such families, and their good intentions not be suspected or resented. The poor people themselves are not so independent, and accept advice or warning more readily; they are not so stamped in public repute with a bad name; less is known of them, and the children, under new influences, break off from the vicious career of their parents, and grow up as honest and industrious persons. Moreover, the existence of so much charitable organi-

8

zation in the cities brings the best talent and character of the fortunate classes to bear directly on the
unfortunate, far more than is the fact in villages.

CHAPTER V.

OVER-CROWDING.

THE source of juvenile crime and misery in New York, which is the most formidable, and, at the same time, one of the most difficult to remove, is the *over-crowding* of our population. The form of the city-site is such—the majority of the dwellings being crowded into a narrow island between two water-fronts—that space near the business-portion of the city becomes of great value. These districts are necessarily sought for by the laboring and mechanic classes, as they are near the places of employment. They are avoided by the wealthy on account of the population which has already occupied so much of them. The result is, that the poor must live in certain wards; and as space is costly, the landlords supply them with (comparatively) cheap dwellings, by building very high and large houses, in which great numbers of people rent only rooms, instead of dwellings.

Were New York a city radiating from a centre over an almost unlimited space—as Philadelphia, for instance—the laborers or the mechanics might take up their abode anywhere, and land would be comparatively cheap, so that the highest blessing of the laboring class would be attainable—of separate homes for each family. But, on this narrow island, business is so peculiarly concentrated, and population is so much forced to one exit—towards the north—and the poor have such a singular objection to living beyond a ferry, that space will inevitably continue very dear in New York, and the laboring classes will be compelled to occupy it.

To add to the unavoidable costliness of ground-room on this island, has come in the effect of bad government.

It is one of the most unpleasant experiences of the student of political economy, that the axioms of his science can so seldom be understood by the masses, though their interests be vitally affected by them. Thus, every thoughtful man knows that each new "job" among city officials, each act of plunder of public property by members of the municipal government, every loss of income or mal-appropriation or extravagance in the city's funds, must be paid for by taxation, and that taxation always falls heaviest on labor. The laboring classes of the city rule it, and through their especial leaders are the great public losses and wastefulness occasioned.

Yet they never know that they themselves continually pay for these in increased rents. Every landlord charges his advanced taxation in rent, and probably a profit on that. The tenant pays more for his room, the grocer more for his shop, the butcher and tailor and shoemaker, and every retailer have heavier expenses from the advance in rents, and each and all charge it on their customers. The poor feel the final pressure. The painful effect has been, that the expense for rent has arisen enormously with the laboring classes of this city during the last five years, while many of the other living expenses have nearly returned to the standard before the war.

The influence of high rents is to force more people into a given space, in order to economize and divide expense.

The latest trustworthy statistics on this important subject are from the excellent Reports of the Metropolitan Board of Health for 1866. From these, it appears that the Eleventh Ward of this city, with a population of 58,953, has a rate of population of 196,510 to the square mile, or $16\frac{1}{5}$ square yards to each person; the Tenth Ward, with 31,587 population, has a rate of 185,512 to the square mile, or $17\frac{1}{5}$ square yards to each; the Seventeenth Ward, with 79,563, has the rate of 153,006; the Fourteenth, with 23,382, has a rate of 155,880; the Thirteenth, with 26,388, has 155,224; and so on with others, though in less proportion.

The worst districts in London do not at all equal

this crowding of population. Thus, East London shows the rate of 175,816 to the square mile; the Strand, 141,556; St. Luke's, 151,104; Holborn, 148,705; and St. James's, Westminster, 144,008.

If particular districts of our city be taken, they present an even greater massing of human beings than the above averages have shown. Thus, according to the Report of the Council of Hygiene in 1865, the tenant-house and cellar population of the Fourth Ward numbered 17,611 packed in buildings over a space less than thirty acres, exclusive of streets, which would make the fearful rate of 290,000 to the square mile.

In the Seventeenth Ward, the Board of Health reports that in 1868, 4,120 houses contained 95,091 inhabitants, of whom 14,016 were children under five years. In the same report, the number of tenement-houses for the whole city is given at 18,582, with an estimate of one-half the whole population dwelling in them—say 500,000.

We quote an extract from a report of Mr. Dupuy, Visitor of the Children's Aid Society of the First Ward, describing the condition of a tenement-house:

"What do you think of the moral atmosphere of the home I am about to describe below? To such a home two of our boys return nightly.

"In a dark cellar filled with smoke, there sleep, all in one room, with no kind of partition dividing them, two men with their wives, a girl of thirteen or fourteen, two men and a large boy of about seventeen years of age, a mother with two more boys, one about ten years old, and one large boy of fifteen; another woman with two boys, nine and eleven years of age—in all, *fourteen persons.*

"This room I have often visited, and the number enumerated probably falls below, rather than above the average that sleep there."

It need not be said that with overcrowding such as this, there is always disease, and as naturally, crime. The privacy of a home is undoubtedly one of the most favorable conditions to virtue, especially in a girl.

If a female child be born and brought up in a room of one of these tenement-houses, she loses very early the modesty which is the great shield of purity. Personal delicacy becomes almost unknown to her. Living, sleeping, and doing her work in the same apartment with men and boys of various ages, it is well-nigh impossible for her to retain any feminine reserve, and she passes almost unconsciously the line of purity at a very early age.

In these dens of crowded humanity, too, other and more unnatural crimes are committed among those of the same blood and family.

Here, too, congregate some of the worst of the destitute population of the city—vagrants, beggars, nondescript thieves, broken-down drunken vagabonds, who manage as yet to keep out of the station-houses, and the lowest and most bungling of the "sharpers." Naturally, the boys growing up in such places become, as by a law of nature, petty thieves, pick-pockets, street-rovers, beggars, and burglars. Their only salvation is, that these dens become so filthy and haunted with vermin, that the lads themselves leave them in disgust, preferring the barges on the breezy docks, or the boxes on the side-walk, from which eventually they are drawn into the neat and comfortable Boys' Lodging-houses, and there find themselves imperceptibly changed into honest and decent boys. This is the story of thousands every year.

The cellar-population alone of this city is a source of incessant disease and crime.

And with the more respectable class of poor who occupy the better kind of tenement-houses, the packing of human beings in those great caravansaries is one of the worst evils of this city. It sows pestilence and breeds every species of criminal habits.

From the eighteen thousand tenement-houses comes seventy-three per cent.* of the mortality of our population, and we have little doubt as much as ninety per cent. of the offenses against property and person.

* In 1865, the deaths in tenement-houses were 14,500 out of 19,813, the total for the city.

The death-rate has, however, been brought down by sanitary improvements from 76 per cent., in 1866, to about 66 per cent. in 1871, or a gain of 2,900 lives in these wretched houses.

Over-crowding is the one great misfortune of New York. Without it, we should be the healthiest large city in the world,* and a great proportion of the crimes which disgrace our civilization would be nipped in the bud. While this continues as it does now, there is no possibility of a thorough sanitary, moral, and religious reform in our worst wards.

Few girls can grow up to maturity in such dens as exist in the First, Sixth, Eleventh, and Seventeenth Wards and be virtuous; few boys can have such places as homes and not be thieves and vagabonds. In such places typhus and cholera will always be rife, and the death-rate will reach its most terrible maximum. While the poorest population dwell in these cellars and crowded attics, neither Sunday-schools, nor churches, nor charities, can accomplish a thorough reform.

What, then, is to be done to remedy this terrible evil?

Experience has proved that our remedial agencies can, in individual cases cure even the evils resulting from this unnatural condensing of population. That

* Our annual death-rate is now 28.79 per 1,000, while some of the clean wards show 15 per 1,000, or about the rate of the Isle of Wight.

The rate of London is about 24, Liverpool has been as high as 40, but is more healthy now, owing to sanitary improvements. Our Sixth Ward reaches 43, and "Gotham Court," in Cherry Street, attains the horrible maximum of 195 per 1,000.

is, we can point to thousands of lads and young girls who were born and reared in such crowded dens of humanity, but who have been transformed into virtuous, well-behaved, and industrious young men and women, by the quiet daily influence of the charitable organization I am about to describe.

Still, these cases of reform are, in truth, exceptions. The natural and legitimate influence of such massing of population is all in the direction of immorality and degeneracy. Whatever would lessen that, would at once, and by a necessary law, diminish crime and poverty and disease.

REMEDIES.

The great remedies are to be looked for in broad, general provisions for distributing population. Thus far, the means of communication between business New York and the suburbs have been singularly defective. An underground railway with cheap workman's trains, or elevated railways with similar conveniences, connecting Westchester County and the lower part of the city, or suburbs laid out in New Jersey or on Long Island expressly for working people, with cheap connections with New York and Brooklyn, would soon make a vast difference in the concentration of population in our lower wards. It is true that English experience would show that laboring-men, after a heavy day's work, cannot bear the jar of railway traveling. There must be, however, many varieties of labor—such as work in factories and the like—where a little movement in a railroad-train at the close of a day would be a refreshment.

Then, as the laboring class was concentrated in suburban districts, the various occupations which attend them, such as grocers, shoemakers, tailors, and others, would follow, and be established near them. Many nationalities among our working class have an especial fondness for gardens and bits of land about their houses. This would be an additional attraction to such settlements; and with easy and cheap communications we might soon have tens of thousands of our laborers and mechanics settled in pleasant and healthy little suburban villages, each, perhaps having his own small house and garden, and the children growing up under far better influences, moral and physical, than they could possibly enjoy in tenement-houses. There are many districts within half an hour of New York, where such plots could be laid out with lots at $500 each, which would pay a handsome profit to the owner, or where a cottage could be let with advantage for the present rent of a tenement attic.

Improved communications have already removed hundreds and thousands of the middle class from the city to all the surrounding neighborhood, to the immense benefit both of themselves and their families. Equal conveniences suited to the wants of the laboring class will soon cause multitudes of these to

live in the suburban districts. The obstacle, however,
as in all efforts at improvement for the working people, is in their own ignorance and timidity, and their
love of the crowd and bustle of a city.

More remote even, than relief by improved communications, is a possible check to high rents by a
better government. A cheap and honest government
of the masses in New York would at once lower taxation and bring down rents. The enormous prices
demanded for one or two small rooms in a tenement-
house are a measure (in part) of the cost of our city
government.

Another alleviation to our over crowding has often
been proposed, but never vigorously acted upon, as we
are persuaded it might be, and that is, the making the
link between the demand for labor in our country districts and the supply in New York, closer. The suc
cess of the charity which we are about describing in
the transfer of destitute and homeless children to
homes in the West, and of the Commissioners of Emigration in their "Labor Exchange," indicate what
might be accomplished by a grand organized movement for transferring our unemployed labor to the
fields of the West. It is true, this would not carry
away our poorest class, yet it would relieve the pressure of population here on space, and thus give more
room and occupation for all.

But admitting that we cannot entirely prevent the

enormous massing of people, such as prevails in our Eleventh and Seventeenth Wards, we can certainly control it by legislation. The recent Sanitary Acts of New York attempt to hold in check the mode of building tenement-houses, requiring certain means of ventilation and exit, forbidding the filling-up of the entire space between the houses with dwellings, and otherwise seeking to improve the condition of such tenement-houses.

There only needs two steps farther in imitation of the British Lodging-house Acts—one removing altogether the cellar-population, when under certain unhealthy conditions; and the other limiting by law the the number who can occupy a given space in a tenement-room. The British Acts assign 240 cubic feet as the lowest space admissible for each tenant or lodger, and if the inspector finds less space than that occupied, he at once enters a complaint, and the owner or landlord is obliged to reduce the number of his occupants, under strict penalties. A provision of this nature in our New York law would break up our worst dens, and scatter their tenants or lodgers. The removal of the cellar-population from a large proportion of their dwellings should also be made. Liverpool removed 20,000 cellar-occupants in one year (1847), to the immense gain, both moral and sanitary, of the city. New York needs the reform quite as much. There would be no real hardship in such a measure,

as the tenants could find accommodations in other
parts of the city or the suburbs; and some would perhaps emigrate to the country.

One often-proposed remedy for the ills of our
tenant-house system—the "Model Lodging-house"—
has never been fairly tried here. The theory of this
agency of reform is, that if a tenement-house can be
constructed on the best sanitary principles, with good
ventilation, with limited number of tenants, no over-
crowding, and certain important conveniences to the
lodgers, all under moral supervision (so that tenants
of notoriously bad character are excluded), and such
a house can be shown to pay, say seven per cent. net,
this will become a "model" to the builders of tenement-houses; some building after the same style, because public opinion and their own conscience require
it, others because competition compels it. Thus, in
time, the mode of structure and occupancy of all the
new tenement-houses would be changed. But to attain
this desirable end, the model houses must first pay a
profit, and a fair one. So long as they do not succeed
in this, they are a failure, however benevolent their
object and comfortable their arrangements. In this
point of view, the "Waterloo Houses," in London,
are a success, and do undoubtedly influence the mode
of building and management of private tenement-
houses; in this, also, the "Peabody Houses" are not
a success, and will have no permanent influence.

The Model Houses in London for lodging single men have, as the writer has witnessed, changed and elevated the whole class of similar private lodging-houses.

The experiment ought to be tried here, on a merely business basis, by some of our wealthy men. The evil of crowded tenement-houses might be immensely alleviated by such a remedy.

CHAPTER VI.

THE CAUSES OF CRIME.

INTEMPERANCE.

THE power of the appetite for alcoholic stimulus is something amazing. A laboring-man feels it especially, on account of the drag on his nervous system of steady and monotonous labor, and because of the few mental stimuli which he enjoys. He returns to his tenement-house after a hard day's work, "dragged out" and craving excitement; his rooms are disagreeable; perhaps his wife cross, or slatternly, and his children noisy; he has an intense desire for something which can take him out of all this, and cause his dull surroundings and his fatigue to be forgotten. Alcohol does this; moreover, he can bear alcohol and tobacco, to retard the waste of muscle, as the sedentary man cannot. In a few steps, he can find jolly companions, a lighted and warmed room, a newspaper, and, above all, a draught which, for the moment, can change poverty to riches, and drive care and labor and the thought of all his burdens and annoyances far away.

The liquor-shop is his picture-gallery, club, reading-

THE FORTUNES OF A STREET WAIF.

(Third Stage.)

room, and social *salon*, at once. His glass is the magic transmuter of care to cheerfulness, of penury to plenty, of a low, ignorant, worried life, to an existence for the moment buoyant, contented, and hopeful. Alas that the magician who thus, for the instant, transforms him with her rod, soon returns him to his low estate, with ten thousand curses haunting him! The one thus touched by the modern Circe is not even imbruted, for the brutes have no such appetite; he becomes a demonized man; all the treasures of life are trampled under his feet, and he is fit only to dwell "among the tombs." But, while labor is what it is, and the liquor-shop alone offers sociality and amusement to the poor, alcohol will still possess this overwhelming attraction. The results in this climate, and under the form of alcoholic stimulus offered here, are terrible beyond all computation. The drunkards' homes are the darkest spots even in the abyss of misery in every large city. Here the hearts of young women are truly broken, and they seek their only consolation in the same magic cup; here children are beaten, or maimed, or half-starved, until they run away to join the great throng of homeless street-rovers in our large towns, and grow up to infest society. From these homes radiate misery, grief, and crime. They are the nests in which the young fledgelings of misfortune and vice begin their flight. Probably two-thirds of the crimes of every city (and a very large portion of its poverty) come from the over-indulgence of this appetite. As an appetite, we do not believe it can ever be eradicated from the human race.

If we look at criminal statistics for the effects of this appetite, we will find that in the New York City prisons, during 1870, there were, out of 49,423 criminals, 30,507 of confessedly intemperate habits, while no doubt, with a large portion of the rest, indulgence in liquor was the cause of their offenses.

In the Albany Penitentiary there were, in 1869-70, 1,093 convicts, of whom 893 admitted they were intemperate. Of this whole number only 563 could read and write, and only 568 were natives of this country.

Among the children of misfortune in our city, the homeless boys and girls, and those compelled by poverty to attend the Industrial Schools (which I shall hereafter describe), it would be safe to say that ninety out of a hundred are the children of drunkards.

As a direct cause of crime in children, drunkenness takes but a small place. This is not an appetite of childhood. Very few boys or girls of the poorest class are addicted to it till they become mature.

The effort for Total Abstinence has been, indeed, an untold blessing to the working class in this country and many parts of Europe. It may be said, in many regions, to have broken the wand of the terrible enchantress. It has introduced a new social habit in drinking. It has connected abstinence with the ceremonial of religion and the pleasures of social organizations. It has addressed the working-man—as, in fact, he often is—as a child, and saved him from his own habits, by a sworn abstinence. Thousands of men could never have freed themselves from this most tyrannical appetite, except by absolute refusal to touch. In fact, it may be said that no vice is ever abandoned by gradual steps. The only hope for any one under the control of any wrong indulgence is in entire and immediate abandonment.

With those, too, who had not fallen under the sway of this appetite, especially if of the working class, abstinence was the safest rule.

The "Total Abstinence Reform" in this country, in Great Britain, and in Sweden, was one of the happiest events that ever occurred in the history of the working classes. Its blessings will descend through many generations. But in its nature it could not last. It was a tremendous reaction against the heavy and excessive drinking of fifty years since. It was a kind of noble asceticism. Like all asceticism, it could not continue as a permanent condition. Its power is now much spent. Wherever it can be introduced now among the laboring classes, it should be; and we believe one of the especial services of the Irish Catholic clergy, at this day, to the world, is in supporting and encouraging this great reform.

All who study the lower classes are beginning, however, now to look for other remedies of the evil of intemperance.

It has become remarkably apparent, during the last few years, that one of the best modes of driving out low tastes in the masses is to introduce higher. It has been found that galleries and museums and parks are the most formidable rivals of the liquor-shops. The experience near the Sydenham Palace, in England, and other places of instructive and pleasant resort for the laboring masses, is, that drinking-saloons do not flourish in opposition. Wherever, in the evening, a laboring-man can saunter in a pleasant park, or, in company with his wife and family, look at interesting pictures, or sculpture, or objects of curiosity, he has not such a craving for alcoholic stimulus.

Even open-air drinking in a garden—as is so common on the Continent—is never so excessive as in an artificial-lighted room. Where, too, a working-man can, in a few steps, find a cheerfully-lighted reading-room, with society or papers, or where a club is easily open to him without drinking, it will also be found that he ceases to frequent the saloon, and almost loses his taste for strong drink.

Whatever elevates the taste of the laborer, or expands his mind, or innocently amuses him, or passes his time pleasantly without indulgence, or agreeably instructs, or provides him with virtuous associations, tends at once to guard him from habits of intoxication. The Kensington Museum and Sydenham Palace, of London; the Cooper Union, the Central Park, and free Reading-rooms of New York, are all temperance-societies of the best kind. The great effort now is to bring this class of influences to bear on the habits of the laboring-people, and thus diminish intemperance.

It is a remarkable fact, in this connection, that, though ninety out of the hundred of our children in the Industrial Schools are the children of drunkards, *not one* of the thousands who have gone forth from them has been known to have fallen into intemperate habits. Under the elevating influences of the school, they imperceptibly grow out of the habits of their mothers and fathers, and never acquire the appetite.

Another matter, which is well worthy of the attention of reformers, is the possibility of introducing into those countries where "heavy drinking" prevails, the taste for light wines and the habit of open-air drinking. The passion for alcohol is a real one. On a broad scale it cannot be annihilated. Can we not satisfy it innocently? In this country, for instance, light wines can be made to a vast extent, and finally be sold very cheaply. If the taste for them were formed, would it not expel the appetite for whisky and brandy, or at least, in the coming generation, form a new habit?

There is, it is true, a peculiar intensity in the American temperament which makes the taking of concen-

trated stimulus natural to it. It will need some time
for men accustomed to work up their nervous system
to a white heat by repeated draughts of whisky or
brandy to be content with weak wines. Perhaps the
present generation never will be. But the laws of
health and morality are so manifestly on the side of
drinking light wines as compared with drinking heavy
liquors, that any effort at social improvement in this
direction would have a fair chance of success. Even
the slight change of habit involved in drinking leis-
urely at a table in the open air with women and children—after the German fashion—would be a great
social reform over the hasty bar-drinking, while standing. The worst intoxication of this City is with the
Irish and American bar-drinkers, not the German frequenters of gardens.

LIQUOR LAWS.

In regard to legislation, it seems to me that our
New York License laws of 1866 were, with a few improvements, a very "happy medium" in law-making.
The ground was tacitly taken, in that code, that it
subserved the general interests of morality to keep
one day free from riotous or public drinking, and
allow the majority of the community to spend it in
rest and worship; and, inasmuch as that day was one
of especial temptation to the working-classes, they
were to be treated to a certain degree like minors,
and liquor was to be refused to them on it. Un-

der this law, also, minors and apprentices, on week-days, were forbidden to be supplied with intoxicating drinks, and the liquor-shops were closed at certain hours of the night. Very properly, also, these sellers of intoxicating beverages, making enormous profits, and costing the community immensely in the expenses of crime occasioned by their trade, were heavily taxed, and paid to the city over a million dollars annually in fees, licenses, and fines. The effects of the law were admirable, in the diminution of cases of arrest and crime on the Sunday, and the checking of the ravages of intoxication.

But it was always apparent to the writer that, with the peculiar constitution of the population of this city, it could not be sustained, unless concessions were made to the prejudices and habits of certain nationalities among our citizens. Our reformers, however, as a class, are exceedingly adverse to con-cessions; they look at questions of habits as absolute questions of right and wrong, and they will permit no half-way or medium ground. But legislation is always a matter of concession We cannot make laws for human nature as it ought to be, but as it is. If we do not get the absolutely best law passed, we must content ourselves with the medium best. If our Temperance Reformers had permitted a clause in the law, excepting the drinking in gardens, or of lager-beer, from the restrictions of the License Law, we should not, indeed, have had so good a state of things as we had for a few years, under the old law, but we might have had it permanently. Now, we have nearly lost all control over drinking, and the Sunday orgies and crimes will apparently renew themselves without check or restraint. If a reform in legislation claim too much, there is always a severe reaction possible, when the final effects will be worse than the evils sought to be corrected.

The true plan of reform for this city would be to cause the License Law of 1866 to be re-enacted with certain amendments. The "intoxicating drinks" mentioned should be held not to include lager-beer or certain light wines; and garden-drinking might be permitted, under strict police surveillance.

The Excise Board should be allowed very summary control, however, even over the German gardens and lager-beer drinking-places, so that, if they were perverted into places of disturbance and intoxication, the licenses could be revoked.

By separating absolutely the licenses for light drinks and those for rum, whisky, and heavy ales, a vast deal of drunkenness might be prevented, and yet the foreign habits not be too much interfered with, and comparatively innocent pleasures permitted.

In small towns and villages, a reasonable compromise would seem to be to allow each municipality to control the matter in the mode it preferred: some

THE FORTUNES OF A STREET WAIF.

(Fourth Stage.)

communities in this way, forbidding all sale of intoxicating liquors, and others permitting it, under conditions; but each being responsible for the evils or benefits of the system it adopted.

If a student of history were reviewing the gloomy list of the evils which have most cursed mankind, which have wasted households, stained the hand of man with his fellow's blood, sown quarrels and hatreds, broken women's hearts, and ruined children in their earliest years, bred poverty and crime, he would place next to the bloody name of War, the black word—INTEMPERANCE. No wonder that the best minds of modern times are considering most seriously the soundest means of checking it. If abstinence were the natural and only means, the noble soul would still say, in the words of Paul: "It is good neither to eat flesh, nor to drink wine, nor anything whereby thy brother stumbleth."

But abstinence is not thoroughly natural; it has no chance of a universal acceptance; and experience shows that other and wider means must be employed. We must trust to the imperceptible and widely-extended influences of civilization, of higher tastes, and more refined amusements on the masses. We must employ the powers of education, and, above all, the boundless force of Religion, to elevate the race above the tyranny of this tremendous appetite.

4

CHAPTER VII.

ORGANIZATION OF A REMEDY.

In New York, we believe almost alone among the great capitals of the world, a profound and sustained effort for many years has been made to cut off the sources and diminish the numbers of the dangerous classes; and, as the records of crime show, with a marked effect.

In most large cities, the first practical difficulty is the want of a united organization to work upon the evils connected with this lowest class. There are too many scattered efforts, aiming in a desultory manner at this and that particular evil, resulting from the condition of the children of the streets. There is no unity of plan and of work. Every large city should form one Association or organization, whose sole object should be to deal alone with the sufferings, wants, and crimes, arising from a class of youth who are homeless, ignorant, or neglected. The injuries to public morals and property from such a class are important enough to call out the best thought and utmost energy and inventiveness of charitable men and women to prevent them. Where an association devotes itself, thus to one great public evil, a thousand remedies or ingenious devices of cure and prevention will be hit upon, when, with a more miscellaneous field of work, the best methods would be overlooked. So threatening is the danger in every populous town from the children who are neglected, that the best talent ought to be engaged to study their condition and devise their improvement, and the highest character and most ample means should be offered to guarantee and make permanent the movements devised for their elevation.

The lack of all this in many European capitals is a reason that so little, comparatively, has been done to meet these tremendous dangers.

Then, again, in religious communities, such as the English and American, there is too great a confidence in *technical religious* means.

We would not breathe a word against the absolute necessity of Christianity in any scheme of thorough social reform. If the Christian Church has one garland on its altars which time does not wither nor skepticism destroy, which is fresh and beautiful each year, it is that humble offering laid there through every age by the neglected little ones of society, whom the most enlightened Stoicism despised and Paganism cast out, but who have been blessed and saved by its ministrations of love. No skeptical doubt or "rationalism" can ever pluck from the Christian Church this, its purest crown.

To attempt to prevent or cure the fearful moral diseases of our lowest classes without Christianity, is like trying to carry through a sanitary reform in a city without sunlight.

But the mistake we refer to, is a too great use of, or confidence in, the old technical methods—such as distributing tracts, and holding prayer-meetings, and scattering Bibles. The neglected and ruffian class which we are considering are in no way affected directly by such influences as these. New methods must be invented for them.

Another obstacle, in American cities, to any comprehensive results of reform or prevention among these classes, has been the too blind following of European precedents. In Europe, the labor-market is fully supplied. There is a steady pressure of population on subsistence. No general method of prevention or charity can be attempted which interferes with the rights of honest and self-supporting labor. The victims of society, the unfortunate, the *enfants perdus*, must be retained, when aided at all, in public institutions. They cannot be allowed to compete with outside industry. They are not wanted in the general market of labor. They must be kept in *Asylums*.

Now, Asylums are a bequest of monastic days. They breed a species of character which is monastic—indolent, unused to struggle; subordinate indeed, but with little independence and manly vigor. If

the subjects of the modern mo ...... ˈ˙˙ˈengaged in
nates—especially if they be already somewhat ....ˈʰᵃᵗ
with vice and crime—the effect is a weakening of
true masculine vigor, an increase of the apparent virtues, and a hidden growth of secret and contagious
vices. Moreover, the life under the machinery of an
"Institution" does not prepare for the thousand petty
hand-labors of a poor man's cottage. But, greatest
of all objections, the asylum system is, of necessity,
immensely expensive, and can reach but a comparatively small number of subjects.

These various obstacles and difficulties, which im-
pede thorough work for the elevation of our worst
classes, can, however, be overcome.

PIONEER WORK.

Some twenty years ago, the then Chief of Police
of New York, Captain Matsell, put forth a report on
the condition of the street-children of the city, which
aroused universal anxiety, and called forth much compassion. The writer of this was then engaged (in 1852)
outside of his professional duties in rather desultory
and despairing labors for the reform of adult prisoners
on Blackwell's Island and the squalid poor in the Five-
Points district. It was a Sisyphus-like work, and
soon discouraged all engaged in it. We seemed in
those infernal regions to repeat the toil of the Da-
naides, and to be attempting to fill the leaky vessel

.y by efforts which left it as empty as before. What soon struck all engaged in those labors was the immense number of boys and girls floating and drifting about our streets, with hardly any assignable home or occupation, who continually swelled the multitude of criminals, prostitutes, and vagrants.

Saddest of all sights was the thin child's face, so often seen behind prison-bars, and the melancholy procession of little children who were continually passing through that gloomy Egyptian portal, which seemed to some of us then always inscribed with the scroll over the entrance of the Inferno, "Here leave all hope behind!"

It was evident soon, to all who thought upon the subject, that what New York most of all needed was some grand, comprehensive effort to check the growth of the "dangerous classes."

The "Social Evil," of course, was pressed continually on the minds of those engaged in these labors. Mr. Pease was then making a most heroic effort to meet this in its worst form in the Five-Points region. No one whom we have ever known was so qualified for this desperate work, or was so successful in it. Still, it was but one man against a sea of crime. The waves soon rolled over these enthusiastic and devoted labors, and the waste of misfortune and guilt remained as desolate and hopeless as before. It was clear that whatever was done there, must be done in the source and origin of the evil—in prevention, not cure.

The impression deepened both with those engaged in these benevolent labors and with the community, that a general Organization should be formed which should deal alone with the evils and dangers threatened from the class of neglected youth then first coming plainly into public view. Those who possessed property-interests in the city saw the immense loss and damage which would occur from such an increasing community of young thieves and criminals. The humane felt for the little waifs of society who thus, through no fault of their own, were cast out on the currents of a large city; and the religious recognized it as a solemn duty to carry the good news of Christianity to these "heathen at home." Everything seemed in readiness for some comprehensive and well-laid scheme of benevolence and education for the street-children of New York.

A number of our citizens, with the present writer threw themselves into a somewhat original method for benefiting the young "roughs" and vagabond boys of the metropolis. This was known as the effort of the

"BOYS' MEETINGS."

The theory of these original assemblages was, that the "sympathy of an audience" might be used to influence these wild and untutored young Arabs when ordinary agencies were of no avail. The street-boys, as is well-known, are exceedingly sharp and

keen, and, being accustomed to theatrical perform-
ances, are easily touched by real oratory, and by
dramatic instruction; but they are also restless, soon
tired of long exhortations, and somewhat given to *chaff*.

The early days of those "Boys' Meetings" were
stormy. Sometimes the salutatory exercises from the
street were showers of stones; sometimes a general
scrimmage occurred over the benches; again, the
visitors or missionaries were pelted by some opposi-
tion-gang, or bitter enemies of the lads who attended
the meeting. The exercises, too, must be conducted
with much tact, or they broke up with a laugh or in a
row. The platform of the Boys' Meeting seemed to
become a kind of chemical test of the gaseous element
in the brethren's brains. One pungent criticism we
remember—on a pious and somewhat sentimental
Sunday-school brother, who, in one of our meetings,
had been putting forth vague and declamatory religious exhortation—in the words "*Gas! gas!*" whis-
pered with infinite contempt from one hard-faced
young disciple to another. Unhappy, too, was the
experience of any more daring missionary who ventured to question these youthful inquirers.

Thus—"In this parable, my dear boys, of the
Pharisee and the publican, what is meant by the
'publican?'"

"Alderman, sir, wot keeps a pot-house!" "Dimo-
crat, sir!" "Black Republican, sir!"

Or—"My boys, what is the great end of man! When is he happiest! How would *you* feel happiest?"

" When we'd plenty of hard cash, sir!"

Or—"My *dear* boys, when your father and your mother forsake you, *who* will take you up!"

" The Purlice, sir (very seriously), the Purlice!"

They sometimes took their own quiet revenge among themselves, in imitating the Sunday-school addresses delivered to them.

Still, ungoverned, prematurely sharp, and accustomed to all vileness, as these lads were, words which came forth from the depths of a man's or woman's heart would always touch some hidden chord in theirs. Pathos and eloquence vibrated on their heart-strings as with any other audience. Beneath all their rough habits and rude words was concealed the solemn monitor, the *Daimōn*, which ever whispers to the lowest of human creatures, that some things are wrong—are not to be done.

Whenever the speaker could, for a moment only, open the hearts of the little street-rovers to this voice, there was in the wild audience a silence almost painful, and every one instinctively felt, with awe, a mysterious Presence in the humble room, which blessed both those who spake and those who heard.

Whatever was bold, or practical, or heroic in sentiment, and especially the dramatic in oratory, was

most intently listened to by these children of misfortune.

The Boys' Meetings, however, were not, and could
not, in the nature of things, be a permanent success.
They were the pioneer-work for more profound labors
for this class. They cleared the way, and showed the
character of the materials. Those engaged in them
learned the fearful nature of the evils they were
struggling with, and how little any moral influence on
one day can do to combat them. These wild gatherings, like meetings for street-preaching, do not seem
suited to the habits of our population; they are too
much an occasion for frolic. They have given way to,
and been merged in, much more disciplined assemblages for precisely the same class, which again are
only one step in a long series of moral efforts in their
behalf, that are in operation each day of every week
and month, and extend through years.

The first of these meetings was opened in 1848,
under the charge of Mr. A. D. F. Randolph by the
members of a Presbyterian church, in a hall on the
corner of Christopher and Hudson Streets. This was
followed by another in a subsequent year in Wooster
Street, commenced by the indefatigable exertions of
the wife of Rev. Dr. G. B. Cheever, and sustained
especially by Mr. B. J. Howland and W. C. Russell.

The writer took more or less part in those, but was
especially engaged in founding one in Sixth Street,

near Second Avenue; another in 118 Avenue D, from
which arose the "Wilson School" and the Avenue D
Mission; one in King Street, near Hudson, from
which came the Cottage-Place Mission; and another
in Greenwich Street, near Vandam Street.

CHAPTER VIII.

A NEW ORGANIZATION.

ALL those who were engaged in these efforts felt their inadequacy, and we resolved to meet at different private houses to discuss the formation of some more comprehensive effort. At length, in 1853, we organized, and, to the great surprise of the writer, his associates suggested that he should take the position of executive officer of the new and untried Association. He was at that time busied in literary and editorial pursuits, but had expected soon to carry out the purpose of his especial training, and to become a preacher. He never dreamed of making a life-pursuit of it in the beginning, or during a number of years; but "the call" of the neglected and outcast was too strong for him, finally, to listen to any other, and the humble charity at length became a moral and educational movement so profound and earnest as to repay the life-endeavors of any man. He has never regretted having cast aside whatever chance he may have had for the prizes and honors of life, for the sake of the forgotten and the unfortunate, and, above all, for

His sake to whom we owe all. Indeed, he holds himself most fortunate in his profession, for it may be said there is no occupation to which man can devote himself, where he can have such unmingled happiness, as when he is assuaging human misery and raising the ignorant and depressed to a higher life.

THE TRUSTEES.

One of the most energetic members of this new body, in the beginning, was a nephew of Dr. Channing—a Unitarian, Mr. Wm. C. Russell—a man of singular earnestness of character, now Professor of History and Vice-President in Cornell University. With him was associated a friend, Mr. B. J. Howland, of peculiar compassion of nature, whose life almost consisted of the happiness it shed on others— he also being a Unitarian. Then, on the other side, theologically, was Judge John L. Mason, one of the pillars of the Presbyterian Church, from an old and honored Presbyterian family. His accurate legality of mind and solidity of character were of immense advantage to the youthful Association, while, under a formal exterior, he had a most merciful heart for all kinds of human misery. He was our presiding officer for many years, and did most faithful and thorough work for the charity. With him representing the Congregationalists, was a very careful and judicious man, engaged for many years in Sunday-schools and similar movements, Mr. Wm. C. Gilman. The Dutch Reformed were represented by an experienced friend of education, Mr. M. T. Hewitt; and the Presbyterians again by one of such gentleness and humanity, that all sects might have called him Brother—Mr. W. L. King. To these was added one who has been a great impelling force of this humane movement ever since— a man of large, generous nature, and much impulse of temperament, with a high and refined culture, who has done more to gain support for this charity with the business community, where he is so influential, than any other one man—Mr. J. E. Williams, also a Unitarian. Mr. W. had also been engaged in similar charities in Boston.

During the first year, we added to our board from the Methodists, Dr. J. L. Phelps; from the Episcopalians, Mr. Archibald Russell (since deceased), who has accomplished so much as the President of the Board of the Five Points House of Industry; Mr. George Bird, and Mr. A. S. Hewitt, who is now the managing head of that great educational institution, the Cooper Union; from the Presbyterians, the celebrated Mr. Cyrus W. Field; and from the "Come-outers," Mr. C. W. Elliott, the genial author of the "New England History." Of all the first trustees, the only ones in office in 1871 are J. E. Williams, B. J. Howland, M. T. Hewitt, and C. L. Brace.

On a subsequent year we elected a gentleman who

especially represented a religious body that has always profoundly sympathized with our enterprise—Mr. Howard Potter, the son of the eminent Episcopal Bishop of Pennsylvania, and nephew of the Bishop of New York. And yet, of all the members of our Board, no one has been more entirely unsectarian than this trustee; and certainly no one has thrown into our charity more heart and a more unbiased judgment. Mr. Potter is still trustee. Through him and Mr. R. J. Livingston, who was chosen a few years after, the whole accounts of the Society were subsequently put in a clear shape, and the duties of the trustees in supervision made distinct and regular.

It is an evidence of the simple desire for doing good which actuated these gentlemen, and of the possibility of a "Christian Union" that, though representing so many different sects, and ardently attached to them, there never was in all the subsequent years the slightest difference among them resulting from their divergent views on speculative topics. Nearly all of them were engaged practically in laboring among the dangerous classes. Mr. Howland and Mr. Russell had struggled most earnestly for a considerable period to reform the morals and elevate the character of the degraded population near "Rotten Row," in Laurens street, and their "Boys' Meeting" had been one of the most spirited efforts in this direction to be seen in the city.

Several of the gentlemen I have mentioned have become distinguished in their various professions, but it may be doubted if they will look back on any action of their public careers with more satisfaction than their first earnest efforts to lay firmly the foundations of a broad structure of charity, education, and reform.

The organization was happily named

"THE CHILDREN'S AID SOCIETY OF NEW YORK."

This association, which, from such small beginnings has grown to so important dimensions, was thus formed in 1853, and was subsequently incorporated in 1856, under the general Act of the State of New York in relation to Charitable Associations.

A small office on the corner of Amity Street was opened, with a single lad in attendance, besides the present writer.

The public, so profound was the sense of these threatening evils, immediately came forward with its subscriptions—the first large gift (fifty dollars) being from the wife of the principal property-holder in the city, Mrs. William B. Astor.

Most touching of all was the crowd of wandering little ones who immediately found their way to the office. Ragged young girls who had nowhere to lay their heads; children driven from drunkards' homes; orphans who slept where they could find a box or a stairway; boys cast out by step-mothers or step-fathers; newsboys, whose incessant answer to our question, "Where do you live?" rung in our ears, "*Don't live nowhere!*" little bootblacks, young peddlers "canawl-boys," who seem to drift into the city every winter, and live a vagabond life; pickpockets and petty thieves trying to get honest work; child beggars and flower-sellers growing up to enter courses of crime—all this motley throng of infantile misery and childish guilt passed through our doors, telling their simple stories of suffering, and loneliness, and temptation, until our hearts became sick; and the present writer, certainly, if he had not been able to stir up the fortunate classes to aid in assuaging these fearful miseries, would have abandoned the post in discouragement and disgust.

The following letter, written at this time by the Secretary, is appended, as showing the feeling of those founding the Society:

"W. L. KING, Esq.:

"MY DEAR SIR—We were very glad to get your first letter to Mr. Russell, giving us your good wishes and your subscription. It was read aloud to our committee, and we have several times expressed ourselves as very much regretting your absence. I should have certainly written you, but I did not know your address. I received yours from Macon yesterday, and hasten to reply.

"Everything goes on well. We have taken Judge Mason and Mr. J. E. Williams (formerly of Boston) into the committee. I enclose a circular, to which, according to the permission which you gave us, we have placed your name. We have opened one room for a workshop in Wooster Street, where we expect to have

Magic Lantern

forty or fifty boys. The work is shoe-making. The boys jump at the chance gladly. Some three 'Newsboys' Meetings' we are just getting under way, though the churches move slowly. Our Meeting in Avenue D is improving every Sunday, and is very full. Next Thursday eve, I have made arrangements for a lecture on the Magic Lantern to the boys of our Meeting. We gave out tickets on Sunday. The Girls' meeting is large, and you know, perhaps, is now widened into an 'Industrial School'* for girls, which meets every day in our Building in Avenue D. They have some fifty girls at work there—the worst vagrant kind. Public attention is arousing everywhere to this matter; and the first two or three days after our Appeal was published, we had some $400 sent in, part in cash, without the trouble of collecting. We shall begin collecting this week. I have been interrupted here by a very intelligent little newsboy, who is here vagrant and helpless—ran away from his step-father. One of the pressmen sent him to me. We shall put him in our workshop.

"I pray with you, dear sir, for God's blessing on our young enterprise. It is a grand one; but without HIM I see how useless it will be. If we succeed even faintly, I shall feel that we have not lived in vain. Surely Christ will be with us in these feeble efforts for his poor creatures.

"Very truly yours,

"CHARLES L. BRACE.

"NEW YORK, March 7, 1853.

"P. S.—I forgot to tell you the name we have chosen—'Children's Aid Society.'

"Office, No. 683 Broadway, 2d floor, New York."

The following is the first circular of

THE CHILDREN'S AID SOCIETY.

"This society has taken its origin in the deeply settled feelings of our citizens, that something must be done to meet the increasing crime and poverty among the destitute children of New York. Its objects are to help this class by opening Sunday

* "The Wilson School."

Meetings and Industrial Schools, and, gradually as means shall
be furnished, by forming Lodging-houses and Reading-rooms for
children, and by employing paid agents whose sole business
shall be to care for them.

"As Christian men, we cannot look upon this great multitude
of unhappy, deserted, and degraded boys and girls without feeling our responsibility to GOD for them. We remember that
they have the same capacities, the same need of kind and good
influences, and the same Immortality as the little ones in our
own homes. We bear in mind that One died for them, even as
for the children of the rich and happy. Thus far, alms-houses
and prisons have done little to affect the evil. But a small part
of the vagrant population can be shut up in our asylums, and
judges and magistrates are reluctant to convict children so young
and ignorant that they hardly seem able to distinguish good and
evil. The class increases. Immigration is pouring in its multitude of poor foreigners, who leave these young outcasts everywhere abandoned in our midst. For the most part, the boys grow
up utterly by themselves. No one cares for them, and they care
for no one. Some live by begging, by petty pilfering, by bold
robbery; some earn an honest support by peddling matches, or
apples, or newspapers; others gather bones and rags in the street
to sell. They sleep on steps, in cellars, in old barns, and in markets, or they hire a bed in filthy and low lodging-houses. They
cannot read; they do not go to school or attend a church. Many
of them have never seen the Bible. Every cunning faculty is
intensely stimulated. They are shrewd and old in vice, when
other children are in leading-strings. Few influences which are
kind and good ever reach the vagrant boy. And, yet, among
themselves they show generous and honest traits. Kindness
can always touch them.

"The girls, too often, grow up even more pitiable and deserted.
Till of late no one has ever cared for them. They are the cross-
walk sweepers, the little apple-peddlers, and candy-sellers of
our city; or, by more questionable means, they earn their scanty
bread. They traverse the low, vile streets alone, and live without mother or friends, or any share in what we should call a
home. They also know little of God or Christ, except by name.
They grow up passionate, ungoverned, with no love or kindness

ever to soften the heart. We all know their short wild life—and the sad end.

"These boys and girls, it should be remembered, will soon form the great lower class of our city. They will influence elections; they may shape the policy of the city; they will, assuredly, if unreclaimed, poison society all around them. They will help to form the great multitude of robbers, thieves, vagrants, and prostitutes who are now such a burden upon the law-respecting community.

"In one ward alone of the city, the Eleventh, there were, in 1852, out of 12,000 children between the ages of five and sixteen, only 7,000 who attended school, and only 2,500 who went to Sabbath School; leaving 5,000 without the common privileges of education, and about 9,000 destitute of public religious influence.

"In view of these evils we have formed an Association which shall devote itself entirely to this class of vagrant children. We do not propose in any way to conflict with existing asylums and institutions, but to render them a hearty co-operation, and, at the same time, to fill a gap, which, of necessity, they all have left. A large multitude of children live in the city who cannot be placed in asylums, and yet who are uncared-for and ignorant and vagrant. We propose to give to these work, and to bring them under religious influence. As means shall come in, it is designed to district the city, so that hereafter every Ward may have its agent, who shall be a friend to the vagrant child. 'Boys' Sunday Meetings' have already been formed, which we hope to see extended until every quarter has its place of preaching to boys. With these we intend to connect 'Industrial Schools,' where the great temptations to this class arising from want of work may be removed, and where they can learn an honest trade. Arrangements have been made with manufacturers, by which, if we have the requisite funds to begin, five hundred boys in different localities can be supplied with paying work. We hope, too, especially to be the means of draining the city of these children, by communicating with farmers, manufacturers, or families in the country, who may have need of such for employment. When homeless boys are found by our agents, we mean to get them homes in the families of respectable, needy persons in the city, and put them in the way of an honest living.

We design, in a word, to bring humane and kindly influences to bear on this forsaken class—to preach in various modes the gospel of Christ to the vagrant children of New York.

"Numbers of our citizens have long felt the evils we would remedy, but few have the leisure or the means to devote themselves personally to this work with the thoroughness which it requires. This society, as we propose, shall be a medium through which all can, in their measure, practically help the poor children of the city.

"We call upon all who recognize that these are the little ones of Christ; all who believe that crime is best averted by sowing good influences in childhood; all who are the friends of the helpless, to aid us in our enterprise. We confidently hope this wide and practical movement will have its full share of Christian liberality. And we earnestly ask the contributions of those able to give, to help us in carrying forward the work.

*　　*　　*　　*　　*　　*　　*

"March, 1853."

DENS OF MISERY AND CRIME.

In investigating closely the different parts of the city, with reference to future movements for their benefit, I soon came to know certain centres of crime and misery, until every lane and alley, with its filth and wretchedness and vice, became familiar as the lanes of a country homestead to its owner. There was the infamous German "Rag-pickers' Den," in Pitt and Willett Streets—double rows of houses, flaunting with dirty banners, and the yards heaped up with bones and refuse, where cholera raged unchecked in its previous invasion. Here the wild life of the children soon made them outcasts and thieves.

Then came the murderous blocks in Cherry and Water Streets, where so many dark crimes were con-

tinually committed, and where the little girls who
flitted about with baskets and wrapped in old shawls
became familiar with vice before they were out of
childhood.

There were the thieves' Lodging-houses, in the
lower wards, where the street-boys were trained by
older pickpockets and burglars for their nefarious
callings; the low immigrant boarding-houses and vile
cellars of the First Ward, educating a youthful population for courses of guilt; the notorious rogues' den
in Laurens Street—"Rotten Row"—where, it was
said, no drove of animals could pass by and keep its
numbers intact; and, farther above, the community
of young garroters and burglars around "Hamersley
Street and Cottage Place." And, still more north,
the dreadful population of youthful ruffians and
degraded men and women in "Poverty Lane," near
Sixteenth and Seventeenth streets and Ninth Avenue,
which subsequently ripened into the infamous "Nineteenth-street Gang."

On the east side, again, was "Dutch Hill," near
Forty-second Street, the squatters' village, whence
issued so many of the little peddlers of the city, and
the Eleventh Ward and "Corlear's Hook," where the
"copper-pickers," and young wood-stealers, and the
thieves who beset the ship-yards congregated; while
below, in the Sixth Ward, was the Italian quarter,
where houses could be seen crowded with children,

monkeys, dogs, and all the appurtenances of the corps of organ-grinders, harpers, and the little Italian street-sweepers, who then, ignorant and untrained, wandered through our down-town streets and alleys.

Near each one of these "fever-nests," and centres of ignorance, crime, and poverty, it was our hope and aim eventually to place some agency which should be a moral and physical disinfectant—a seed of reform and improvement amid the wilderness of vice and degradation.

It seemed a too enthusiastic hope to be realized; and, at times, the waves of misery and guilt through these dark places appeared too overwhelming and irresistible for any one effort or association of efforts to be able to stem or oppose them.

How the somewhat ardent hope was realized, and the plan carried out, will appear hereafter.

The first special effort that we put forth was the providing of work for these children, by opening

WORKSHOPS.

These experiments, of which we made many at different times, were not successful. Our object was to render the shops self-supporting. But the irregularity of the class attending them, the work spoiled, and the necessity of competing with skilled labor and often with machinery, soon put us behind. We had one workshop for pegging boots and shoes in Wooster

Street, where we soon got employment for numbers of street-boys; but a machine was suddenly invented for pegging shoes, which drove us out of the field. We tried then paper box and bag-making, carpentering, and other branches; but it may be set down as an axiom, that "Benevolence cannot compete with Selfishness in business." Philanthropy will never cut down the expenses of production, as will individual self-interest.

Moreover, these artificial workshops excite the jealousy of the trades, while they are not so necessary in this country as in Europe, because the demand is so great here for children's labor.

We soon discovered that if we could train the children of the streets to habits of industry and self-control and neatness, and give them the rudiments of moral and mental education, we need not trouble ourselves about anything more. A child in any degree educated and disciplined can easily make an honest living in this country. The only occasional exception is with young girls depending on the needle for support, inasmuch as the competition here is so severe. But for these we often were enabled to provide instruction in skilled labor, which supported them easily; and, if taught cleanliness and habits of order and punctuality, they had no difficulty in securing places as upper servants, or they soon married into a better class.

LODGING-HOUSES FOR HOMELESS BOYS—AS THEY ARE.

(The Newsboys' House.)

No. 2.

CHAPTER IX.

HOMELESS BOYS.

THE NEWSBOYS' LODGING-HOUSE.

THE spectacle which earliest and most painfully arrested my attention in this work, were the *houseless boys* in various portions of the city.

There seemed to be a very considerable class of lads in New York who bore to the busy, wealthy world about them something of the same relation which Indians bear to the civilized Western settlers. They had no settled home, and lived on the outskirts of society, their hand against every man's pocket, and every man looking on them as natural enemies; their wits sharpened like those of a savage, and their principles often no better. Christianity reared its temples over them, and Civilization was carrying on its great work, while they—a happy race of little heathens and barbarians—plundered, or frolicked, or led their roving life, far beneath. Sometimes they seemed to me, like what the police call them, "street-rats," who gnawed at the foundations of society, and scampered away when light was brought near them. Their life was, of course, a painfully hard one. To sleep in boxes, or under stairways, or in hay-barges on the coldest

5

winter-nights, for a mere child, was hard enough; but
often to have no food, to be kicked and cuffed by the
older ruffians, and shoved about by the police, standing barefooted and in rags under doorways as the
winter-storm raged, and to know that in all the great
city there was not a single door open with welcome
to the little rover—this was harder.

Yet, with all this, a more light-hearted youngster
than the street-boy is not to be found.   He is always
ready to make fun of his own sufferings, and to
"chaff" others.   His face is old from exposure and
his sharp "struggle for existence;" his clothes flutter
in the breeze; and his bare feet peep out from the
broken boots.   Yet he is merry as a clown, and always
ready for the smallest joke, and quick to take "a
point" or to return a repartee.   His views of life are
mainly derived from the more mature opinions of
"flash-men," engine-runners, cock-fighters, pugilists,
and pickpockets, whom he occasionally is permitted
to look upon with admiration at some select pot-house;
while his more ideal pictures of the world about him,
and his literary education, come from the low theatres,
to which he is passionately attached.   His morals are,
of course, not of a high order, living, as he does, in a
fighting, swearing, stealing, and gambling set.   Yet
he has his code; he will not get drunk; he pays his
debts to other boys, and thinks it dishonorable to sell
papers on their beat, and, if they come on his, he

administers summary justice by "punching;" he is generous to a fault, and will always divide his last sixpence with a poorer boy. "Life is a strife" with him, and money its reward; and, as bankruptcy means to the street-boy a night on the door-steps without supper, he is sharp and reckless, if he can only earn or get enough to keep him above water. His temptations are, to cheat, steal, and lie. His religion is vague. One boy, who told me he "didn't live nowhere," who had never heard of Christ, said he had heard of God, and the boys thought it "kind o' lucky" to say over something to Him which one of them had learned, when they were sleeping out in boxes.

With all their other vices, it is remarkable how few. of these smaller street-boys ever take liquor. And their kindness to one another, when all are in the utmost destitution, is a credit to human nature.*

Their money is unfortunately apt to slip away, especially for gambling and petty lotteries, called "policy-tickets." A tradition in the remote past of some boy who drew a hundred dollars in these lotteries still pervades the whole body, and they annually sink a considerable portion of their hard-earned pennies in "policy-tickets."

* Only recently, a poor hump-backed lad in the Newsboys' Lodging-house gave his dollar, and collected nine more from the boys, for the family of the children who were lost in New Jersey.

The choice of these lads of a night's resting-place is sometimes almost as remarkable as was Gavroche's in "Les Misérables." Two little newsboys slept one winter in the iron tube of the bridge at Harlem; two others made their bed in a burned-out safe in Wall Street. Sometimes they ensconced themselves in the cabin of a ferry-boat, and thus spent the night. Old boilers, barges, steps, and, above all, steam-gratings, were their favorite beds.

In those days the writer would frequently see ten or a dozen of them, piled together to keep one another warm, under the stairs of the printing-offices.

In planning the alleviation of these evils, it was necessary to keep in view one object, not to weaken the best quality of this class—their sturdy independence—and, at the same time, their prejudices and habits were not too suddenly to be assailed. They had a peculiar dread of Sunday Schools and religious exhortations—I think partly because of the general creed of their older associates, but more for fear that these exercises were a "pious dodge" for trapping them into the House of Refuge or some place of detention.

The first thing to be aimed at in the plan was, to treat the lads as independent little dealers, and give them nothing without payment, but at the same time to offer them much more for their money than they could get anywhere else. Moral, educational, and religious influences were to come in afterward. Securing them through their interests, we had a permanent hold of them.

Efforts were made by the writer among our influential citizens and in various churches, public meetings were held, articles written, the press interested, and at length sufficient money was pledged to make the experiment. The board of the new Society gave its approval, and a loft was secured in the old "Sun Buildings," and fitted up as a lodging-room, and in March, 1854, the first Lodging-house for street-boys or newsboys in this country was opened.

An excellent superintendent was found in the person of a carpenter, Mr. C. C. Tracy, who showed remarkable ingenuity and tact in the management of these wild lads. These little subjects regarded the first arrangements with some suspicion and much contempt. To find a good bed offered them for six cents, with a bath thrown in, and a supper for four cents, was a hard fact, which they could rest upon and understand; but the motive was evidently "gaseous." There was "no money in it"—that was clear. The Superintendent was probably "a street preacher," and this was a trap to get them to Sunday Schools, and so prepare them for the House of Refuge. Still, they might have a lark there, and it could be no worse than "bumming," i. e., sleeping out. They laid their plans for a general scrimmage in the school-room—first cutting off the gas, and then a row in the bedroom.

The superintendent, however, in a bland and benevolent way, nipped their plans in the bud. The gas-pipes were guarded; the rough ring-leaders were politely dismissed to the lower door, where an officer looked after their welfare; and, when the first boots began to fly from a little fellow's bed, he found himself suddenly snaked out by a gentle but muscular hand, and left in the cold to shiver over his folly. The others began to feel that a mysterious authority was getting even with them, and thought it better to nestle in their warm beds.

Little sleeping, however, was there among them that night; but ejaculations sounded out—such as, "I say, Jim, this is rayther better'an bummin'—eh?" "My eyes! what soft beds these is!" "Tom! it's 'most as good as a steam-gratin', and there ain't no M. P.'s to poke neither!" "I'm glad I ain't a bummer to-night!"

A good wash and a breakfast sent the lodgers forth in the morning, happier and cleaner, if not better, than when they went in. This night's success established its popularity with the newsboys. The "Fulton Lodge" soon became a boys' hotel, and one loft was known among them as the "Astor House."

Quietly and judiciously did Mr. Tracy advance his lines among them.

"Boys," said he, one morning, "there was a gentleman here this morning, who wanted a boy in an office, at three dollars a week."

"My eyes! Let *me* go, sir!" And—"*Me*, sir!"

"But he wanted a boy who could write a good hand."

Their countenances fell.

"Well, now, suppose we have a night-school, and learn to write—what do you say, boys?"

"Agreed, sir."

And so arose our evening-school.

The Sunday Meeting, which is now an "institution," was entered upon in a similarly discreet manner. The lads had been impressed by a public funeral, and Mr. Tracy suggested their listening to a little reading from the Bible. They consented, and were a good deal surprised at what they heard. The "Golden Rule" struck them as an altogether impossible kind of precept to obey, especially when one was "stuck and short," and "had to live." The marvels of the Bible—the stories of miracles and the like—always seemed to them natural and proper. That a Being of such a character as Christ should control Nature and disease, was appropriate to their minds. And it was a kind of comfort to these young vagabonds that the Son of God was so often homeless, and that he belonged humanly to the working classes. The petition for "daily bread" (which a celebrated divine has declared "unsuited to modern conditions of civilization") they always rolled out with a peculiar unction. I think that the conception of a Superior Being, who

knew just the sort of privations and temptations that
followed them, and who felt especially for the poorer
classes, who was always near them, and pleased at
true manhood in them, did keep afterward a considerable number of them from lying and stealing and
cheating and vile pleasures.

Their singing was generally prepared for by taking
off their coats and rolling up their sleeves, and was
entered into with a gusto.

The voices seemed sometimes to come from a dif-
erent part of their natures from what we saw with the
bodily eyes.   There was, now and then, a gentle and
minor key, as if a glimpse of something purer and
higher passed through these rough lads. A favorite
song was, "There's a Rest for the Weary," though
more untiring youngsters than these never frisked
over the earth; and "There's a Light in the Window
for Thee, Brother," always pleased them, as if they
imagined themselves wandering alone through a great
city at night, and at length a friendly light shone in
the window for them.

Their especial vice of money-wasting the Superintendent broke up by opening a Savings-bank, and
allowing the boys to vote how long it should be closed.
The small daily deposits accumulated to such a degree that the opening gave them a great surprise at
the amounts which they possessed, and they began to
feel thus the "sense of property," and the desire of

accumulation, which, economists tell us, is the base of all civilization. A liberal interest was also soon allowed on deposits, which stimulated the good habit. At present, from two hundred to three hundred dollars will often be saved by the lads in a month.

The same device, and constant instruction, broke up gambling, though I think policy-tickets were never fairly undermined among them.

The present Superintendent and Matron of the Newsboys' Lodging-house, Mr. and Mrs. O'Connor (at Nos. 49 and 51 Park Place), are unsurpassed in such institutions in their discipline, order, good management, and excellent housekeeping. The floors, over which two hundred or two hundred and fifty street-boys tread daily, are as clean as a man-of-war's deck. The Sunday-evening meetings are as attentive and orderly as a church, the week-evening school quiet and studious. All that mass of wild young humanity is kept in perfect order, and brought under a thousand good influences.

The Superintendent has had a very good preliminary experience for this work in the military service—having been in the British army in the Crimea. The discipline which he maintains is excellent. He is a man, too, of remarkable generosity of feeling, and a good "provider." One always knows that his boys will have enough to eat, and that everything will be managed liberally—and justly. It is truly remarkable during how many years he controlled that great multitude of little vagabonds and "roughs," and yet with scarcely ever even a complaint from any source against him. For such success is needed the utmost kindness, and, at the same time, the strictest justice. His wife has been almost like a mother to the boys.

In the course of a year the population of a town passes through the Lodging-house—in 1869 and '70, *eight thousand eight hundred and thirty-five* different boys. Many are put in good homes; some find places for themselves; others drift away—no one knows whither. They are an army of orphans—regiments of children who have not a home or friend—a multitude of little street-rovers who have no place where to lay their heads. They are being educated in the streets rapidly to be thieves and burglars and criminals. The Lodging-house is at once school, church, intelligence-office, and hotel for them. Here they are shaped to be honest and industrious citizens; here taught economy, good order, cleanliness, and morality; here Religion brings its powerful influences to bear upon them; and they are sent forth to begin courses of honest livelihood.

The Lodging-houses repay their expenses to the public ten times over each year, in preventing the growth of thieves and criminals. They are agencies of pure humanity and almost unmingled good. Their only possible reproach could be, that some of their wild subjects are soon beyond their reach, and have been too deeply tainted with the vices of street-life to be touched even by kindness, education, or religion. The number who are saved, however, are most encouragingly large.

The Newsboys' Lodging-house is by no means, however, an entire burden on the charity of the community. During 1870 the lads themselves paid $3,349 toward its expense.

The following is a brief description of the rooms during the past five years:

The first floor is divided into various compartments —a large dining-room, where one hundred and fifty boys can sit down to a table; a kitchen, laundry, store-room, servants' room, and rooms for the family of the superintendent. The next story is partitioned into a school-room, gymnasium, and bath and wash rooms, plentifully supplied with hot and cold water. The hot water and the heat of the rooms are supplied by a steam-boiler on the lower story. The two upper stories are filled with neat iron bedsteads, having two beds each, arranged like ships' bunks over each other; of these there are two hundred and sixty. Here are also the water-vats, into which the many barrelsful used daily are pumped by the engine. The rooms are high and dry, and the floors clean.

It is a commentary on the housekeeping and

accommodations that for eighteen years no case of contagious disease has ever occurred among these thousands of boys.

The New York Newsboys' Lodging-house has been in existence eighteen years. During these years it has lodged 91,326 different boys, restored 7,278 boys to friends, provided 5,126 with homes, furnished 576,-485 lodgings and 469,461 meals. The expense of all this has been $132,888. Of this amount the boys have contributed $32,306.

That the Lodging-house has had a vigorous growth, is shown by the following table:

TABULAR STATEMENT SINCE ORGANIZATION OF NEWSBOYS' LODGING-HOUSE.

YEAR.	No. of Boys.	No. of Lodgings.	No. of Meals.	Returned to friends.	Expenses.	Paid by Boys.	No. of Boys using Bank.	Am'nt saved by them.
1854 to 1855	408	6,872	.....	.....	$1,199 76	$397 56	.....	.....
1855 to 1856	374	7,599	.....	.....	1,431 82	391 26	16	$643 58
1856 to 1857	387	5,157	.....	.....	1,762 56	262 56	116	270 70
1857 to 1858	500	8,026	11,923	.....	1,925 03	298 03	.....	.....
1858 to 1859	3,000	14,000	13,114	.....	2,199 34	807 15	.....	.....
1859 to 1860	4,500	19,747	13,341	.....	2,113 56	955 44	23	110 10
1860 to 1861	4,000	27,390	16,873	100	3,420 57	1,036 98	230	1,259 77
1861 to 1862	3,875	32,954	19,809	247	2,736 08	1,138 88	388	1,376 59
1862 to 1863	3,000	29,409	20,000	396	3,402 82	1,102 33	347	1,315 10
1863 to 1864	6,325	36,572	25,506	437	5,758 16	1,559 10	405	2,080 06
1864 to 1865	6,793	42,446	30,137	576	7,159 95	1,944 22	499	2,515 92
1865 to 1866	7,256	43,797	32,867	633	10,058 13	2,127 44	599	2,486 43
1866 to 1867	8,192	49,519	33,033	719	10,847 79	2,718 79	542	2,121 76
1867 to 1868	8,599	51,740	35,617	819	12,094 00	3,177 69	703	2,203 45
1868 to 1869	8,944	53,610	54,092	896	23,333 45	3,644 49	796	2,057 76
1869 9 months	7,383	39,077	33,207	642	13,445 24	3,180 85	659	1,688 22
1869 to 1870	8,655	55,565	56,128	713	15,102 11	4,214 42	1,107	2,433 60
1870 to 1871	8,835	53,005	53,214	1,100	14,895 03	3,349 77	1,065	2,588 31
Total	91,326	576,485	469,461	7,278	$132,888 40	$32,306 96	7,495	$25,141 35

Extracts from the journal of a visitor from the country:

A VISIT TO THE NEWSBOYS.

"It requires a peculiar person to manage and talk to these boys. Bullet-headed, short-haired, bright-eyed, shirt-sleeved, go-ahead boys. Boys who sell papers, black boots, run on errands, hold horses, pitch pennies, sleep in barrels, and steal their bread. Boys who know at the age of twelve more than the children of ordinary men would have learned at twenty; boys who can cheat you out of your eye-teeth, and are as smart as a steel-trap. They will stand no fooling; they are accustomed to gammon, they live by it. No audience that ever we saw could compare in attitudinizing with this. Heads generally up; eyes full on the speaker; mouths, almost without an exception, closed tightly; hands in pockets; legs stretched out; no sleepers, all wide-awake, keenly alive for a pun, a point, or a slangism. Winding up, Mr. Brace said: 'Well, boys, I want my friends here to see that you have the material for talkers amongst yourselves; whom do you choose for your orator?'

"'Paddy, Paddy,' shouted one and all. 'Come out, Paddy. Why don't you show yourself?' and so on.

"Presently Paddy came forward, and stood upon a stool. He is a youngster, not more than twelve, with a little round eye, a short nose, a lithe form, and chuck-full of fun.

"'Bummers,' said he, 'smoozers, and citizens, I've come down here among ye to talk to yer a little! Me and my friend Brace have come to see how ye'r gittin' along, and to advise yer. You fellers what stands at the shops with yer noses over the railin', smellin' ov the roast beef and the hash—you fellers who's got no home—think of it how we are to encourage ye. [Derisive laughter, "Ha-ha's," and various ironical kinds of applause.] I say, bummers—for you're *all* bummers (in a tone of kind patronage)—*I was a bummer once* [great laughter]—I hate to see you spendin' your money on penny ice-creams and bad cigars. Why don't you save your money? You feller without no boots, how would you like a new pair, eh? [Laughter from all the boys but the one addressed.] Well, I hope you may get 'em, but I

THE NEWSBOY.

(From a Photograph.)

rayther think you won't. I have hopes for you all. I want you to grow up to be rich men—citizens, Government men, lawyers, generals, and influence men. Well, boys, I'll tell you a story. My dad was a hard 'un. One beautiful day he went on a spree, and he came home and told me where's yer mother? and I axed him I didn't know, and he clipt me over the head with an iron pot, and knocked me down, and me mither drapped in on him, and at it they went. [Hi-hi's, and demonstrative applause.] Ah! at it they went, and at it they kept—ye should have seen 'em—and whilst they were fightin', I slipped meself out the back door, and away I went like a scart dog. [Oh, dry up! Bag your head! Simmer down!] Well, boys, I wint on till I kim to the 'Home' [great laughter among the boys], and they took me in [renewed laughter], and did for me, without a cap to me head or shoes to me feet, and thin I ran away, and here I am. Now boys [with mock solemnity], be good, mind yer manners, copy me, and see what you'll become.'

"At this point the boys raised such a storm of hifalutin applause, and indulged in such characteristic demonstrations of delight, that it was deemed best to stop the youthful Demosthenes, who jumped from his stool with a bound that would have done credit to a monkey.

"At this juncture huge pans of apples were brought in, and the boys were soon engaged in munching the delightful fruit, after which the Matron gave out a hymn, and all joined in singing it, during which we took our leave."

A NEWSBOY'S SPEECH. (FROM OUR JOURNAL.)

"Some of these boys, in all their misfortunes, have a humorous eye for their situation—as witness the following speech, delivered by one of them at the Newsboys' Lodginghouse, before the departure of a company to the West. The report is a faithful one, made on the spot. The little fellow mounted a chair, and thus held forth:

"'Boys, gintlemen, chummies: Praps you'd like to hear summit about the West, the great West, you know, where so many of our old friends are settled down and growin' up to be great men, maybe the greatest men in the great Republic. Boys, that's the place for growing Congressmen, and Governors, and Presidents. Do you want to be newsboys always, and shoeblacks, and timber-merchants in a small way by sellin' matches? If ye do you'll stay in New York, but if you don't you'll go out West, and begin to be farmers, for the beginning of a farmer, my boys, is the making of a Congressman, and a President. Do you want to be rowdies, and loafers, and shoulder-hitters? If ye do, why, ye can keep around these diggins. Do you want to be gentlemen and independent citizens? You do—then make tracks for the West, from the Children's Aid Society. If you want to be snoozers, and rummeys, and policy-players, and Peter Funks men, why you'll hang up your caps and stay round the groceries and jine fire-engine and target companies, and go firin' at haystacks for bad quarters; but if ye want to be the man who will make his mark in the country, ye will get up steam, and go ahead, and there's lots on the prairies a waitin' for yes.

"'You haven't any idear of what ye may be yet, if you will only take a bit of my advice. How do you know but, if you are honest, and good, and industerous, you may get so much up in the ranks that you won't call a gineral or a judge your boss. And you'll have servants ov all kinds to tend you, to put you to bed when you are sleepy, and to spoon down your vittles when you are gettin' your grub. Oh, boys! won't that be great! Only think—to have a feller to open your mouth, and put great slices of punkin pie and apple dumplings into it. You will be lifted on hossback when you go for to take a ride on the prairies, and if you choose to go in a wagon, or on a 'scursion, you will find that the hard times don't touch you there; and the best of it will be that if 'tis good to-day, 'twill be better to-morrow.

"But how will it be if you don't go, boys? Why, I'm afeard when you grow too big to live in the Lodging-house any longer, you'll be like lost sheep in the wilderness, as we heard of last Sunday night here, and you'll maybe not find your way out any more. But you'll be found somewhere else. The best of you will be something short of judges and governors, and the feller as has the worst luck—and the worst behaver in the groceries—will be very sure to go from them to the prisons.

"I will now come from the stump. I am booked for the

West in the next company from the Lodging-house. I hear they have big school-houses and colleges there, and that they have a place for me in the winter time; I want to be somebody, and somebody don't live here, no how. You'll find him on a farm in the West, and I hope you'll come to see him soon and stop with him when you go, and let every one of yous be somebody, and be loved and respected. I thank yous, boys, for your patient attention. I can't say more at present, I hope I haven't said too much.' "

THE BUILDING FUND.

An effort was made in the Legislature, a few years since, to obtain a building-fund for the Newsboys' Lodging-house. This was granted from the Excise Fund of the city for the legitimate reason, that those who do most to form drunkards should be compelled to aid in the expense and care of the children of drunkards. Thirty thousand dollars were appropriated from these taxes, provided a similar amount was raised by private subscription. This sum was obtained by the kindness and energy of the friends of the enterprise, and the whole amount ($60,000) was invested in good securities.

In 1872 it had accumulated to $80,000, and the purchase was made of the "Shakespeare Hotel," on the corner of Duane and Chambers Streets, which is now being fitted up and rebuilt as a permanent Lodging-house for Homeless Boys. The building has streets on three sides, and, plenty of air and light. Shops will be let underneath, so that the payments of the boys and the rents received will nearly defray the annual expenses of this charity, thus insuring its permanency.

CHAPTER X.

A GIRL street-rover is to my mind the most painful figure in all the unfortunate crowd of a large city. With a boy, "Arab of the streets," one always has the consolation that, despite his ragged clothes and bed in a box or hay-barge, he often has a rather good time of it, and enjoys many of the delicious pleasures of a child's roving life, and that a fortunate turn of events may at any time make an honest, industrious fellow of him. At heart we cannot say that he is much corrupted; his sins belong to his ignorance and his condition, and are often easily corrected by a radical change of circumstances. The oaths, tobacco-spitting, and slang, and even the fighting and stealing of a street-boy, are not so bad as they look. Refined influences, the checks of religion, and a fairer chance for existence without incessant struggle, will often utterly eradicate these evil habits, and the rough, thieving New York vagrant make an honest, hard-working Western pioneer. It is true that sometimes the habit of vagrancy and idling may be too deeply worked in him for his character to speedily reform; but, if of tender years, a change of circumstances will nearly always bring a change of character.

With a girl-vagrant it is different. She feels homelessness and friendlessness more; she has more of the feminine dependence on affection; the street-trades, too, are harder for her, and the return at night to some lonely cellar or tenement-room, crowded with dirty people of all ages and sexes, is more dreary. She develops body and mind earlier than the boy, and the habits of vagabondism stamped on her in childhood are more difficult to wear off.

Then the strange and mysterious subject of sexual vice comes in. It has often seemed to me one of the most dark arrangements of this singular world that a female child of the poor should be permitted to start on its immortal career with almost every influence about it degrading, its inherited tendencies overwhelming toward indulgence of passion, its examples all of crime or lust, its lower nature awake long before its higher, and then that it should be allowed to soil and degrade its soul before the maturity of reason, and beyond all human possibility of cleansing!

For there is no reality in the sentimental assertion that the sexual sins of the lad are as degrading as those of the girl. The instinct of the female is more toward the preservation of purity, and therefore her fall is deeper—an instinct grounded in the desire of preserving a stock, or even the necessity of perpetuating our race.

Still, were the indulgences of the two sexes of a similar character—as in savage races—were they both following passion alone, the moral effect would not perhaps be so different in the two cases. But the sin of the girl soon becomes what the Bible calls " a sin against one's own body," the most debasing of all sins. She soon learns to offer for sale that which is in its nature beyond all price, and to feign the most sacred affections, and barter with the most delicate instincts. She no longer merely follows blindly and excessively an instinct; she perverts a passion and sells herself. The only parallel case with the male sex would be that in some Eastern communities which are rotting and falling to pieces from their debasing and unnatural crimes. When we hear of such disgusting offenses under any form of civilization, whether it be under the Rome of the Empire, or the Turkey of to-day, we know that disaster, ruin, and death, are near the State and the people.

This crime, with the girl, seems to sap and rot the whole nature. She loses self-respect, without which every human being soon sinks to the lowest depths; she loses the habit of industry, and cannot be taught to work. Having won her food at the table of Nature by unnatural means, Nature seems to cast her out, and henceforth she cannot labor. Living in a state of unnatural excitement, often worked up to a high pitch of nervous tension by stimulants, becoming weak in body and mind, her character loses fixedness of purpose and tenacity and true energy. The diabolical women who support and plunder her, the vile society she keeps, the literature she reads, the business she has chosen or fallen into, serve continually more and more to degrade and defile her. If, in a moment of remorse, she flee away and take honest work, her weakness and bad habits follow her; she is inefficient, careless, unsteady, and lazy; she craves the stimulus and hollow gayety of the wild life she has led; her ill name dogs her; all the wicked have an instinct of her former evil courses; the world and herself are against reform, and, unless she chance to have a higher moral nature or stronger will than most of her class, or unless Religion should touch even her polluted soul, she soon falls back, and gives one more sad illustration of the immense difficulty of a fallen woman rising again.

The great majority of prostitutes, it must be remembered, have had no romantic or sensational history, though they always affect this. They usually relate, and perhaps even imagine, that they have been seduced from the paths of virtue suddenly and by the wiles of some heartless seducer. Often they describe themselves as belonging to some virtuous, respectable, and even wealthy family. Their real history, however, is much more commonplace and matter-of-fact. They have been poor women's daughters, and did not want to work as their mothers did; or they have grown up in a tenement-room, crowded with boys and men, and lost purity before they knew what it was; or they have liked gay company, and have had no good influences around them, and sought pleasure in criminal indulgences; or they have been street-children, poor, neglected, and ignorant, and thus naturally and inevitably have become depraved women. Their sad life and debased character are the natural outgrowth of poverty, ignorance, and laziness. The number among them who have "seen better days," or have fallen from heights of virtue, is incredibly small. They show what fruits neglect in childhood, and want of education and of the habit of labor, and the absence of pure examples, will inevitably bear. Yet in their low estate they always show some of the divine qualities of their sex. The physicians in the Blackwell's Island Hospital say that there are no nurses so tender and devoted to the sick and dying as these girls. And the honesty of their dealings with the washerwomen and shopkeepers, who trust them while in their vile houses, has often been noted.

The words of sympathy and religion always touch their hearts, though the effect passes like the April cloud. On a broad scale, probably no remedy that man could apply would ever cure this fatal disease of society. It may, however, be diminished in its ravages, and prevented in a large measure. The check to its devastations in a laboring or poor class will be the facility of marriage, the opening of new channels of female work, but, above all, the influences of education and Religion.

An incident occurred during our early labors, which is worth preserving:

EXTRACTS FROM JOURNAL DURING 1854.

THE TOMBS.

"Mrs. Forster, the excellent Matron of the Female Department of the prison, had told us of an interesting young German girl, committed for vagrancy, who might just at this crisis be rescued. I entered these soiled and gloomy Egyptian archways, so appropriate and so depressing, that the sight of the low columns and lotus capitals is to me now inevitably associated with the somber and miserable histories of the place.

"After a short waiting, the girl was brought in—a German girl, apparently about fourteen, very thinly but neatly dressed, of slight figure, and a face intelligent and old for her years, the eye passionate and shrewd. I give details because the conversation which followed was remarkable.

"The poor feel, but they can seldom speak. The story she told, with a wonderful eloquence, thrilled to all our hearts; it seemed to us, then, like the first articulate voice from the great poor class of the city.

"Her eye had a hard look at first, but softened when I spoke to her in her own language.

"'Have you been long here?'

"'Only two days, sir.'

"'Why are you here?'

"'I will tell you, sir. I was working out with a lady. I had to get up early and go to bed late, and I never had rest. She worked me always; and, finally, because I could not do everything, she beat me—she beat me like a dog, and I ran away; I could not bear it.'

"The manner of this was wonderfully passionate and eloquent.

"'But I thought you were arrested for being near a place of bad character,' said I.

"'I am going to tell you, sir. The next day I and my father went to get some clothes I left there, and the lady wouldn't give them up; and what could we do? What can the poor do? My father is a poor old man, who picks rags in the streets, and I have never picked rags yet. He said, "I don't want you to be a rag-picker. You are not a child now—people will look at you —you will come to harm." And I said, "No, father, I will help you. We must do something now, I am out of place;" and so I went out. I picked all day, and didn't make much, and I was cold and hungry. Towards night, a gentleman met me—a very fine, well-dressed gentleman, an American, and he said, "Will you go home with me?" and I said, "No." He said, "I will give you twenty shillings," and I told him I would go. And the next morning I was taken up outside by the officer.'

"'Poor girl!' said some one, 'had you forgotten your mother? and what a sin it was!'

"'No, sir, I did remember her. She had no clothes, and I had no shoes; and I have only this (she shivered in her thin dress), and winter is coming on. I know what making money is, sir. I am only fourteen, but I am old enough. I have had to take care of myself ever since I was ten years old, and I have never had a cent given me. It may be a sin, sir (and the tears rained down her cheeks, which she did not try to wipe away). I do not ask you to forgive it. Men can't forgive, but God will forgive. I know about men.

"'The rich do such things and worse, and no one says anything against them. But I, sir—*I am poor!* (This she said with a tone which struck the very heart-strings.) I have never had any one to take care of me. Many is the day I have gone hungry from morning till night, because I did not dare spend a cent or two, the only ones I had. Oh, I have wished sometimes so to die! Why does not God kill me?'

"She was choked by her sobs. We let her calm herself a moment, and then told her our plan of finding her a good home, where she could make an honest living. She was mistrustful. 'I will tell you, *meine Herren ;* I know men, and I do not believe any one, I have been cheated so often. There is no trust in any one. I am not a child. I have lived as long as people twice as old.'

"' But you do not wish to stay in prison?'

"' O God, no! Oh, there is such a weight on my heart here. There is nothing but bad to learn in prison. These dirty Irish girls! I would kill myself if I had to stay here. Why was I ever born? I have such *Kummerniss* (woes) here (she pressed her hand on her heart)—I am poor!'

"We explained our plan more at length, and she became satisfied. We wished her to be bound to stay some years.

"' No, 'said she, passionately, 'I cannot; I confess to you, gentlemen. I should either run away or die, if I was bound.'

"We talked with the matron. She had never known, she said, in her experience, such a remarkable girl. The children there of nine or ten years were often as old as young women, but this girl was an experienced woman. The offense, however, she had no doubt was her first.

"We obtained her release; and one of us, Mr. G., walked over to her house or cabin, some three miles on the other side of Williamsburgh, in order that she might see her parents before she went to her new home.

"As she walked along, she looked up in Mr. G.'s face, and asked, thoughtfully, Why we came there for her? He explained. She listened, and after a little while, said, in broken English, 'Don't you think better for poor little girls to die than live?' He spoke kindly to her, and said something about a good God. She shook her head, 'No, no good God. Why am I so? It always was so. Why much suffer, if good God?' He told her they would get her a supper, and in the morning she should start off and find new friends. She became gradually almost ungoverned—sobbed—would like to die, even threatened suicide in this wild way.

6

"Kindness and calm words at length made her more reasonable. After much trouble, they reached the home or den of the poor rag-picker. The parents were very grateful, and she was to start off the next morning to a country home, where, perhaps finally, the parents will join her.

"For myself, the evening shadow seemed more somber, and the cheerful home-lights less cheerful, as I walked home, remembering such a history.

"Ye who are happy, whose lives have been under sunshine and gentle influences around whom Affection, and Piety, and Love have watched, as ye gather in cheerful circles these autumn evenings, think of these bitter and friendless children of the poor, in the great city. But few have such eloquent expressions as this poor girl, yet all inarticulately feel.

'There are sad histories beneath this gay world—lives over which is the very shadow of death. God be thanked, there is a Heart which feels for them all, where every pang and groan will find a sympathy, which will one day right the wrong, and bring back the light over human life.

"The day is short for us all; but for some it will be a pleasant thought, when we come to lay down our heads at last, that we have eased a few aching hearts, and brought peace and new hope to the dark lives of those whom men had forgotten or cast out."

THE STREET-GIRL'S END.

CHAPTER XI.

THE question of the best mode of legally control-
ling the great evil of prostitution, and confining its
bad physical effects, is a very difficult one.

The merely philosophical inquirer, or even the physician, regarding humanity "in the broad," comes
naturally to the conclusion that this offense is one of
the inevitable evils which always have followed, and
always will follow, the track of civilization; that
it is to be looked upon, like small-pox or scarlet
fever, as a disease of civilized man, and is to be
treated accordingly, by physical and scientific means,
and must be controlled, as it cannot be uprooted,
by legislation. Or they regard it as they do intoxication, as the effect of a misdirected natural desire,
which is everywhere thought to be a legitimate object
both of permission or recognition by government, as
well as of check by rigid laws.

If medical men, their minds are almost exclusively
directed toward the frightful effects on society and
upon the innocent, of the diseases which attend this

offense. They see that legislation would at once check the ravages from these terrible maladies, and that a system of licenses such as is practiced in the Continental cities would prevent them from spreading through society and punishing those who had never sinned. As scientific healers of human maladies, they feel that anything is a gain which lessens human suffering, controls disease, and keeps up the general health of the community.

Their position, too, has been strengthened by the foolish and superstitious arguments of their opponents. It has been claimed that syphilitic disorders are a peculiar and supernatural punishment for sin and wrong-doing; that by interfering with their legitimate action on the guilty, we presume to diminish the punishments inflicted by the Almighty; and, in so far as we cure or restrain these diseases, we lessen one great sanction which nature and Providence have placed before the infraction of the law of virtue.

The medical man, however, replies very pertinently that he has nothing to do with the Divine sanctions; that his business is to cure human diseases and lessen human suffering wherever he find them; and that gout, or rheumatism, or diphtheria, or scarlet fever, are as much "punishments" as the diseases of this vice. If he refused to visit a patient whenever he thought that his sins had brought upon him his diseases, he would have very little occupation, and mankind would receive very little alleviation from the medical art. Nor is he even called upon to refuse to cure a patient who, he knows, will immediately begin again his evil courses. The physician is not a judge or an executioner. He has nothing to do but to cure and alleviate. Influenced by this aspect of his duty, the medical man almost universally advocates licenses to prostitutes, based on medical examination, and a strict legal control of the participants in this offense.

On the other hand, those of us who deal with the moral aspects of the case, and who know the class that are ruined body and soul by this criminal business, have a profound dread of anything which, to the young, should appear to legalize or approve, or even recognize it. The worst evil in prostitution is to the woman, and the worst element in that is moral rather than physical.

The man has the tremendous responsibility on his soul of doing his part in helping to plunge a human being into the lowest depths of misery and moral degradadation. He has also all the moral responsibility which the Divine law of purity places on each individual, and the further burden of possibly causing disease hereafter to the innocent and virtuous.

But the woman who pursues this as a business has seldom any hope in this world, either of mental or moral health. The class, as a class, are the most desperate and unfortunate which reformatory agencies ever touch. Now, any friend of the well-being of society, knowing the strength of men's passions, and the utter misery and degradation of these victims of them, will dread any public measure or legislation which will tend to weaken the respect of young men for virtue, or to make this offense looked upon as permissible, or which will add to the number of these wretched women by diminishing the public and legal condemnation of their debasing traffic.

Among the large class of poor and ignorant girls in a large city who are always just on the line between virtue and vice, who can say how many more would be plunged into this abyss of misery by an apparent legal approval or recognition of the offense through a system of license? Among the thousand young men who are under incessant temptations in a city like this, who can say how many are saved by the consciousness that this offense is looked upon both by morality and law as an offense, and is not even recognized as permissible and legal? A city license constitutes a profession of prostitutes. The law and opinion recognize them. The evil becomes more fixed by its public recognition.

It is true that prostitution will always, in all probability, attend civilization; but so will all other sins and offenses. It may be possible, however, to diminish and control it. It is already immensely checked in this country, as compared with continental countries, partly through economical and partly through moral causes. It has been diminished among the daughters of the lowest poor in this city by the " Industrial Schools." Why should it be increased and established by legal recognition ?

We admit that the present condition of the whole matter in New York is terrible. The humanity and science which ought to minister to the prostitute as freely as to any other class, are refused to her by the public, unless she apply as a pauper. The consequence is, that the fearful diseases which follow this offense, like avenging Furies, have spread through not only this class of women, but have been communicated to the virtuous and innocent, and are undermining the health of society. This fact is notorious to physicians.

Now we think a reasonable "middle course" might be pursued in this matter;-that, for instance, greater conveniences for medical attendance and advice in the city (and not on Blackwell's Island) might be afforded by our authorities to this class, both as a matter of humanity and as a safeguard to the public health. If there was a hospital or a dispensary for such cases within the city, it would avoid the disgrace and publicity of each patient reporting herself to the court as a pauper, and then being sent to the Island Hospital. Hundreds more would present themselves for attendance and treatment than do now, and the public health be proportionately improved. No moral sanction.

would thus be given to this demoralizing and degrading business. The simple duties of humanity would be performed.

The advocates of the license system would still reply, however, that such a hospital would not meet the evil; that Law only can separate the sickly from the healthy, and thus guard society from the pestilence; and the only law which could accomplish this would be a strict system of license. The friend of public order, however, would urge that a wise legislator cannot consider physical well-being alone: he must regard also the moral tendencies of laws; and the influence of a license system for prostitution is plainly toward recognizing this offense as legal or permissible. It removes indirectly one of the safeguards of virtue.

Perhaps the *reductio ad-absurdum* in the relation of the State with a criminal class, and of the Church with the State, was never so absurdly shown as in the Berlin license laws for prostitutes, twenty years since. According to these, in their final result, no woman could be a prostitute who had not partaken of the communion!—that is, the *Schein*, or license, was never given to this business any more than to any other, except on evidence of the person's having been "confirmed," or being a member of the State Church, that is, a citizen! This classing, however, the trade of prostitution with peddling, or any other business needing a license, did not in the least tend, so far as we have ever heard, to elevate the women, or save them from moral and mental degradation. On the contrary, the universal law of Providence that man or woman must live by labor, and that any unnatural substitute for it saps and weakens all power and vigor, applies to this class in Continental cities as much as here. Without doubt, too, wherever the Germanic races are, no degree of legalizing this traffic can utterly do away with the public sentence of scorn against the female participants in it; and the contempt of the virtuous naturally depresses the vicious.

The "public woman" has a far greater chance of recovery in France or Italy than in Germany, England, or America. Still, the wise legislator, though regretting the depression which this public sentiment causes to the vicious classes, cannot but value it as a safeguard of virtue, and will be very cautious how he weakens it by legislation.

There is, no doubt, some force in the position that the non-licensing of these houses is in some degree a terror to the community, and that the cautious and prudent are kept from the offense through fear of possible consequences in disease and infection. This, however, does not seem to us an object which legislators can hold before them as compared with the duties of humanity in curing and preventing disease and pestilence. They have nothing to do with adding to the natural penalties of sin, or with punishing sinners. They are concerned only with human law. But they have the right, and, as it seems to us, the duty, so to legislate as not to encourage so great an evil as this of prostitution. And licensing, it seems to us, has that tendency. It certainly has had it in Paris, where it has been tried to its full extent, and surely no one could claim the population of that city as a model to any nation, whether in physical or moral power.

Bad as London is in this matter—not, however, so much through defect of licensing as through want of a proper street-police—we do not believe there is so wide-spread a degradation among poor women as in Berlin.

New York, in our judgment, is superior to any great city in its smaller prostitute class, and the virtue of its laboring poor. Something of this, of course, is due to our superior economical conditions; something to the immense energy and large means thrown into our preventive agencies, but much also to the public opinion prevailing in all classes in regard to this vice. Our wealthy classes, we believe, and certainly our middle classes, have a higher sentiment in regard to the purity both of man and woman than any similar classes in the civilized world. More persons relatively marry, and marriages are happier. This is equally true of the upper laboring classes. If it is not true of the lowest poor, this results from two

great local evils—Overcrowding, and the bad influences of Emigration. Still, even with these, the poor
of New York compare favorably in virtue with those
of Paris, Berlin, or Vienna. Now, how large a part
of the public opinion which thus preserves both ends
of society from vice may be due to the fact that we
have not recognized the greatest offense against purity
by any permissive legislation ? The business is still
regarded, in law, as outside of good morals and not
even to be tacitly allowed by license.

CHAPTER XII.

THE BEST PREVENTIVE OF VICE AMONG CHILDREN.

INDUSTRIAL SCHOOLS.

As a simple, practical measure to save from vice the girls of the honest poor, nothing has ever been equal to the INDUSTRIAL SCHOOL.

Along with our effort for homeless boys, I early attempted to found a comprehensive organization of Schools for the needy and ragged little girls of the city.

Though our Free Schools are open to all, experience has taught that vast numbers of children are so ill-clothed and destitute that they are ashamed to attend these excellent places of instruction; or their mothers are obliged to employ them during parts of the day; or they are begging, or engaged in street occupations, and will not attend, or, if they do, attend very irregularly. Very many are playing about the docks or idling in the streets.

Twenty years ago, nothing seemed to check this evil. Captain Matsell, in the celebrated report I have alluded to, estimated the number of vagrant children as 10,000, and subsequently in later years, the esti-

mate was as high as 30,000. The commitments for
vagrancy were enormous, reaching in one year (1857),
for females alone, 3,449; in 1859, 5,778; and in 1860,
5,880. In these we have not the exact number of
children, but it was certainly very large.

What was needed to check crime and vagrancy
among young girls was some School of Industry and
Morals, adapted for the class.

Many were ashamed to go to the Public Schools;
they were too irregular for their rules. They needed
some help in the way of food and clothing, much
direct moral instruction and training in industry;
while their mothers required to be stimulated by earnest appeals to their consciences to induce them to
school them at all. Agents must be sent around to
gather the children, and to persuade the parents to
educate their offspring. It was manifest that the Public Schools were not adapted to meet all these wants,
and indeed the mingling of any eleemosynary features
in our public educational establishments would have
been injudicious. As our infant Society had no
funds, my effort was to found something at first by
outside help, with the hope subsequently of obtaining a
permanent support for the new enterprises, and bringing them under the supervision of the parent Society.

The agencies which we sought to found were the
INDUSTRIAL SCHOOLS, which I shall now attempt to
describe.

Each one of these humble charities has a history of its own—a history known only to the poor—of sacrifice, patience, and labor.

Some of the most gifted women of New York, of high position and fortune, as well as others of remarkable character and education, have poured forth without stint their services of love in connection with these ministrations of charity.

THE WILSON SCHOOL.

The School to which allusion has already been made on page 83, as growing out of the Boys' Meeting in Sixth Street, and afterwards in Avenue D, was the first of these Schools, and owes its origin especially to a lady of great executive power, Mrs. Wilson, wife of the Rev. Dr. Wilson. It has always been an exceedingly successful and efficient School. It was formed in February, 1853, the writer assisting in its organization, and was carried on outside of the Society whose history I am sketching.

THE ROOKERIES OF THE FOURTH WARD—A REMEDY.

In visiting from lane to lane and house to house in our poorest quarters, I soon came to know one district which seemed hopelessly given over to vice and misery—the region radiating out from or near to Franklin Square, especially such streets as Cherry, Water, Dover, Roosevelt, and the neighboring lanes. Here were huge barracks—one said to contain some 1,500

persons—underground cellars, crowded with people,
and old rickety houses always having "a double" on
the rear lot, so as more effectually to shut out light
and air.   Here were as many liquor-shops as houses,
and those worst dens of vice, the "Dance-Saloons,"
where prostitution was in its most brazen form, and
the unfortunate sailors were continually robbed or
murdered.   Nowhere in the city were so many murders committed, or was every species of crime so rife.
Never, however, in this villainous quarter, did I experience the slightest annoyance in my visits, nor did
any one of the ladies who subsequently ransacked
every den and hole where a child could shelter itself.

My own attention was early arrested by the number
of wild ragged little girls who were flitting about
through these lanes; some with basket and poker
gathering rags, some apparently seeking chances of
stealing, and others doing errands for the dance-
saloons and brothels, or hanging about their doors.
The police were constantly arresting them as "vagrants," when the mothers would beg them off from
the good-natured Justices, and promise to train them
better in future.   They were evidently fast training,
however, for the most abandoned life.   It seemed to
me if I could only get the refinement, education, and
Christian enthusiasm of the better classes fairly to
work here among these children, these terrible evils
might be corrected at least for the next generation.

I accordingly went about from house to house among ladies whom I had known, and, representing the condition of the Ward, induced them to attend a meeting of ladies to be held at the house of a prominent physician, whose wife had kindly offered her rooms.

For some months I had attempted to prepare the public mind for these labors by incessant writing for the daily papers, by lectures and by sermons in various pulpits. Experience soon showed that the most effective mode of making real the condition of the poorest class, was by relating incidents from real life which continually presented themselves.

The rich and fortunate had hardly conceived the histories of poverty, suffering, and loneliness which were constantly passing around them.

The hope and effort of the writer was to connect the two extremes of society in sympathy, and carry the forces of one class down to lift up the other. For this two things were necessary—one to show the duty which Christ especially teaches of sacrifice to the poor for His sake, and the value which He attaches to each human soul; and the other to free the whole, as much as possible, from any sectarian or dogmatic character. Nothing but "the enthusiasm of humanity" inspired by Christ could lead the comfortable and the fastidious to such disagreeable scenes and hard labors as would meet them here. It was necessary to feel that many comforts must be foregone, and much leisure given

up, for this important work. Very unpleasant sights
were to be met with, coarse people to be encountered,
and rude children managed; the stern facts of filth,
vice, and crime to be dealt with.

It was not to be a mere holiday-work, or a sudden
gush of sentiment; but, to be of use, it must be patiently continued, week by week, and month by
month, and year by year, with some faint resemblance
to that patience and love which we believed a Higher
One had exercised towards us. But, with this inspiration, as carefully as possible, all dogmatic limitation
must be avoided. All sects were invited to take a
share in the work, and, as the efforts were necessarily
directed to the most palpable and terrible evils, the
means used by all would be essentially the same.
Even those of no defined religious belief were gladly
welcomed if they were ready to do the offices of
humanity. The fact that ninety-nine hundredths of
these poor people were Roman Catholics compelled us
also to confine ourselves to the most simple and fundamental instructions, and to avoid, in any way, arousing religious bigotry.

In the meeting, gathered at the house of Dr. P.,
were prominent ladies from all the leading sects.

An address was delivered by the writer, and then
a constitution presented, of the simplest nature, and
an association organized and officers appointed by the
ladies present. This was the foundation of the

"FOURTH WARD INDUSTRIAL SCHOOL."

In the meanwhile, we went forth through the slums of the ward, and let it be widely known that a School to teach work, and where food was given daily, and clothes were bestowed to the well-behaved, was just forming.

Our room was in the basement of a church in Roosevelt Street. Hither gathered, on a morning in December, 1853, our ladies and a flock of the most ill-clad and wildest little street-girls that could be collected anywhere in New York. They flew over the benches, they swore and fought with one another, they bandied vile language, and could hardly be tamed down sufficiently to allow the school to be opened.

Few had shoes, all were bonnetless, their dresses were torn, ragged, and dirty; their hair tangled, and faces long unwashed; they had, many of them, a singularly wild and intense expression of eye and feature, as of half-tamed creatures, with passions aroused beyond their years.

The dress and ornaments of the ladies seemed to excite their admiration greatly. It was observed that they soon hid or softened their own worst peculiarities. They evidently could not at first understand the motive which led so many of a far higher and better class to come to help them. The two regular and salaried teachers took the discipline in hand gently and firmly. The ladies soon had their little classes, each gathered quietly about the one instructing. As a general thing, the ladies took upon themselves the industrial branches—sewing, knitting, crocheting, and the like; this gave them also excellent opportunities for moral instruction, and winning the sympathy of .the children.

As these ladies, many of them of remarkable character and culture, began to show the fruits of a high civilization to these poor little barbarians, the thought seemed to strike them—though hardly capable of being expressed—that here was a goodness and piety they had never known or conceived. This offspring of poverty and crime vailed their vices and bad habits before these angels. They felt a new impulse—to be worthy of their noble friends. The idea of unselfish Love dawned on their souls; they softened and became respectful. So it continued; each day the wild little beggars became more disciplined and controlled; they began to like study and industry; they were more anxious to be clean and neatly dressed; they checked their tongues, and, in some degree, their tempers; they showed affection and gratitude to their teachers; their minds awakened; most of all, their moral faculties. The truths of Religion or of morals, especially when dramatized in stories and incidents, reached them.

And no words can adequately picture the amount of loving service and patient sacrifice which was poured out by these ladies in this effort among the poor of the Fourth Ward. They never spared themselves or their means. Some came down every day to help in the school; some twice in the week; they were there in all weathers, and never wearied. Three of the number offered up their lives in these labors of humanity, and died in harness.

A most gifted intellectual family, the S——s, supplied some of our most devoted workers; the wife, since deceased, of one of our leading merchants and public men, himself a man much loved for his generosity, occupied the place of one of the Directresses; the wife of a prominent physician was our Treasurer. A young lady of fortune, since dead, Miss G., took the hardest labors upon herself. The wife of a gentleman since Governor and United States Senator, was in especial charge of the house, and dreaded no labor of humanity, however disagreeable. Two others, sisters, who represented one of our most honored historical families, but whose characters needed no help of genealogy to make them esteemed by all, threw themselves into the work with characteristic earnestness. Another of that family, which has furnished the pioneer of all reform-work among the youthful criminals, and in criminal law, and which in the early days of our history so often led public affairs, visited from house to house among the miserable poor of the ward, and twice found herself face to face with small-pox in its most virulent form.

The effects of this particular School upon the morals of the juvenile population of the Fourth Ward were precisely what they have always been in similar schools. These little girls, who might be said to be almost the inmates of the brothels, and who grew up in an atmosphere of crime and degradation, scarcely ever, when mature, joined the ranks of their sisters and neighbors. Though living in the same houses with the gay dance-saloons, they avoided them as they would pestilential places. Trained to industry and familiar with the modest and refined appearance of pure women in the schools, they had no desire for the society of these bold girls, or to earn their living in this idle and shameful manner. They felt the disgrace of the abandoned life around them, and were soon above it. Though almost invariably the children of drunkards, they did not inherit the appetites of their mothers, or if they did, their new training substituted higher and stronger desires. They were seldom known to have the habit of drinking as they grew up. Situations were continually found for them in the country, or they secured places for themselves as servants in respectable families; and, becoming each day more used to better circumstances and more neatly dressed, they had little desire to visit their own wretched homes and remain in their families. Now and then there would be a fall from virtue among them, but the cases were very few indeed. As they grew up they married young mechanics or farmers, and were soon far above the class from which they sprang. Such were the fruits in general of the patient, self-denying labors of these ladies in the Fourth Ward School.

One most self-sacrificing and heroic man, a physician, Dr. Robert Ray, devoted his education and something of his fortune to these benevolent efforts, and died while in the harness. Singularly enough, I never knew, in twenty years' experience, an instance of one of these volunteer teachers contracting any contagious disease in these labors, though repeatedly they have entered tenement rooms where virulent typhoid or small-pox cases were being tended. They made it a rule generally to bathe and change their clothing after their work.

For a more exact account of the results of the Fourth-Ward labors, it is difficult to obtain precise statistics. But when we know from the Prison Reports that soon after the opening of this school there were imprisoned 3,449 female vagrants of all ages, and that last year (1870), when the little girls who then attended such schools would have matured, there were only 671; or when we observe that the Prison in that neighborhood inclosed 3,172 female vagrants in 1861 and only 339 in 1871, we may be assured that the sacrifices made in that Ward have not been without their natural fruit.

Extracts from our Journal:

A VISIT IN THE FOURTH WARD

" We started out a wintry afternoon to see some of our scholars in the Industrial School of the Fourth Ward. A number of ragged little girls, disdaining to enter, were clustered about the door of the School. As they caught a glimpse of some one coming out, the cry of 'Lie low! lie low!' passed among them, and they were off, capering about in the snow-storm like so many little witches.

" We passed up Oak Street and Cherry. Here is the entrance, a narrow doorway on the side. Wind through this dark passage and you are at the door of a little back room; it is the home of a German rag-picker who has a child in the school. A filthy, close room, with a dark bedroom; there is one window, and a small stove, and two or three chairs. The girl is neat and healthy-looking. 'I pick rags, sir,' says the mother, 'and I can't send her to Public School. I am away all day, and she would have to be in the streets, and it's very hard to live this winter. It's been a great help to send her to that school.' I told her we wanted none who could go to Public School, but if it was so with her she might continue to send. A miserable hole for a home, and yet the child looked neatly.

" Here, beyond, is an old house. We climb the shaking stairs, up to the attic—a bare front room with one roof-window. The only furniture a bed and stove and a broken chair. Very chill and bare, but the floor is well swept. A little hump-backed child is reading away very busily by the light of the scuttle window, and another is cleaning up the floor. The mother is an Irish woman. 'Shure! an' its nivir none of the schools I could sind 'em to. I had no clo'es or shoes for 'em and, it's the truth, I am jist living, an' no more. Could ye help us?' We told her we meant to help her by helping her children, and asked about the little deformed one. 'Och! she is sich a swate won! She always larned very quick since her accidint, and I used to think, maybe she wont live, and God will take her away—she was so steady and good. Yes, I am thankful to those ladies for what they are teaching her. She never had no chance before. God bless ye, gintlemen!'

"We climbed again one of these rookeries. It is a back garret. A dark-eyed, passionate-looking woman is sitting over the little stove, and one of our little scholars is standing by— one of the prettiest and brightest children in the school. One of those faces you see in the West of Ireland, perhaps with some Spanish blood in them ; a little oval face, with soft brown complexion, quick, dark eyes and harsh, black hair. The mother looked like a woman who had seen much of the worst of life. 'No, sir, I never did send 'em to school. I know it, they ought to learn, but I couldn't. I try to shame him some- times—it's my husband, sir—but he drinks, and then bates me. Look at that bruise!' and she pointed to her cheek ; 'and I tell him to see what's comin' to his children. There's Peggy, goes sellin' fruit every night to those cellars in Water Street, and they're *hells*, sir. She's learnin' all sorts of bad words there, and don't get back till eleven or twelve o'clock.' She spoke of a sister of the little girl, about thirteen years old, and the picture of that sweet, dark-eyed little thing, getting her education, uncon- sciously, every night in those vile cellars of dancing prostitutes, came up to my mind. I asked why she sent her there, and spoke of the dangers. 'I must, sir; he makes nothing for me, and if it wasn't for this school, and the help there, and her earning of a shilling or two shilling in them places, I should starve. Oh, I wish they was out of this city! Yes, it's the truth, I would rather have them dead than on the street, but I can't help it.' I told her of some good families in the country, where we could place the children. 'Would they git schoolin, sir?' 'Certainly, that is the first condition. We always look especially to that.' The little dark eyes sparkled, and she '*should* like to take care of a baby so!' The sister now came in, and we talked with her. 'Oh! no, she didn't like to go to those places; but they only buy there at nights'—and she seemed equally glad to get a place. So it was arranged that they were to come up to the office next day, and then get a home in the country. The little girl now wrapped her thin shawl about her head, and ran along before us, through the storm, to some of the other children. The harder it snowed, the more the little eyes sparkled and the prettier she looked.

"Another home of poverty—dark, damp, and chill. The

mother an Englishwoman; her child had gone to the school barefooted. This girl was engaged in the same business—selling fruit at night in the brothels. 'I know it, sir,' she said; 'sho ought to have as good a chance as other people's children. But I'm so poor! I haven't paid a month's rent, and I was sick three weeks.'

"'Yes, you're right. I know the city, sir; and I would rather have her in her grave than brought down to those cellars. But what can I do, sir?'

"We arrange, again, to find a situation in the country, if she wishes—and engage her, at least, to keep the child at school.

"Our little sprite flies along again through the snow, and shows us another home of one of our scholars—a prostitute's cellar. The elder sister of the child is there, and meets us pleasantly, though with a shame-faced look. 'Yes, she shall go to school every day, sir. We never sent her before, nowheres; but she's learnin' very fast there now.'

"We tell her the general objects of the school, and of the good, kind home which can be found for her sister in the country. She seems glad and her face, which must have been pretty once, lights up, perhaps, at the thought for her sister, of what she shall never more have—a pure home. Two or three sailors, sitting at their bottles, say, 'Yes, that's it! git the little gal out of this! it ain't no place for her.'

"They are all respectful, and seem to understand what we are doing.

"The little guide has gone back, and we go now to another address—a back cellar in Oak Street—damp, dark, so that one at mid-day could hardly see to read; filthy, chilly, yet with six or eight people living there. Every one has a cold; and the oldest daughter, a nice girl of fourteen, is losing her eyes in the foul atmosphere. The old story: 'No work, no friends, rent to pay, and nothing to do.' The parents squalid, idle, intemperate, and shiftless. There they live, just picking up enough to keep life warm in them; groaning, and begging, and seeking work. There they live, breeding each day pestilence and disease, scattering abroad over the city seeds of fearful sickness—raising a brood of vagrants and harlots—retorting on society its neglect

7

by cursing the bodies and souls of thousands whom they never knew, and who never saw them.

"Yet it is cheering—it cheered me even in that squalid hole—that the children are so much superior to their parents. It needs time for vice and beggary and filth to degrade childhood. God has given every fresh human soul something which rises above its surroundings, and which even want and vice do not wear away. For the old poor, for the sensual who have stooped themselves in crime, for the drunkard, the thief, the prostitute who have run a long course, let those heroically work who will. Yet, noble as is the effort, one's experience of human nature is obliged to confess, the fruits will be very few. The old heart of man is a hard thing to change. In any comprehensive view, the only hopeful reform through society must begin with childhood, basing itself on a change of circumstances and on religious influences."

The average expense of a school of this nature, with one hundred scholars and two salaried teachers, where a cheap meal is supplied, and garments and shoes are earned by the scholars, we reckon usually at $1,500, or at $15 per head annually for each scholar.

CHAPTER XIII.

THE GERMAN RAG-PICKERS.

OUR next great effort was among the Germans. On the eastern side of the city is a vast population of German laborers, mechanics, and shop-keepers. Among them, also, are numbers of exceedingly poor people, who live by gathering rags and bones.

I used at that time to explore these singular settlements, filled with the poor peasantry of the "Fatherland," and being familiar with the German *patois*, I had many cheery conversations with these honest people, who had drifted into places so different from their mountain-homes. In fact, it used to convey to me a strange contrast, the dirty yards piled with bones and flaunting with rags, and the air smelling of carrion; while the accents reminded of the glaciers of the Bavarian Alps or the fresh breezes and wild scenes of the Harz. The poor people felt the contrast terribly, and their children most of all.

From ignorance of the language and the necessity of working at their street-trades, they did not attend our schools, and seldom entered a church. They were growing up without either religion or education. Yet they were a much more honest and hopeful class than the Irish. There seemed always remaining in them something of the good old German *Biederkeit*, or solidity. One could depend on the children if they were put in places of trust, and in school they seemed to grasp knowledge with much more tenacity and vigor. The young girls, however, coming from a similar low class were weaker in virtue than the Irish.

The number of the Germans in the poor quarters may be somewhat measured by the population of the Wards which they inhabited. The Eleventh Ward at that time (1854) was reckoned to contain 50,000 inhabitants; at present (1870) it contains 64,372, and the Sixteenth Ward, another strong German district, has 99,375.

The Association of ladies which we called together for labors among this population happened to be composed mainly of Unitarians, a religious body that has always felt a peculiar interest in the moral condition of our German poor. The moving spirit in the association was a lady of such singular grace and delicacy of character, that I hardly venture, even after these many years, to make public her name. She occupied then one of the foremost positions in New York society—a position accorded in part to her name, honored for intellectual services to the Republic, beyond almost any other in our history, but above all due to her own singular sweetness and dignity of manner and a very highly cultivated and strong intellect. Her power, whether with rich or poor, was her wonderful consideration for others, and her quick sympathy. The highest inspiration of Christian faith breathed through her life and animated her in laboring with these children of poverty. The same inspiration sustained her subsequently in a prolonged and terrible trial of months under a fearful disease, and made her death a sun-set of glory to all who knew her. Never did the faith in immortal union with God through Christ attain a more absolute certainty in any human being. Her death, even to many skeptics who were intimate with her, became a new and astonishing argument for Immortality.

She numbered among her friends many of the leading intellects of the country, as well as those among the poor who depended on her advice, sympathy, and aid.

Into this labor of love among the Germans, Mrs. S. threw herself, in company with a few friends, with profound earnestness.

In view of the peculiar temptations of the young German girls, one of our objects in this school was to offer a social as well as educational resort in the evenings. We furnished the rooms pleasantly and tastefully, and proposed to vary our school exercises by games or an occasional dance and frolic. Mrs. S. and other ladies consented to be often present, to instruct and talk with the girls. Our visitors and myself at once gathered in a needy-looking assembly of the poor German girls of the Eleventh Ward, not as ragged or wild as the Irish throng in the Fourth Ward, but equally poor and quite as much exposed to temptation. The School went on day by day in its ministrations of love and its patient industry, and gradually produced the same effects as have been experienced under all these Schools. The wild became tamer, the wayward more docile. The child of the rag-picker soon began to like in-door industry better than the vagrant business of the streets, and to lose something of her boldness and correct her slovenliness.

After laboring thus for some years with a board of ladies, a strong effort was made to secure the assistance of the German merchants of the city.

In 1859, a subscription of about $1,000 was obtained from them, and the School was enlarged and made still more attractive, so as to reach the young working German girls in the evening. At this time a young lady of high culture, from one of the prominent intellectual families of New England, offered herself for this difficult task, and she was placed at the head of the School. For two years she labored unceasingly for this wild, uncontrolled class, being present every evening in the school, and bringing all her education and earnestness of character to bear upon them. They never forgot her, and she left an indelible im-

pression on these children, and aided in saving them
from the temptations which have ruined so many of
their companions.

Our German patrons gradually left us, and it was
only in 1870 that their assistance was secured again
for a charity which was saving so many thousand
children of their countrymen.

The School is now held at No. 272 Second Street,
and contains some four hundred children.

"DUTCH HILL" AND THE SWILL-GATHERERS.

ON the eastern side of the city, in the neighborhood of Fortieth Street, is a village of squatters,
which enjoys the title of "Dutch Hill." The inhabitants are not, however, "Dutch," but mainly poor
Irish, who have taken temporary possession of unused
sites on a hill, and have erected shanties which serve
at once for pig-pens, hen-coops, bed-rooms, and living-
rooms. They enjoy the privilege of squatters in
having no rent to pay; but they are exposed to the
penalty of being at any moment turned out from their
dens, and losing land and house at once. Usually
they remain while the quarrymen who are opening
streets almost undermine their shanties, and then if
the buildings are not blown away, they pull them
down and pack them away like tents to another dwell-
ing-place.

The village is filled with snarling dogs, which aid

in drawing the swill or coal carts, for the children are mainly employed in collecting swill and picking coals through the streets.

The shanty family are never quite so poor as the tenement-house family, as they have no rent to pay. But the filth and wretchedness in which they sometimes live are beyond description.

It happened that for many years (not wishing to scatter my efforts too much), I made this quarter my special "parish" for visitations; and very discouraging visits they were, many of them. The people had very little regular occupation, many being widows who did occasional "chores" in families; others lived on the sale of the coal their children gathered, or on the pigs which shared their domicile; others kept fowls, and all had vast flocks of goats, though where the profits from these latter came I could never discover, as no one seemed to buy the milk, and I never heard of their killing them. Money, however, in some way they did procure, and one old red-faced swill-gatherer I knew well, whose bright child we tried so long to save, who died finally, it was said, with a large deposit in the Savings-Bank, which no one could claim; yet one corner of her bed-chamber was filled with a heap of smelling bones, and the pigs slept under her bed.

Another old rag-picker I remember whose shanty was a sight to behold; all the odds and ends of a great city seemed piled up in it,—bones, broken dishes, rags, bits of furniture, cinders, old tin, useless lamps, decaying vegetables, ribbons, cloths, legless chairs, and carrion, all mixed together, and heaped up nearly to the ceiling, leaving hardly room for a bed on the floor where the woman and her two children slept. Yet all these were marvels of health and vigor, far surpassing most children I know in the comfortable classes. The woman was German, and after years of effort could never be induced to do anything for the education of her children, until finally I put the police on their track as vagrants, and they were safely housed in the "Juvenile Asylum."

Many a time have I come into their shanties on a snowy morning and found the people asleep with the snow lying thick on their bed-clothes. One poor creature was found thus one morning by the police, frozen stiff. They all suffered, as might be expected, terribly from rheumatism. Liquor, of course, "prevailed." Every woman drank hard, I suppose to forget her misery; and dreadful quarrels raged among them.

The few men there worked hard at stone-quarrying, but were often disabled by disease and useless from drunkenness. Many of the women had been abandoned by their husbands, as their families increased and became burdensome, or as they themselves grew plain and bad-tempered. Some of these poor creatures drank still more to heal their wounded affections. The children, of course, were rapidly following the ways of their parents. The life of a swillgatherer, or coal-picker, or *chiffonnier* in the streets soon wears off a girl's modesty and prepares her for worse occupation.

Into this community of poor, ignorant, and drunken people I threw myself, and resolved, with God's aid, to try to do something for them. Here for years I visited from cabin to cabin, or hunted out every cellar and attic of the neighboring tenement-houses; standing at death-beds and sick-beds, seeking to administer consolation and advice, and, aided by others, to render every species of assistance.

In returning home from these rounds, amidst filth and poverty, I remember that I was frequently so depressed and exhausted as to throw myself flat upon the rug in front of the fire, scarcely able to move. The discouraging feature in such visits as I was making, and which must always exist in similar efforts, is that one has no point of religious contact with these people.

Among all the hundreds of families I knew and visited I never met but two that were Protestants. To all words of spiritual warning or help there came the chilling formalism of the ignorant Roman Catholic in reply, implying that certain outward acts made the soul right with its Creator. The very inner ideas of our spiritual life of free love towards God, true repent-

ance and trust in a Divine Redeemer, seemed wanting
in their minds. I never had the least ambition to be
a proselytizer, and never tried to convert them, and I
certainly had no prejudice against the Romanists; on
the contrary, it has been my fortune in Europe to enjoy
the intercourse of some most spiritual-minded Catholics. But these poor people seemed stamped with the
spiritual lifelessness of Romanism. At how many a
lonely death-bed or sick-bed, where even the priest
had forgotten to come, have I longed and tried to say
some comforting word of religion to the dull ear,
closing to all earthly sounds; but even if heard and
the sympathy gratefully felt, it made scarcely more
religious impression than would the chants of the
Buddhists have done. One sprinkle of holy water
were worth a volume of such words.

A Protestant has great difficulty in coming into
connection with the Romanist poor. I was often
curious to know the exact influence of the priests
over these people. The lowest poor in New York are
not, I think, much cared for by the Romanist priesthood. One reason, without doubt, is that their attention has thus far been mainly (and wisely) directed to
building handsome churches, and that they have not
means to do much for these persons. Another and
more powerful reason is, probably, that the old "enthusiasm of humanity" which animated a Guy, a
Vincent de Paul, or Xavier, has died out among them.

I have known, however, individual cases in our city, where a priest has exercised a marked influence in keeping his charge from intoxication. There were also occasionally, in this very region, something like "Revivals of Religion" among the people, stimulated by the priests, in which many young girls joined religious societies, and did lead, to my knowledge, for a time more pure and devout lives.

When one thinks what a noble-minded and humane Priest might accomplish among the lowest classes of New York, how many vices he could check, and what virtues he might cherish, and what public blessings on the whole community he might confer, by elevating this degraded population; and then as one looks at the moral condition of the Roman Catholic poor, one can only sigh, that that once powerful body has lost so much of the inspiration of Christ which once filled it.

The plan which I laid out in working in this quarter was in harmony with all our previous efforts; it was especially to influence and improve the children.

It so happened that near "Dutch Hill" was another hill covered with handsome houses and inhabited by wealthy people, "Murray Hill." The ladies in this prosperous quarter were visited, and finally assembled in a public meeting; and, with the same preliminaries as in the other Schools, we at length organized in 1854.

THE EAST RIVER INDUSTRIAL SCHOOL.

Early in the history of this School, we secured the services of a lady, Miss Spratt, now Mrs. Hurley, who has been ever since the main-stay of that most useful charity.

For seventeen years this woman of refinement and education has spent her days in this School of poor children, and her hours of leisure in those wretched shanties—an angel of mercy and sympathy to every unfortunate family for miles around. Whatever woman falls into misfortune, loses husband or child, is driven from home by poverty, or forced from work by depression of business, or meets with troubles of mind or body, at once comes to her for sympathy and relief. She has become so used to scenes of misery, that to her, she says, "the house of mourning" is more natural than "the house of feasting."

The present writer, for his own part, confesses that he could not possibly have borne the harrowing and disagreeable scenes with which he has been so long familiar, without making a strict rule never to think or speak of the poor when he was away from his work, and immediately absorbing himself in some entirely different subject. The spring of the mind would have been broken.

But Mrs. Hurley lived in and for the poor; her only relaxation was hearing Mr. Beecher on Sunday; and yet, when she occasionally visited us in the country, she devoured books—her great favorite being a trans-lation I had of Plato.

The children, of course, became passionately at-tached to this missionary of charity. During her labors, she was married to a physician, Dr. Hurley, who subsequently was killed in the army during the War of the Rebellion. While she was temporarily absent, and a strange teacher employed, six of the wildest girls were expelled, so unmanageable were they. When she came back, they returned and welcomed her eagerly, behaving perfectly well; and it was dis-covered that so attached were they to her, they had each carried fragments of her dress as mementos in their bosom!

The peculiar value of our common experience in this School was, that we were enabled through so many years to follow carefully the results of the School on a large class of very destitute little girls. We know personally what was here accomplished. A very hopeful feature appeared soon in the work. The children rose above the condition of their parents; sometimes they improved, by their own increasing neatness and good behavior, the habits and appear-ance of their fathers and mothers. More often they became ashamed of their paternal piggeries and nasty dens, and were glad to get away to more decent homes or new occupations. One great means of in-fluence here was, as in the other Schools, through the regular assistance of volunteer teachers, the ladies of the Association.

It happened that there was among them more of a certain tenacity of character, of the old Puritan faithfulness, than was manifested by some of our co-laborers; having put their hands to the plow, they never thought of turning back. They gave time and labor, and money freely, and they continued at their posts year after year.

The children felt their refining and elevating influence. We soon found that the daughters of the drunkards did not follow their mothers' footsteps, simply because they had acquired higher tastes. We hardly ever knew of one who indulged in drinking; indeed, one old red-faced tippler, Mrs. McK., who was the best chore-woman on the Hill when sober, eventually was entirely reformed by her children. No child seemed to fall back into the degradation of the parents. And recalling now the rank foul soil from which so many sweet flowers seemed to spring, one can only wonder and be grateful that efforts so imperfect bore such harvest.

I remember the F. family—such a cheery, healthy-looking family living in a damp, dark basement, and almost always half-starved, wretchedly poor, but very industrious! The youngest daughter passed through our School, and is now becoming a teacher; another married a mechanic (these girls never marry day-laborers). Still another proved herself a heroine. We sent her as nursery-maid to a family, and as they were all sailing down the Hudson in the *St. John*, the boiler burst; amid the horrible confusion and panic where so many perished, this girl had the courage to rush through the steam and boiling water, and save the three children entrusted to her charge. Of course, after this, she was no longer a servant, but a "sister beloved" in the family. A gentleman of fortune, attracted by her appearance and intelligence, ultimately married her. He died, and she was left with a nice fortune. She bore her change of fortune beautifully.

The following is another similar incident from our Journal:

A ROMANTIC INCIDENT IN AN INDUSTRIAL SCHOOL,

"A few years ago I remember an old shanty on 'Dutch Hill,' where a wretched-looking man lived with his pigs and goats, called K——. He was considered a bad man even among his bad neighbors, and the story of him was (I do not know how true), that he had committed murder, and had escaped the law by some legal quibble. He was a swill-gatherer, and had two little bright daughters to assist him at home. These came to our Fortieth-street School. They improved very fast, and one used to attract much attention from the ladies by her pretty face and intelligent answers. Nellie finally left the school, and was sent by us to the West. She improved much there, and, after some time spent in different families, came back to the city, where she became an 'operator' on the sewing-machine. While at this business and living in a respectable boarding-house, she attracted the attention of a gentleman of some means and position, much older than herself, who, at length, offered himself to her in marriage.

She declined, on the ground that she was so much inferior in position to him, and that his family would object. He insisted, and declared that 'he wished to please himself, not his family,' and they were married.

"He took his wife away to a foreign country, where his business lay, and there she has been a number of years, gradually improving in manners, taste, and education, living like a lady of fortune, with her maid and carriage, and making herself, in every way, a most suitable wife for one who had been so much above her. We had often heard of her good fortune. But during our Christmas Festival at the East River School, she herself came in to see it again and thank those who had been so kind to her. We all knew her at once; and yet she was so changed— a pretty, tasteful-looking young lady, with a graceful manner and a Spanish accent now—all the old stamp of 'Dutch Hill' quite gone, even the *brogue* lost and replaced by foreign intonations. She was perfectly simple and unaffected, and thanked us all for our former kindness with the utmost heartiness; and told her story very simply, and how anxious she still was to improve her education, seemingly not ashamed of her poor origin. It is a pleasant circumstance that she has taken out her beloved teacher, Mrs. Hurley, a number of times to drive in her carriage."

Several changes of fortune of this kind have made it quite a natural question, when I visit Mrs. Hurley's School, "What about the heiresses ?"

Another girl, I remember, in one of these shanties, who came to school in an old petticoat, and barefooted, a most destitute-looking child. She was subsequently employed in our own family. I doubt whether many girls of the highest classes show a greater natural refinement; and she was as clever in every part of household work as she was nice. She finally married a hotel-keeper in San Francisco, and is doing well.

Generally, the girls married mechanics and people above their rank of life. Some became Protestants; those who married Catholics were never bigoted. A number went to the West, and have done well there.

Mrs. Hurley reckons over at least two thousand different girls who have been in this school and under its influence, since she has been there during the past eighteen years. The condition of all these we know probably pretty well. We count *but five* who have become drunkards, prostitutes, or criminals! Such a wonderful result can be shown by hardly any preventive efforts in the world. Yet, there were certain cases which we used to call

'OUR FAILURES."

There was the D. family—they lived on the lucrative spoils of their infant, who sold toilet-covers to compassionate ladies. This little Julia was an imp of deceit and mischief. She had, fortunately for her, a worn, sad face, and a capacity and imagination for lying unequaled at her years. With inarticulate sobs, and the tears coursing down her thin cheeks, she told of her dying mother and her labors to get her bread; or, again, she was an orphan supporting herself and her deformed little brother; or her disabled father depended on her feeble efforts for his slender support. The addresses she gave of her house were always wrong; and so, year by year, she gathered in a plenteous harvest from the pity of the ladies.

At home, a little band of able-bodied, slatternly sisters were living mainly on the money thus begged· They naturally became each day more lazy and dissolute; and little Julia more bold and brazen-faced. We tried to bribe the young beggar to go to school, we paid her rent, we offered the sisters work, we remonstrated and threatened, we even set the police on her track, but nothing could check or turn her; she eluded the police as easily as she did the ladies. If she came to school, she stayed but a day; all effort failed against the ingrained slovenliness and vagrancy of the family; day by day they sank; one daughter was seduced, and to their number was now added an illegitimate child. They grew dirtier and more miserable; and here, years ago, we left them. No doubt, Julia is still pursuing her profitable vocation from house to house, and the girls are in yet lower depths.

A STREET-CHILD. (FROM OUR JOURNAL.)

"Some ten years ago, I made many efforts to save a little homeless girl, who was floating about the quarter near East Thirty-second Street. Her drunken mother had thrown her out of doors, and she used to sleep under stairways or in deserted cellars, and was a most wretched, half-starved little creature. I talked with her often, but could not induce her to go to school, or to seek a home in the country. She grew up steadily vagrant. At length we succeeded in getting her away to the family of an excellent lady in Buffalo. There she speedily gave up her roving habits, became neat and orderly under the influence of the lady, attended church and Sabbath School, and altogether seemed quite a changed child. Unfortunately, the lady was obliged to move to this city, and instead of placing the little girl in another family in the country, she brought her with her to New York, and, no longer having room for her in her house, let her go to her old associates. In a few weeks, the nice, tidy little girl began to look like the idle and vagrant young girls who were her companions. She became slatternly in her habits, and instead of seeking a place in some family, she joined a company of poor working-girls, who earned their living by manufacturing children's torpedoes. She lodged in the crowded tenement-houses, and gradually fell into all their low associations. The next I knew of her, I heard that she had been seduced under a promise of marriage, and that she was about to be a mother. Again I knew of her, with her unfortunate little babe, driven about from one low lodging-house to another, dependent upon charity for support. Finally, the child was adopted by the parents of her seducer, and she was left free again. Though in extreme destitution, she would not take a situation away from the city. She resumed her work at torpedoes, and lived about in the tenement-houses, a poor, bedraggled-looking creature. Again, after some time, I heard of her as having married a low fellow in that district. She had only been married a few days when her husband abandoned her, and never returned to her. She now hangs about the low lodging-houses between First and Second Avenues, in East Thirty-first and Thirty-second Streets, a forlorn-looking, slovenly woman, who will almost certainly end in the lowest vice and penury."

Thus far in the Journal. Our constant pursuit of this girl did tend, I think, to keep her from utter ruin.

She fell no lower; and subsequently connected herself with one of the charitable institutions, where she is living a virtuous life.

CHAPTER XIV.

SCENES AMONG THE POOR.

EFFECTS OF DRUNKENNESS. (FROM OUR JOURNAL.)

"It sometimes seems in our Industrial Schools as if each wretched, blear-eyed, half-starved, filthy little girl was a living monument of the curses of Intemperance. The rags, the disease, the ignorance, the sunny looks darkened, the old faces on young shoulders, are not necessarily the pitiable effects of overwhelming circumstances. The young creatures are not always cursed by poverty principally, but by the ungoverned appetites, bad habits and vices of their parents. On 'Dutch Hill' one can hardly enter a shanty where is a sober family. The women all drink; the men work, and then carouse. The hard earnings go off in alcohol. No savings are laid up for the winter. The children are ragged and unprotected, and, but for the Industrial School, uneducated. It is sometimes the saddest sight to see a neat little shanty grow day by day more filthy; the furniture sold, the windows broken, the children looking more thin and hungry, the parents falling out of honest work—all the slow effects of ungoverned passion for liquor.

"I entered, yesterday, a little hut on the 'Hill,' where a middle-aged woman lived, whom I knew. She was sitting near the door, weeping violently. I asked her the reason, and, after a little time, she told me. Her eldest daughter, a girl of twenty, had just been in drunk, and had struck her over the eye; and when her mother was looking at her bruise in the glass, she had dashed her fist through the glass.

"There was no safety there, the mother said, when she came in. If they were away she would burst open the doors and break the furniture, and cut her sewing-work to pieces. 'She is a devil, sir, when she's in liquor!' *Three times* the mother had had her arrested and sent to Blackwell's Island; 'but somehow, sir, she's always worse when she comes out, and I niver heard her use bad words till she'd been there.

"'Now, God knows where she lives—they say it's in a bad house; and it's I who am afraid she's gittin' Tommy, her broder, into the same way, for he doesn't come home now. O God! *I might as well be in hell!*' Nothing can convey the tone of despair with which that was said. She told me how the girl had been such a bright little one. 'She was so pretty, sir; and maybe we flattered her, and made too much of her. And her father, he thought she ought to learn the dressmakin' trade, but she felt somehow above it, and she went to be a book-folder downtown. And one day we missed her till late o' night; and thin the next night it was later, and at last her father—bless his poor soul!—he said she shouldn't be out so, and whipt her. And thin she niver came back for three nights, and we thought, maybe, she's at her work, and has to stay late; and we niver suspected how it was, when, suddenly, Mrs. Moore came and said as how Maggy said she was at Mrs. Rooney's—the ould divil—and my husband wouldn't belave it at all; but I wint and bust open the door wid a stone, and found *her*—my own child—there wid a lot of men and women; and I swore at 'em, and the M. P.'s they come and cleared 'em all out, and there was the last of her. She's niver been an honest woman since, when she's in liquor. It broke her father's heart. He died the next Saturday; people said it was some sort of dysentry, but I know it was this. God help me! And, now, sir (almost fiercely), can't you get me out of this? All I want is, to sell my shanty, and wid my two little ones, git away from *her*. I don't care how far!'

"The mother fleeing her daughter. The pretty child becomes a drunken outcast! So ends many a sad history in our city."

THE DYING SEWING-WOMAN.

"In East Thirty-fourth Street, in a tenement-house, a poor sewing-woman has lived for the last two years. She had formerly been in very good circumstances, and her husband, a respectable mechanic, earned a support for her and her children, until at length he fell into intemperate drinking. With the appetite for liquor on him, everything that he made was spent, and he himself was gradually becoming worse and worse. The poor wife was forced to the hardest work to keep her children and herself alive. Last winter, in a moment of desperation, the husband put his name down for a three-years' whaling voyage, and was taken off to sea, leaving the woman with an old father and three children to care for. Many a night, the old man says, has the poor creature walked up from the lower part of the city (some three or four miles) with four dozen shirts on her back, through snow and wet, and then, without fire or food, in her wet clothes, has worked till the dawn of day for the poor little ones dependent on ·her. He has seen *the blood* come from her mouth and nose after some of these efforts. Still more bitter than all this, was the sense of desertion by her husband. But it was all in vain. · The children for whom she had slaved, and whom she loved more than her own life, were attacked with scarlet fever, and two of them died in the mother's arms. One only, a sweet little girl, was left. With them went the spring of hope and courage which had sustained the hard-working mother. Her father says she never shed a tear, but she lost heart; and, though never doubting of the goodness of her Great Father, she had not the spirit for the remaining work of life. Her exposures and hard labor had brought on a cough, and finally a disease of the lungs. She was at last unable to work, and could only lie upon her bed and depend on the chance charities of strangers.

"The teacher of our Fortieth-street School, who, in a way unseen and unknown to the world, is a minister of mercy and goodness to all that quarter of the city, first discovered her, and has managed, with a little aid here and there, to lighten her dying hours.

"I was called in the other day and held a long conversation with her. She has no more fears or anxieties; she is not even troubled about her little one. God will care for her. 'Once,' she said, 'I felt it so hard to lose the children, but now I am glad they are gone! They will be much better where they are than here. I have put everything away now,' she added, with an expression of sublime faith and hope on a face whose worn features the hectic flush made almost beautiful again. 'I trust all to my Redeemer. Through him alone I hope. He will forgive me and receive me.' She spoke of her many trials and sorrows—they were all over, and she was glad she was soon to be at rest.

"We asked about her food. She said she could not relish many things, and she often thought if she could only get some of the good old plain things she had in Ireland at her brother's farm she should feel so much better.

"I told her we would get her some good genuine oat-meal cake from an Irish friend. Her face lighted up at once, and she seemed cheered by the promise.

"'Oh, sir! I have thought so much of my mother in this sickness, and those happy, happy days. I was such a happy girl! How little she thought I would come to this! We lived in the North, you know, and had everything very comfortable, as all the Protestant Irish do. But it's all gone, gone,' she said, dreamily, 'and I wouldn't have it back again, for God is the best friend—He knows,

> "'Oh, how glad I am to die!
> His rod and His staff they comfort me.'

"The words were simple, but the whole was touching beyond description, forcing tears whether one would or not.

"We were glad to find that her clergyman, the Missionary of the Calvary Church, had administered the sacraments to her that day. May she soon be where the sting of poverty, the rubs and blows of hard circumstances, the loneliness of desertion, the anxiety and care, and hopelessness, and disappointment which have followed her unhappy path, shall cease forever, and the unfortunate one shall enter on her new and blissful life of peace and abiding love!"

DISCOURAGEMENT.

"I was lately visiting a poor woman, who had seen better circumstances, the wife of a worker in an iron-foundry. The room was bare but clean, and the woman was neatly dressed, though her face looked thin and worn, and her eyes had an unusual expression of settled, sad discouragement. A little girl of ten or eleven sat near her tending a baby, with the same large sad blue eyes, as if the expression of the mother had come to receive a permanent reflection in the child's face. Her husband had been sick for several months, which put them all behind, though now he was getting work enough.

"'You know how it is, sir,' she said, ' with working people: if a man falls out of work for a day, the family feels it for a week after. We can hardly make the two ends meet when he's well, and the moment he is sick it comes hard upon us. Many's the morning he's gone down to the foundry without his breakfast, and I've had to send out the little Maggy there, to the neighbors, for bits of bread, and then she's taken it down to him.'

"' She is a beggar, then?'

"'Yes, sir, and sorrow of it. We never thought we could come to that. My mother brought me up most dacently, and my husband, he's a very good scholard, and could be a clark or anything, but we can't help it! We must have bread. I would be willing to do anything, wash, scrub, or do plain sewing; and I keep trying, but I never find anything. There seems no help for us; and I sometimes feel clean gone and down-hearted: and I'm troubled at other things, too."

"'What other things?'

"'At my sin, ye see.'

"'What do you mean?'

"' Well, sir, if I could only have peace of mind! But I work on from Monday morn to Saturday night, and I never hear or see anything good; and when Sunday comes, I can't go out; I haven't any bonnet for my head, or any dress fit for a dacent church. I just walk the floor, and I don't dare to think of ever meeting God."

"' Are you a Catholic?'

"'Yes, sir; I was brought up one, and so was my husband, but now it's little we know, as they say, of mass, meeting, or church; we ain't neither Catholics or Protestants; I might as well be a haythen. We haven't any books, nor a prayer-book, or anything. I know it, sir, we ought to pray," she continued, "but I kneel down sometimes, and I get up and say to my husband, ' It's no use my praying, I am too much distracted.' If I could only get some good to my soul, for I think of dying often,

and I see I should not be at all ready. *Life is a burden to me.'*
I spoke of the hopes and consolations which can come to
poor as well as rich, and of her children. ' Yes, sir; no one
can tell the patience of the Lord. How much He has borne
from me! Oh, if I could only have peace of mind, and see
those children getting on well, I should be glad to die. That
little girl cries every time we send her out to beg, and she's
learning nothing good. But I am afraid nothing will ever come
lucky to us; and oh, sir, if you could have seen how we started
in Ireland, and what a home my mother had; she was a very
different woman from what I am.'

"We spoke of her attending the mission meeting in Fortieth
Street, and reading a Testament given by us. She seemed glad
to do both.

"'Oh, sir, if I could only feel that friendship with God you
spoke of, I shouldn't care; I could bear anything; but to work
as we are doing, and to have such trouble, and see the poor wee
thing grow thinner and poorer, and my man almost down
broken, and then to get no nearer—no, we keep getting farther
from the Lord! Oh, if I was only ready to die! I haven't
nothing in this world.'

"Let us hope that the peace-giving words of Christ, the love
of the Redeemer, may at length plant in that poor, weary discouraged soul the seeds of hope and immortal faith, even as
they have done in so many thousands weary and heavy-laden!"

THE SWILL-GATHERER'S CHILD.

"Most of those familiar with the East River Industrial School
will remember a poor widow—a swill-gatherer—who lived in the
notorious village of shanties near Forty-second Street, known as
'Dutch Hill.' She owned a small shanty, which had been put
up on some rich man's lot as a squatter's hut, and there, with
her pigs and dogs and cat in the same room, she made her home.
From morning till evening she was trailing about the streets,
filling up her swill-cans, and at night she came back to the little
dirty den, and spent her evenings—we hardly know how. She
had one smart little girl who went to the Industrial School. As
the child came back day by day, improving in appearance, sing-

ing her sweet songs, and with new ideas of how ladies looked and lived, the mother began to grow ashamed of her nasty home. And I remember entering one day, and finding, to my surprise, pigs and rubbish cleared out, the walls well scrubbed, and an old carpet on the floor, and the mother sitting in state on a chair! It was the quiet teachings of the school coming forth in the houses of the poor.

"After a while the little girl began to get higher ideas of what she might become, and went out with another girl to a place in the West. She did well there, and was contented, but her mother was continually anxious and unhappy about her, and finally, after some years, forced her to return to the city. She was now a very neat, active young girl, far above her mother's condition, and the change back to the pig-shanty and Dutch Hill was anything but pleasant. The old woman hid away her best clothes to prevent her going back, and seemed determined to make her a swill-gatherer like herself. Gradually, as might be expected, we began to hear bad stories about our old scholar. The people of the neighborhood said, she drank and quarreled with her mother, and that she was frequenting houses where low company met. Another of the worst Dutch Hill girls—the daughter of a drunkard—was constantly with her. Soon we heard that the other young girl had been sent to Blackwell's Island, and that this one must be saved now, or she would be utterly lost. I went up at once to the old woman's shanty, though with but the feeblest hopes of doing anything, yet with many unuttered prayers. For who that knows the career before the street-girl of the city can help breathing out his soul in agony of prayer for her, when the time of choice comes?

"When I entered the shanty, the young girl was asleep on the bed, and the mother sat on a box, crooning and weeping.

"'Och, and why did I iver tak ye from that swate place—ye that was makin' an honest woman of yoursel'! Ach, God bless your honor! can ye help her? She's a'most gone. Can't ye do somethin'?'

"'Well, how is she doing now?'

"'Och (in a whisper), your honor, she brought three bad fellers last night, and she brake my own door in, and I tould 'em—says I, I'm an honest woman, and I never had ony sich in my kin—and she was drunk—yes, yer honor, she, my own darlint, strak me, and wanted to turn me out—and now there she's been sleepin' all the mornin'. Ach, why did I tak her out of her place!'

"Here the girl woke up, and sat up on the bed, covering her face in shame. I said some few sober words to her, and then the mother threw herself down on the floor, tears pouring down her cheeks.

"'Ach, darlint! my own swate darlint! will ye not list to the gintleman? Sure an' ye wouldn't bring disgrace to yer ould mither and yer family! We've had six generations of honest people, and niver wan like this! Ach, to think of comin' to your ind on the Island, and be on the town! For the love of the blessed Vargin, *do* give them all up, and say ye won't taste a drop—do, darlint!'

"The girl seemed obdurate; so I took up the sermon, and we both pleaded, and pictured the shame and pain and wretched life and more wretched death before her. There is no need of delicacy in such cases, and the strongest old Bible Saxon words come home the deepest. At last, her tears began to flow, and finally she gave her full assent to breaking off from liquor and from her bad company (it should be remembered she was only about sixteen); and she would show her repentance by going back to the place where she was, if they would receive her. I hardly expected she would do so; but in a day or two she was in the office, and started for her old situation. Since that we have had a letter from her and her mistress, and sho seems to be getting on wonderfully well. May God uphold her!

"The following is a letter we have received from her since:

"'B——, PENN., October 11.

"'MY DEAR MOTHER—I have the pleasure of writing a few lines to you, to let you know that I am well. I got safe back to my place; kind friends took me back again; I have got into the country, where there is plenty of everything to live on. Dear mother, I would like very much to hear from you. I hope you are all well; please write soon. I want you to show this letter to Miss Spratt.* Good-by, dear mother.   M.

* Now Mrs. Hurley.

"'DEAR MISS SPRATT—As I was writing to my mother, I thought I would like to write a few lines to you. Now that I am so far away, I feel a grateful remembrance of your kindness. I am very sorry I did not have a chance of going to see you before I left the city. Please tell Mr. Brace I am much obliged to him for his kindness: tell him I got safe back to Mr. M.'s, and have a very good home. Good-by, Miss Spratt.'"

The East River Industrial School (at No. 206 East Fortieth Street) still continues its humble but profound labors of love. Mrs. Hurley is still there, the "friend of the poor" for miles around, carrying sympathy, advice, and assistance to thousands of unbefriended creatures, and teaching faithfully all day in the School. Two gentlemen have especially aided her in providing food and clothing for her little ones; and the lady-volunteers still give liberally of their means and time. May the School long shine as a light in one of the dark places of the city.

CHAPTER XV.

IT is not often that our efforts carry us among Protestant poor, but it happens that on the west side of the city, near Tenth Avenue and Twenty-seventh Street, is a considerable district of English and Scotch laboring people, who are mainly Protestants.

A meeting of ladies was called in the western part of the city, in like manner with the proceedings at the formation of the other Schools; and a School was proposed. The wife of a prominent property-holder in the neighborhood, a lady of great energy of character, Mrs. R. R., took a leading part, and greatly aided the undertaking; other ladies joined, and the result was the formation of the

HUDSON RIVER INDUSTRIAL SCHOOL,

the fourth of our Schools founded in 1854. With all these Schools, in the beginning, the ladies themselves raised all the funds for their support, and, as I have related, devoted an incredible amount of time to aiding in them, there being usually, however. two salaried teachers.

The experience in the Edinburgh Ragged Schools, I was assured, when there, was, that you cannot depend on volunteer help after the first enthusiasm has passed by. This is not our experience.

As one set of "volunteers" have withdrawn or leave the work, others appear, and there are still in this and some of our other Industrial Schools, most active and efficient voluntary helpers. Gradually, however, the support and supervision of the Schools fell more and more into the hands of the central authority—The Children's Aid Society.

The obtaining a share in the Common School Fund enabled the Society to do more for these useful charities and to found new ones.

In the Hudson River School, it cannot be said that the Protestant poor proved much better than the Catholic; in fact, it has often seemed to me that when a Protestant is reduced to extreme poverty, and, above all, a Yankee, he becomes the most wretched and useless of all paupers. The work and its results were similar on the west side to those in the other districts which I have already described.

"MUSCULAR ORPHANS."

Our attention had thus far been directed mainly to girls in these Industrial School efforts. They seemed the class exposed to the most terrible evils, and besides, through our other enterprises, we were sheltering, teaching, and benefiting for life vast numbers of lads.

We determined now to try the effect of industry and schooling on the roving boys, and I chose a district where we had to make head against a "sea of evils." This was in the quarter bordering on East Thirty-fourth Street and Second Avenue. There seemed to be there a society of irreclaimable little vagabonds. They hated School with an inextinguishable hatred; they had a constitutional love for smashing windows and pilfering apple-stands. They could dodge an "M. P." as a fox dodges a hound; they disliked anything so civilized as a bed-chamber, but preferred old boxes and empty barns, and when they were caught it required a very wide-awake policeman, and such an Asylum-yard as hardly exists in New York, to keep them.

I have sometimes stopped, admiringly, to watch the skill and cunning with which the little rascals, some not more than ten years old, would diminish a load of wood left on the docks; the sticks were passed from one to another, and the lad nearest the pile was apparently engaged eagerly in playing marbles. If the woodman's attention was called to his loss, they were off like a swarm of cockroaches.

We opened a School with all the accessories for reaching and pleasing them; our teacher was a skillful mechanic, a young man of excellent judgment and

STREET ARABS.

hearty sympathy with boys; he offered to teach them carpentering and box-making and pay them wages. Common-school lessons were given, also, and a good warm meal provided at noon. We had festivals and magic-lantern exhibitions and lectures. We taught, and we fed and clothed. In return, they smashed our windows; they entered the premises at night and carried off everything they could find; they howled before the door, and yelled "Protestant School!" We arrested one or two for the burglary, as a warning, but the little flibbertigibbets escaped from the police like rats, and we let them go with the fright they had had. Some few of the worst we induced to go to the country, and others we had arrested as vagrants, without appearing ourselves, until a kind of dark suspicion spread among them against the writer that he had the power of spiriting away bad boys to distant regions by some mysterious means. Those that did go to the country proved of the kind called by a Western paper "muscular orphans," for an unfortunate employer undertaking to administer corporal punishment to two of them, the little vagabonds turned and chastised him and then fled.

The following case is noted in our Journal of these up-town boys:

A HARD CASE REFORMED.

"MR. BRACE—*Dear Sir:* You request me to send you some reminiscences of the early life of Michael S———n. My most vivid recollection of him is his taking the broomstick to me

once, as I was about to punish him for some misdemeanor.
Being the first and last of my pupils who ever attempted anything of the kind, it stands out in bold relief in my memory. I
soon conquered the broomstick, but on the first opportunity he
ran out, thus ending his Industrial School career.

"His most marked characteristic was a desire to travel, and
he presented himself with the freedom of the city at a very
early age, going off for weeks at a time, sleeping in entries and
around engine-houses, and disdaining bolts and bars when they
were turned upon him. One of your visitors calling to consult
with his mother as to what could be done with him, found him
vigorously kicking the panels out of the door, she having locked
him in for safe-keeping till she came home from work. The
Captain of Police, tired of having him brought in so frequently,
thought one day of a punishment that he expected would effectually frighten him, which was—to hang him. His mother con-
senting, he was solemnly hung up by the feet to a post, till he
promised reformation. This failing to produce the desired effect,
she placed him with "the Brothers," who put him in a kind of
prison, where he had to be chained by the leg to prevent him
from scaling the walls. Taking him from there, after some
months of pretty severe discipline, he very soon went back to
his old habits, when she had him sent to Randall's Island. Here
he was discovered in a plan to swim to the opposite shore
(something of a feat for a boy of twelve). Fearing he would
attempt it and be drowned, she took him away and put him in
the Juvenile Asylum, where he remained several months, and
finally seemed so much tamed down that she ventured on taking
him out and sending him to a place which you procured for him
at Hastings. But, pretty soon, the ruling passion, strong as ever,
took possession of him, and he started on a tour through the
surrounding villages.

"Being brought home again, he told his mother very delibe-
rately, one morning, that she need not expect him home any
more; he was going to live with a soldier's wife. Knowing
that if he went he would be in a very den of wickedness, she
came to the resolution to give him to your care, and let him be
sent to the West.

"It would require a volume to tell of all his freaks and wanderings; his scaling of fences, and breaking out of impossible places. Towards the last of his New York life he began to add other vices to his original stock—such as drinking, smoking, and swearing; yet strange to say, he disdained to lie, and was never known to steal; and his face would glow with satisfaction when he could take charge of an infant. His mother hears, with trembling hope, the good accounts of him from the West, scarcely daring to believe that her wild and vagrant son will ever make a steady, useful man.

"Truly yours,

"MRS. E. S. HURLEY."

The young rovers gradually became softened and civilized under the combined influences of warm dinners, carpentering, and good teaching; but we found the difficulty to be that we did not have sufficient hold over them out of school hours; we needed more appliances for such habitual vagabonds. What was wanted was a Lodging-house and all its influences, as well as School, for the former gives a greater control than does a simple Industrial School.

We accordingly transferred the whole enterprise to a still worse quarter, where I had done my first work in visiting, and which I thoroughly knew, the the region on East River, at the foot of Eleventh Street. Here was a numerous band of similar boys, who slept anywhere, and lived by petty pilferings from the iron-works and wood-yards and by street jobs.

In this place we combined our carpenters' shop with Day-school, Night-school, Reading-room, and Lodging-house, and exerted thus a variety of influences over the "Arabs," which soon began to reform and civilize them. Here we had no difficulties, and made a steady progress as we had done everywhere else.

At present, some gentle female teachers guide the Industrial School. We have dropped the carpentering, as what the boys need is the habit of industry and a primary school-training more than a trade; and we have found that a refined woman can influence these rough little vagabonds even more than a man.

Subsequently, another school was founded in the quarter from which we removed this, and is now held in East Thirty-fourth Street.

One of the benefactions which we hope for in the future is the erection of a suitable building for a Lodging-house, Reading-room, Day-school, and Mission, in the miserable quarter on East River, near Thirty-fourth Street.

CHAPTER XVI.

NEW METHODS OF TEACHING.

A LADY of high culture and position, who felt peculiarly the responsibilities of the fortunate toward the unfortunate, conceived the idea of doing something to elevate the condition of the destitute classes in the quarter of the city between the East River and Avenue B. She accordingly made the proposition to us of an Industrial School in that neighborhood.

We gladly accepted, and soon secured a room, and gathered a goodly company of poor children, mostly Germans. Fortunately for our enterprise, we chanced on a teacher of singular ability and earnestness of purpose, a graduate of the best Normal School in the country, the Oswego Training School, and thoroughly versed in the " Object System "—Miss Jane Andrews.

The founder of our school proved as earnest in carrying out, as she had been generous in forming, her benevolent plan.

She took part herself, several times each week, in teaching the children, and was indefatigable in promoting their pleasures, as well as aiding their instruction. For many years now, this kind friend of the poor has supported this school and labored among its children. They all know and love her, and her memory will not die among them.

The great peculiarity of this school has now been adapted in the other Industrial Schools, under the name of the "Object System of Teaching"—a method which has proved so singularly successful with the children of the poor, that I shall describe it somewhat at length.

THE OBJECT SYSTEM.

"I began with children," says Pestalozzi, "as nature does with savages, first bringing an image before their eyes, and then seeking a word to express the perception to which it gives rise." This statement of the great reformer of education expresses the essential principle of the Object System. The child's mind grasps first things rather than names; it deals with objects before words; it takes a thing as a whole rather than in parts. Its perceptive and observing faculties are those first awakened, and should be the first used in education; reflection, analysis, and comparison must come afterward. The vice of the former systems of education has been, that words have so much taken in the child's intellect the place of things, and its knowledge has become so often a mere routine, or a mechanical memorizing of names. The scholar was not taught to look beneath words, and to learn the precise thing which the word symbolized. He was trained to repeat like a machine. He did not observe closely, he had not been educated to apply his own faculties, and therefore he could not think afterward. The old system reversed the natural order. It began with what is the ripest fruit of the mature intellect—definitions, or the learning of rules and statements of principles, and went on later to observing facts and applying principles. It analyzed in the beginning, and only later in the course regarded things each as a whole.

The consequence was, that children were months and years in taking the first steps in education—such as learning to read—because they had begun wrong. They had no accurate habits of observation, and, as a natural result, soon fell into loose habits of thinking. What they knew they knew vaguely. When their acquirements were tested they were found valueless. The simplest principles of mathematics were almost unknown to them, because they had learned the science by rote, and had never exercised their minds on it. They could apply none of them. Algebra, instead of being an implement, was of no more practical use to them than Sanscrit would be. Geometry was as abstract as metaphysics. They had never learned it by solid figures, or studied it intelligently. Grammar was a memorized collection of dry abstract rules and examples. Natural history was only a catalogue, and geography a dictionary learned by heart.

Our manufacturers, who had occasion in former years
to employ these youths from our Public Schools, found
them utterly incompetent for using their faculties on
practical subjects. Nor did they go forth with minds
expanded, and ready to receive the germs of knowledge which might be, as it were, floating in the atmosphere. Their faculties had not been aroused.

The "Object System" attempts to lay down the
principles which have been tested in primary education, in the form of a Science; so that the teacher not
gifted with the genius of invention and the talent for
conveying knowledge shall be able to awaken and
train the child's intellect as if he were.

Its first principle is to exercise the senses, but
never during any long period at once. The play of
the children is so contrived as to employ their sense
of touch, of weight, and of harmony. Colors are
placed before them, and they are trained in distinguishing the different delicate shades—in the recognition of which children are singularly deficient. Numbers are taught by objects, such as small beans or
marbles, and then when numerals are learned, regular
tables of addition and substraction are written on the
board by the teacher at the dictation of the scholar.

The great step in all education is the learning the
use of that wonderful vehicle and symbol of human
thought, the printed word.

Here the object system has made the greatest advance. The English language has the unfortunate peculiarity of a great many sounds to each vowel, and of an utter want of connection between the name and the sound of the letter. No mature mind can easily appreciate the dark and mysterious gulf which, to the infant's view, separates the learning the letters and reading. The two seem to be utterly different acquirements. The new methods escape the difficulty in part by not teaching the names, but the sounds, of the letters first, and then leading the child to put his sounds together in the form of a word, and next to print the word on the black-board, the teacher calling on the scholar to find a similar one in a card or book. By this ingenious device, the modern infant, instead of being whipped into reading, is beguiled into it pleasantly and imperceptibly, and makes his progress by a philosophical law. He reads before he knows it. But here the obstacle arises that each vowel, printed in the same type, has so many sounds. One ingenious teacher, Dr. Leigh, obviates this by printing on his charts each vowel-sound in a slightly different form, and giving the silent letters in hair-lines. The objection here might be that the scholar learns a type different from that in common use. Still, the deviation from the ordinary alphabet is so slight as probably not to confuse any young mind, and the learner can go on by a philosophical classification of sounds. Other teachers indicate the different vowel-sounds by accents.

One well-known writer on the "Object System," Mr. Caulkins, seems to approve of what we are inclined to consider even more philosophical still—the learning the word first, and the letters and spelling afterward.

Most children in cultivated families learn to read in this way. The word is a symbol of thought—a thing in itself—first, perhaps, connected with a picture of the object placed at its side, but afterward becoming phonetic, representing arbitrarily any object by its sound. Then other words are learned—not separately, but in association, as one learns a foreign language. Further on, the pupil analyzes, spells, considers each letter, and notes each part of speech.

An objection may occur here, that the habit of correct and careful spelling will not be so well gained by this method as by the old.

Mr. Caulkins's remarks on this topic in his Manual on "Object Lessons" are so sensible that we quote them *in extenso* :—

THE A B C METHOD.

"This old, long, and tedious way consists in teaching, first, the name of each of the twenty-six letters, then in combining these into unmeaning syllables of 'two letters,' 'three letters,' and, finally, into words of 'two syllables' and 'three syllables.' Very little regard is had to the meaning of the words. Indeed, it

seems as if those who attempt to teach reading by this
method supposed that the chief object should be to
make their pupils fluent in oral spelling; and it ends
in spelling, usually, since children thus taught go on
spelling out their words through all the reading lessons, and seldom become intelligent readers. They
give their attention to the words, instead of the ideas
intended to be represented by them. When the child
has succeeded in learning the names of the twenty-six
letters, he has gained no knowledge of their real use
as representatives of sounds, and, consequently, little
ability in determining how to pronounce a new word
from naming its letters. Besides, the names of the
letters constantly mislead him when formed into
words.

"He may have made the acquaintance of each of
the twenty-six individual letters, so as to recognize
their faces and be able to call them by name singly;
but when these same letters change places with their
fellows, as they are grouped into different words, he is
frequently unable to address many of them in a proper
manner, or to determine what duties they perform in
their different places.

"Again, the words that are learned by naming
over the letters which compose them seldom represent any ideas to the young learner; indeed, too many
of the words learned by this method are only mean-
ingless monosyllables. The children begin to read

without understanding what they read, and thus is laid the foundation for the mechanical, unintelligible reading which characterizes most of that heard in schools where the A B C method is used. This plan is in violation of fundamental laws of teaching; it attempts to compel the child to do two things at the same time, and to do both in an unnatural manner, viz., to learn reading and spelling simultaneously, and reading through spelling. Reading has to deal with sounds and signs of thought.

"Spelling rests on the habit of the eye, which is best acquired as the result of reading. In attempting to teach reading through spelling, the effort of the pupil in trying to find out the word by naming the letters that compose it distracts the attention from the thought intended to be represented by it; the mind becomes chiefly absorbed with spelling instead of reading. When properly taught, reading furnishes natural facilities for teaching spelling; but spelling does not furnish a suitable means for teaching reading. Thus it will be seen that the usual plans for teaching reading by the A B C method compel children to do that for which their minds are not fitted, and thus cause a loss of power by restraining them from attending to the thoughts represented by the words, and to other things which would greatly promote their development. The results are that a love for reading is not enkindled, good readers are not produced. The few cases in which the results are different owe both the love for reading and the ability in this art to other causes.

"The pupils learned to love reading, and became able to read well, in spite of poor teaching during their first lessons. There is consolation in believing that this method, which produced so many halting, stumbling readers, is now abandoned by all good teachers of reading. May the number of such teachers be greatly increased.

*　　*　　*　　*　　*　　*

"The 'word method' begins at once with teaching the words in a manner similar to that by which children learn to distinguish one object from another, and learn the names. It proposes to teach words as the signs of things, acts, and qualities, etc. It does not propose to teach children the alphabet, but to leave them to learn this after they have become familiar with enough words to commence reading."

The Object System teaches geography very ingeniously. The pupil begins by getting into his mind the idea of a map. This is by no means so simple an idea as might be supposed, as witness the impossibility almost of making a savage understand it. The child is first told to point to the different points of the compass; then he marks them down on a blackboard; next he draws a plan of the room, and each scholar attempts to locate an object on the plan, and is corrected by the school, if wrong. Next comes a plan of the district or town; then a globe is shown, and the idea of position on the globe given, and of the outlines of different countries. Soon the pupil learns to draw maps on the board, and to place rivers, bays, lakes, and oceans. The book-questions now to be presented will not be on purely political greography or merely arbitrary lists of names. The child is taken on imaginary journeys up rivers, over mountains, by railroads, and must describe from the lesson he has learned the different productions, the animals, the character of the scenery, the vegetation, and the occupations of the people. Thus geography becomes a kind of natural science, deeply interesting to the pupil, and touching his imagination. Certain dry geographical names are forever after associated in his mind with certain animals and plants and a peculiar scenery.

Natural history is also taught in this system, but not by the usual dry method. The teacher brings in a potato, for instance, and carries the pupil along by questions through all its growth and development. Or she takes flowers, or leaves, or seeds, and stamps the most important phenomena about them on the scholar's mind by an objective lesson. Prints of animals are presented, and the teacher begins at the lowest orders, and rises up in regular gradation, questioning the children as to the uses and purposes of every feature and limb. They work out their own natural philosophy. They observe, and then reason; and what they learn is learned in philosophical order, and imprinted by their own efforts on their memories. It is astonishing how much, in these simple methods, may be learned in natural science by very young children; and what nutritive but simple food may be supplied to their minds for all future years.

From lessons in science thus given, the teacher rises easily to lessons of morality and religion. Nothing even in moral teaching impresses a child's mind like pictures, stories, or parables, or some form of "object-teaching." The modern charts and books are extremely ingenious in giving religious lessons through the senses.

The beginning of the higher mathematics may be taught children perfectly well under this method. Straight lines and angles are drawn, or constructed with little sticks, and named, and various figures thus formed. With blocks, the different geometrical figures are constructed and named—all being finished by the pupils themselves. On the blackboard certain lines are given, and with them "inventive drawing" goes on under the pupil's own suggestion.

Weights and measures are learned by practical illustrations with real objects, and are thus not easily forgotten.

Definition is very agreeably taught by the teacher's producing some object, say, an apple, and then making each scholar describe some quality of it, in taste, color, form, or material, and then write this word on the board. Very difficult adjectives, such as "opaque," or "pungent," or "translucent," or "aromatic," may thus be learned, besides all the simpler, and learned permanently.

The old bugbear to children, spelling, is by no means so terrible under these methods. The teacher writes two initial consonants, say, "th," and each scholar makes a new word with them, and it is written on the board; or a terminal consonant is given, or certain combinations of letters are written down—say, *ough*, in "though," and words of corresponding sound must be written underneath, or the different sounds of each vowel must be illustrated by the scholar, and the varying sounds of consonants, and so on endlessly —spelling becoming a perfect amusement, and, at the same time, training the pupil in many delicate shades of sound, and in analyzing and remembering words.

Grammar is conveyed, not by that farce in teaching, and that cross to all children, grammatical rules, which are, in fact, the expressions of the final fruit of knowledge, but the teacher writes incorrectly on the blackboard, both in spelling, punctuation, and grammar, and the children must correct this; thus learning from the senses and usage, instead of from abstract rules.

Reading is given as nearly as possible in conversational tones, and the old loud, mechanical sing-song is forbidden.

The principle most insisted on in all this system is, that the child should teach himself, as far as possible; that his faculties should do the work, and not the teacher's; and the dull and slow pupil is especially to be led on and encouraged. But, as might be supposed, the teacher's task, under the object method, is no sinecure. She can no longer slip along the groove of mechanical teaching. She must be wide-awake, inventive, constantly on the *qui vive* to stir up her pupils' minds. The droning over lessons, and letting children repeat, parrot-like, long lists of words, is not for her. She must be always seeking out some new thing and making her pupils observe and think for themselves. Her duty is a hard one. But this is the only true teaching; and we trust that no Primary School in New York will be without a well-trained "Object-teacher."

CHAPTER XVII.

THE LITTLE ITALIAN ORGAN-GRINDERS.

AMONG the various rounds I was in the habit of
making in the poorest quarters, was one through the
Italian quarter of the "Five Points." Here, in large
tenement-houses, were packed hundreds of poor Italians, mostly engaged in carrying through the city
and country "the everlasting hand-organ," or selling
statuettes. In the same room I would find monkeys,
children, men and women, with organs and plaster-
casts, all huddled together; but the women contriving
still, in the crowded rooms, to roll their dirty maca-
roni, and all talking excitedly; a bedlam of sounds,
and a combination of odors from garlic, monkeys, and
most dirty human persons. They were, without exception, the dirtiest population I had met with. The
children I saw every day on the streets, following
organs, blackening boots, selling flowers, sweeping
walks, or carrying ponderous harps for old ruffians.
So degraded was their type, and probably so mingled
in North Italy with ancient Celtic blood, that their
faces could hardly be distinguished from those of Irish

poor children—an occasional liquid dark eye only
betraying their nationality.

I felt convinced that something could be done for
them. Owing to their ignorance of our language and
their street-trades, they never attended school, and
seldom any religious service, and seemed growing up
only for these wretched occupations. Some of the
little ones suffered severely from being indentured by
their parents in Italy to a "Bureau" in Paris, which
sent them out over the world with their "*padrone*,'
or master, usually a villainous-looking individnal with
an enormous harp. The lad would be frequently sent
forth by his *padrone*, late at night, to excite the compassion of our citizens, and play the harp. I used to
meet these boys sometimes on winter-nights half-
frozen and stiff with cold.

The bright eyes among these children showed that
there was mind in them; and the true remedy for
their low estate seemed to be our old one, a School.

Rev. Dr. Hawks, at this time, brought to my attention a very intelligent Italian gentleman of education,
a Protestant and patriot, who had taken refuge here—
Signor A. E. Cerqua. I will let him tell his own story
of the formation and success of the School:

THE ITALIAN SCHOOL—THE FIVE POINTS SETTLEMENT.

"Coming up Chatham Street and bending your course to the
left, you turn into Baxter Street, a dark, damp, muddy street,
forming one of the Five Points. On each side of the way are

stores of old clothes and heterogeneous articles, kept by Polish and German Jews. Numerous ' Unredeemed Goods for Sale,' in the shape of coats, vests, and other unmentionable garments, are suspended on wooden stands in front of the doorways. There are also junk-stores, rags, bones, and old metal depots, and two Italian groceries, one opposite the other. Advancing further, you reach the centre of the Five Points, synonymous of whatever is degraded and degrading, loathsome and criminal. Here Park Street runs parallel to Chatham Street and crosses Baxter Street at right angles, thus forming four of the Five Points. The fifth point is formed by the junction of Worth Street, leading from this common centre in a northerly direction. This locality is very dimly lighted, and the few lamps scattered around only add to the repulsive nature of the place. The pestiferous exhalations of the filthy streets, and not less filthy shanties, inhabited by the lowest and most disreputable characters, are disgusting beyond any description. Scattered over this neighborhood, densely settled by the most depraved classes of all nationalities, there lived, and still live, some fifteen hundred of the poorest class of Italians, who traditionally cling to that locality. They are generally from the Ligurian coasts, which are over-populated. When the farms require working, the inhabitants usually have something to do ; but, at some seasons, want of employment compels them to turn elsewhere. Men, women, and lads went in ordinary times to the largest cities of Northern Italy for temporary occupation, leaving behind their children to the care of relatives or acquaintances, who, owing to their business, inability, or carelessness, neglected in most cases to exercise over them parental duties. When the hand-organ came into vogue, they found it the easiest way to employ their unoccupied time. Seeing, afterward, that they could realize more by the organ than by the shovel, they went *grinding* all the year, and spread all over Italy at first, then over Europe and America. Some of the children left were sent for, while others were hired out to those who proposed a grinding-tour to America. Those who arrived here first having done well, others followed, and the tide of the organ-grinding emigration set in on a gradual rise. The failure of the Revolutionary movements of 1848 and 1849 having impoverished, to a greater or smaller extent, the several Italian provinces, gave a great impetus to this emigation, and it was not long before the Five Points were crowded to overflowing. Accustomed as they were to agricultural pursuits and out of the reach of better social influences, and totally ignorant of the language, they formed a separate colony, associating only with those of their own country in the Five Points. Had they displayed the vices or criminal inclinations which prevail to a deplorable extent among the low classes of other nationalities, they would soon have been brought to public notice and taken care of by our benevolent and religious societies; but they cannot be reproached with intoxication, prostitution, quarreling, stealing, etc.; and thus, escaping the unenviable notoriety of the criminal, they fell into a privacy that deprived them of the advantages of American benevolence; and there is no instance of any visitor having ever been appointed to explore this fruitful field of operation.

OPENING OF THE SCHOOL.

" Early in December, 1855, the writer, with Mr. Brace, visited several families. Our reception was not such as to promise success, although, considering their distrustful and suspicious disposition, consequent upon their isolated existence, they did not treat us disrespectfully. Having thus prepared and informed them, on the evening of the tenth of the same month we opened our School in a room kindly furnished by Rev. Mr. Pease, on the north side of the Five Points' square.

" On the first night of our operation we had an attendance of ten boys, six girls, seven young men, four young women, two men, and one woman (thirty in all), attracted, as may be evident by the age of the attendants, more by the novelty of the undertaking than by any definite purpose. Of that number, only two could read a little in Italian—not one in English; hence I formed a single class of the whole in the alphabet.

" By more frequent visiting, the attendance was, after a little while, nearly doubled; but toward spring it dwindled to such an insignificant number, that it was deemed expedient to close the School.

" Instead of being deterred by this discouraging feature, we determined to examine the field more carefully, and endeavor to discover the immediate cause of the unexpected check our hopes had experienced. Proper exertions in visiting, and cautious and timely investigations, soon brought out the fact that some absurd rumors had been circulated among them to the effect that our purpose was to turn them away from their own church, alleging, as conclusive evidence, that our school-room was used for Sunday religious meetings. These mischievous insinuations called for the utmost prudent activity on our part, for, although these people are not fanatics in religion, they, at that time, still clung with tenacity to the infallibility of their priest. I say at that time, because the unnatural and unchristian attitude assumed since by their spiritual guides toward Italy has forced even the uneducated class into a certain use of comparative rational freedom, and, beyond the spiritual, they will not follow their religious leaders. Meeting with only partial success by persuasion, I then promised shoes and clothing to pupils who would attend for three months consecutively; and having thus prepared the way, and without ever failing to visit the most unapproachable, it was deemed advisable to reopen the School in November, 1856. The attendance increased by some thirty, with a minor sprinkling of men and women. Shoes and clothes were distributed in March, but the number soon after commenced diminishing, until June, 1857, when the School, as in the previous year, had to be closed for a second time. Two great advantages had, however, been developed. Their ready acceptance of shoes and clothes given and distributed in our room was a powerful argument in my hands to answer their objection to the room; and among the floating attendance I had noticed a score or so of regular pupils upon whom I concentrated my best attention and every possible encouragement, in the conviction that the result of my efforts in that direction would prove efficacious to attract others. And, in fact, when the improvement of these twenty attendants became known, it was found comparatively easy to persuade others to school.

" It had now become evident to me that, with adequate exertions and inducements, the School could be established on a permanent and working order; and on the following September we recommenced operations with better promise. But a narrow-minded opposition partially marred our success this year. [An

Italian priest, called Rebiccio, from the confessional and from the pulpit, flung ferocious anathemas at all who permitted their children to attend our School. He even went from house to house to use his influence in the same direction. I sent a deputation of my oldest scholars to remonstrate with him and correct his misapprehensions by assuring him that we had no sectarian teachings. These same boys I took with me in visiting a number of the most superstitious families, and for the same purpose, but in both cases of no avail ; only, instead of justifying myself, I found that these boys were equally suspected of complicity, some even assuming that they had already been converted. I felt disheartened, not because I did not hope to overcome all obstacles by patience, prudence, and perseverance, but because I could scarcely realize the actual occurrence of such un unflinching, unprincipled, and unjust persecution, or, what was still worse, of such credulous stupidity as was shown by the very people we intended to elevate.

Prompted by these feelings, I then wrote a letter to that worthy priest, inviting him to assist me in teaching, to take my place, to teach these poor children himself—in short, to do what he pleased, provided they were furnished with proper means to better their condition. The letter was couched in the most unexceptionable terms, and closed by entreating him to desist from his unjust attacks, and not to compel me to appeal to the public through the daily press, the last resort in this free country. Discouraged by the suspicious reception I met with from the majority of these people, and by the fruitless result of my aforesaid letter, I was then preparing a statement for the newspapers, when the whole opposition scheme exploded. Under the false pretext that he was going to hire a building to open a school for these children, in connection with a church, which he proposed also to build for them, this worthy priest had collected considerable money in the Five Points, when all at once he disappeared, and it was only after months that he was heard of in affluent circumstances in Italy. A natural and desirable reaction then took place among our people, and since then the School has been yearly in operation for eleven months, and with gradual prosperity. In June, 1866, desiring to extend our work and absorb all children exposed to the bad influences and examples of the streets that attended no day-school, we added also successfully a day-session, so that now, with two hundred and twenty-eight (228) names on our books since October 1, 1867, we have a daily average of sixty-five (65), and one hundred and eighty-six (186) for day and evening sessions respectively. By these figures it will be seen that, while in other schools the proportion of the average to the names entered is, at the best, seventy-five per cent., nearly all our pupils on the roll-book attend regularly one of the two, and several both sessions. The attendants vary from five to twenty-two years of age, averaging about nine and a half. A little less than one-half of the whole are females.

MENTAL IMPROVEMENT.

" Whoever has not associated with this class of Italians before our School was opened cannot form an adequate idea of the result attained both in moral and mental improvement. Out of the whole number entered since the commencement of operations, say, in round numbers, eight hundred and fifty (850), not over forty had a little and imperfect knowledge of reading the Italian, and only about ten had a slight acquaintance with the English. My first endeavors were directed to induce them to attend day-schools, and during the first three years over twenty became pupils of Public Schools. Later on, this number received accessions, amounting at one time to about fifty.

" Our course of study comprises the gradual series of English reading, spelling, and writing adopted in most of the Public Schools ; geography, arithmetic, history, and grammar. The class in the last two branches this year is very small, as the students thereof, being mostly adults, cannot well attend regularly.

" Some twelve years ago, and for a time after, there were only two among them who had some knowledge of letters, and on them the whole colony had to depend for writing and reading letters in Italian and interpreting in English, on payment of charges varying from twenty-five to fifty cents. On becoming acquainted with this fact, I resolved upon teaching also the Italian to the most advanced in the English, which addition met with general favor, for, a year after, the pupils who could and did gratuitously perform the offices of the two literati increased to such an extent that one was usually found within each family or a circle of relatives. The time being limited, these studies are, of course, taught alternately, and the progress therein is not as speedy as would be desirable; but, everything considered, they show remarkable intelligence, aptitude, and willingness to learn. I might quote from reports of the principal press of this city on our last examination; but, as the School is free and always open to visitors, I will content myself with inviting our friends to look into the subject for themselves.

How gratifying when I enter the School to see the oldest of the attendants, but a few years ago illiterate and totally ignorant of everything around them, reading papers, and quoting, discriminating, and discussing the topics of the day, and forming a more or less correct idea of the state of things in the land of their adoption and in other parts of the world! Gratifying, indeed, to see these children, but a few years age without any idea of patriotism, without any other principle to guide their judgment and actions than the natural impulses of a degraded selfishness, exchange intelligent views upon the moral standing and tendency of the political parties in this and in their native country! Many times I have been astonished at the extensive information and sound opinions they display in commenting upon contemporaneous events. The

MORAL IMPROVEMENT.

which has been accomplished is still more extensive and sensible. At first sight the visitor is enabled to draw a line between old and new pupils by noticing the intelligent and clean appearance, quick perception, and admirable behavior of the former, and the dull, downcast, rough, and thoughtless countenances of the latter. It is surprising that all these children were accustomed to wash their faces only on Sundays, and it takes even now some time to induce them to do it daily. Still, it is undeniable that, as a class, they possess an earnest appreciation of good habits, only it is, to say so, an abstract idea as yet with them, and needs development.

"When the School opened, and for some time after, the attendance was generally composed of organ-grinders and beggars, which vocations they indifferently acknowledged to follow, whenever asked, by analogous gestures. To redeem them from those ignoble vocations was, in my opinion, of paramount importance, and to that end I devoted part of my time in visiting their parents, to impress them with a sense of self-respect and human dignity, and talk them into the apprenticing into trades their offspring. As, however, these boys brought home from fifty cents to a dollar per day, it was quite a difficult task to persuade them to give up this source of income for comparatively nominal wages. With guardians and relatives my efforts remained entirely fruitless. I then concluded that if we could show them practically that trades in the end would pay better, it would become easy to accomplish our purpose. I concentrated, therefore, my exertions on three families, the most approachable, and succeeded. One consented to place a boy of fourteen in the Printing Department of the American Tract Society; another soon followed in the same line; the third, a boy of thirteen, entered a machine-shop. All three did very well, and at the end of two years they were earning five and six dollars per week. Their success caused a moral revolution, and had I been able to place all, not one would at this day be blacking boots, which many do for want of better employment. It is a fact that speaks very highly of these Italians, that in every instance, whenever one has been employed, Italians are preferred. I have seen certificates given by manufacturers to some of them, speaking enthusiastically of their honesty, industry, and faithfulness. There are also instances of extraordinary interest taken by employers in their behalf, and in no case has any ever been discharged for any other reason than for want of work. A large number of girls also find occupation in artificial flowers and confectionery. All now look with scorn upon their former vocations, and the term *'pianist'* is ironically applied to newly-landed organ-grinders. Now it is a fact that can stand the strictest scrutiny, that *all* those who follow decent vocations or attend day-schools, public or otherwise, either are or have been our regular attendants for years and that *all grinders, beggggars, and vagrants,* in general, are not and have not, attended at all, or at most a few weeks, attracted only by the hope of getting shoes or clothes.

"Without mentioning the many present pupils who are engaged in honorable pursuits, I can readily name about fifty old attendants who have left school, now employed in this or other States as printers, confectioners, jewelers, shoemakers, machinists, carpenters, waiters, carvers, and farm-hands. To these must be added two who keep and own a neat confectionery and ice-cream saloon in Grand Street; a shoemaker in business for himself; another, one of the first three above-mentioned, a foreman in the very machine-shop in which he served as an apprentice; one a patented machinist in a steam chocolate manufactory; and, lastly, one who for the last three years has been foreman in a wholesale confectionery. I omit to mention those who have gone back to Italy and are doing well. As a rule, they all remember with gratitude their friends, to whose efforts and liberality they acknowledge they owe their present position. From every State in which they settle we receive now and then encouraging news from some boy; and not long ago we heard, for the second time, from a boy in Italy, who, after having mentioned that he was studying Latin, etc., gives vent to his feelings by conveying his most hearty thanks to all the teachers, mentioning them one by one—to Mr. Brace, to Mr. Macy, and, not remembering the name of our good friend, John C. Havemeyer, Esq., he adds, "also to that kind gentleman who has an office at No. 175 Pearl Street." His letter is very touching, and reveals noble feeling and mind.

"Nor are parents less grateful and ready to acknowledge the good of American benevolence. I was conversing one evening with a widow woman, while her boy was writing to her father in Italy, and called her attention to the advantage her son had derived from our School, adding that I still remembered how indifferently she received at first my advices. She felt a little mortified and replied: 'Caro Maestro (Dear Teacher), having never received any good from anybody, but plenty of harm, we could not believe that all at once we had become worthy of so much kindness. We used to have hard treatment at the hand of everybody, had no friends; even our countrymen in better circumstances despised us, and, to tell you the truth, we had made up our mind that we would find charity only in the other world.'

VISITING.

"I will not attempt to give an idea of the difficulty attending visiting in the Five Points, nor can I dwell at length on the extensive suffering and wretchedness that have fallen under my observation. Notwithstanding my comparative familiarity with those places, I cannot dispense yet with a guide and a light, and, in many instances, two of both. The rickety shanties, with crumbling stairs and broken steps, undergo as many changes in the interior as may be suggested by the wants of the successive inmates. The rooms have been partitioned and sub-partitioned a good number of times, and now and then I have found even part of the hall, and the whole thereof on top floors, taken in by new partitions. Small wooden rear buildings are mostly tenanted entirely by Italians, but in large tenement-houses there is generally found a good Irish or Jewish mingling. Visiting, in the latter case, is often attended by most unpleasant occurrences, owing to intoxicated and troublesome persons that are usually found in the stairs and halls. But to relate some of my experience:

"On Christmas-day (1866) a woman with five children—the oldest three our pupils—coming from church, fell, breaking her arm and giving premature birth to a sixth. Hearing of this sad case, I took a few yards of red flannel and went to see her. I found the poor woman in the deepest agony and almost frantic from suffering. Her husband kept a fruit-stand in Nassau Street, but this accident, as she expressed it, had entirely stupified him, and she suffered to a great extent, also, morally, from the hopeless condition of her young family. The stove was as warm (or cold) as every piece of furniture in the room, and the poor patient and the two smallest children had to manage to keep warm by lying on the same bed, with a pile of old clothes and carpets over them. Presently, however, the three elder children came in, half-frozen and barefooted, scarcely able to talk, and discharged near the stove the contents of their aprons and bags, the result of their coal-picking tour. Leaving to their father the care of reviving the fire, they, as of a common consent, started for a closet, and drawing out a good-sized tin pan full of boiled corn-meal, commenced a furious onslaught thereon. The outer room measured some twelve by fourteen feet, and had no beds, but its floor afforded sleeping accommodations to the five children. The inner room was scarcely large enough to admit a middle-sized bedstead used by the parents. When I left, the young ones had taken their places for the night, and the man, having made a good fire, proceeded to assort a barrel of apples, and his wife said it was the fourth time '*that stupid man had gone through the same process without having done anything.*'

"Among guardians, especially, the custom was prevalent of fixing the amount the boy or girl had to bring home in the evening. But not seldom fathers were prompted by avarice to act still more cruelly against their own offspring, and while the former punished the shortcomings of their wards by furnishing them with meals of microscopic proportions, the latter, on the presumption, I suppose, of paternal right, went so far as to whip and even expel from home the son or sons who failed to come up to their greedy expectations. At present, however, such cases are almost unknown, owing to the sense of independence felt by the growing generation and to our influence on the parents. But as late as three years ago I had observed that a boy of twelve, who was very anxious to learn, now and then was absent. One evening I called on him for explanations, and he related tha he was '*taxed*' for eighty cents a day, and every cent short of that amount was balanced by a proportionate dose of cowhiding on his bare body. He entreated me most earnestly not to say a word to his father on the subject, otherwise he would fare still worse. Whenever, therefore, he failed to earn the eighty cents by his boot-blacking vocation, he would not go home. This unnatural father did not stop here; he did not care in the least how long his son would remain out sleeping under market-stands and in newspaper rooms, but he insisted on the boy paying over to him, when he would return, at the rate of eighty cents per day for all the time of his absence, without any allowance for food, etc.

"The case was really heart-rending, especially as the boy was developing fine moral and intellectual qualities, and had to be treated with uncommon prudence. At first I told the boy to call on me for whatever he was short, and he did so on two occasions; but somehow or other the transaction was reported to the father, who, rather than desist from his pretension, as any other man would certainly have done, increased the *tax* to one dollar, with the remark that '*it would make no difference to the teacher, twenty cents, more or less.*' The very same night this happened, seeing the impossibility of curing this man in any other way, I paid him a visit, which seemed to have surprised him to a great extent. I spoke to him calmly but determinedly, as I never had occasion to do before, but without eliciting any answer, and I left him with the assurance that if he did not desist at once from the vile abuse of parental authority I would have him arrested. After a few days he moved to Laurens street, and in about six months from this occurrence returned, with the whole family, to Italy. I never could learn anything afterward concerning his interesting son.

"The filth prevalent in some of their abodes is really appalling, and in some cases incredible. In —— Baxter Street there is a bedroom, nine by twelve feet, occupied by four children and their parents. The door, hindered by the bed behind it, opens scarcely enough to give admittance to a person of ordinary size. At the foot of the bed there is, and was, and will be as long as they stay therein, a red-hot stove, between which and the window stands an old chest; opposite the stove a table. The fetid air inside I would have thought to be beyond human endurance. The woman, at my request, opened the window, remarking 'that she did not see the use of burning coal inside, if the freezing air was to be permitted to come in freely.' The children sleep on the floor; that is to say, one nearly under the bed, another under the table, a third by the stove, and the fourth is at liberty to roll over any of her sisters. I could not help noticing an old greasy piece of print, of no distinguishable color, hanging around the bed, and performing, as I learned with satisfaction, the function of a curtain to keep out of view its occupants.

"During the last ten years some fifteen of our girls, and nearly as many boys, married—mostly, I ought to say, intermarried—and as the greater portion of them have children, say from four to eight years of age, in our school, I visit also occasionally among them, the new generation. And how different in their habits of cleanliness! Floors, walls, ceiling, windows, everything faultlessly clean, their persons neat, so that their rooms are really an oasis in that desert called tenement-houses; and the cordial civility they extend to me carries still farther the comparison by making me realize in their apartments, after a visiting tour at the Five Points, all the satisfaction the traveler derives by the fertile spot after a fatiguing journey across the burning sand.

"I will omit many sad scenes witnessed at the death-bed of several of our pupils, it being my aim to dwell only on such facts as may convey an idea of the nature of the difficulties we had to overcome. But the monotonous scenes of suffering under its various forms are, however, succeeded now and then by others peculiarly exciting.

"Often, of my own choice, but sometimes entreated by the pupils' parents, I paid visits to billiard-rooms. These are placed in the back-room of groceries, of which there are three in that neighborhood, and have, therefore, communication with the yard. Whenever I deemed it necessary to go on such errands, I had to organize previously an expedition of ten or twelve of our oldest scholars, who, in accordance with my instructions, would at a signal prevent all means of egress from windows and doors. I would then go in from the front, and a wild rush for the rear would ensue; but, finding themselves surrounded, all the boys I was looking for, had no other choice but to follow us to school, escorted as deserters. Now, it is more than probable that ninety-nine out of one hundred of billiard-keepers in New York would not allow such proceedings against their interests, for our *descents* did not particularly improve their profits. Still, these Italian grocers not only countenanced and aided my endeavors, but gave me also all the information I previously demanded. Little by little, by repeated expeditions and an occasional *peeping* in these places before going to school, I succeeded in nearly breaking up their vicious habits in this respect, and it is only a rare occurrence that one of our boys on Saturday nights will go in to *look* on a game. In corroboration of which success I may mention that early last winter (1867), one Saturday evening, the police made a regular and truly formidable descent on these billiard-saloons, arresting, among others, in all twenty-seven Italians, I believe, of whom eleven were boys from seven to fifteen. Next evening I had an application to interfere for their release, as it is usual for me to do whenever circumstances warrant it, and in looking into the subject carefully I found that of them only two—namely, the youngest and the oldest—belonged to our school, and that both had gone to buy groceries, and, while the grocer was weighing and wrapping the provisions, they had walked to the door between the store and the saloon to look in, and were under that circumstance arrested. Upon my conviction that such was really the case, I applied for and obtained their discharge. The other boys mostly belonged to families newly arrived from Italy and directed for California, to which State these people generally move if unable to make a living in New York.

"Now I will only add that the Maestro (teacher) at the Five Points has become an indispensable personage among them. He is assumed to be a lawyer, medical doctor, theologian, astronomer, banker—everything as well as a teacher. A boy is arrested for throwing stones in the street; the Maestro is applied to and the boy is released. One has fifty dollars to deposit; the Maestro is consulted as to the soundness of the savings-banks- and so on. But, to better appreciate their feelings on this subject, it must be known that these poor foreigners have for a long while been victimized by the grossest impositions. I have heard of as much as one thousand dollars lost by one family, through the sharp practice of a man (an Italian) who, taking advantage of their ignorance of the English, and of their confidence, deposited and drew in his name the money which was intended as part payment for a farm they had bought in Massachusetts, and gave them to understand that the bank had failed. And this is one of the many cases they had related to me on the subject. Nor less shameful imposition they suffered at the hands of the "shysters" whenever some juvenile delinquent was arrested for trifles. They had to pay from fifty to one hundred dollars, and, what was worse, often without obtaining their release. In order to explain the process by which poor people possess such cash amounts, I must say that in extraordinary circumstances they help each other with the most disinterested and prompt liberality. Some of those who go to California, having borrowed the money here, remit it generally in drafts payable to order of lenders, who, being unknown to the bank, are refused payment. The Maestro then, of course, is applied to, and for the first two or three cases I found it hard to make them understand that I did not do it for money. They would insist on my receiving *something* for my trouble in procuring payment by the drawees, and one, especially, on having paid a draft of one hundred and sixty dollars gold, followed me for a block, with a coin piece in his hand, insisting that I should take it. ' My dear man, keep your money,' I would say ; ' I am very glad to have been able to render you this service.' ' No, Maestro, no. Well, take *at least* these five dollars ' (gold). That *at least* struck me that he must have been laboring under the impression that my services were worth considerably more, and I addressed him in that sense. In answer, he explained that an Italian, who has gone away from New York, charged him and others ten per cent. for cashing drafts to order.

" In conclusion, the Maestro is called upon for every emergency. Questions undecided between two or more dissentient parties are referred to my arbitration. Family quarrels are submitted to my adjustment. It is no exaggeration to say that the good which could be effected by thus visiting among this class is immense—in fact, far beyond the expectation of those who might take as a basis of comparison the result of visiting among the low classes of other nationalities.

OUR FRIENDS.

" As the work was done in a most quiet way, our patrons were at first few, and for six years all Americans. After that period, the few distinguished Italians in this city were applied to with favorable result. But it was not until the end of 1868 that their co-operation proved efficient, and relieved considerably the Children's Aid Society of the pecuniary burden. Previous to that time, five or six of them, headed by the Italian Consul-General, Signor Anfora, visited us, to look into the working of the School, and, becoming satisfied that a great good was being accomplished, later on, at the invitation of the Trustees of the Society, organized themselves into a *Co-operative Sub-Committee*, consisting of Prof. V. Botta, President ; E. P. Fabbri, Treasurer ; G. Albinola and V. Fabbricotti, Esqs., and Dr. G. Cecarini.

The Treasurer, Signor Fabbri, with that kind and unassuming liberality for which he is distinguished, to his annual subscription has added fifty tons of coal to the most deserving, thus relieving their sufferings to a great extent, and establishing a powerful inducement for indifferent parents. The Committee also reported to the Italian Government what was taking place for the advantage of its destitute and ignorant subjects in this city, and obtained some subsidy and other encouragement from that quarter. At the head of the Ministerial Department for Foreign Affairs was, at that period, Cav. M. Cerruti, a gentleman of learning and most enlightened views, who has done much in Italy to popularize public instruction as the speediest and surest means of promoting the prosperity of the nation. This gentleman having lately been appointed Minister Plenipotentiary from his to this country, visited, last October, our School, and met with the hearty reception he deserves as one of our patrons. His visit elicited the following letter from the distinguished Italian statesman to Rev. C. L. Brace, Secretary of the Children's Aid Society :—

> "' CLARENDON HOTEL, October 29, 1867.

> "'DEAR SIR—I beg leave to be allowed to express, in behalf of the Italian Government and nation I have the honor to represent at Washington, the most heartfelt thanks for the Christian and noble undertaking unpretentiously assumed and most successfully prosecuted by the Children's Aid Society for the improvement of the poor class of the Italian population in your city. My visit to the Italian School under your charge, on the 23d instant, was to me a source of high gratification, and convinced me that, by your efficient and humane exertions, hundreds of poor Italian children have been redeemed from vagrancy and turned into industrious and useful members of the community. The cleanliness, mental training, and admirable behavior of the one hundred and fifty pupils assembled on that occasion, impressed me with a deep sense of gratitude toward the friends of the Children's Aid Society, and to you personally, for your unsparing efforts in devising and forwarding such a useful institution. I can only hope that your Society may ever

prosper and continue its charitable work in the vast field of its operations with that truly Christian and benevolent spirit which distinguishes this glorious undertaking.

> "' Believe me, dear sir,
> '"' Yours respectfully,
> [Signed]   "' MARCEL CERRUTI,
> "' *Minister Plenipotentiary from Italy at Washington.'*

GENERAL REMARKS.

" For brevity's sake I had to omit mentioning incidents which speak very highly of our pupils. Nor have I space to describe the many cases of articles and money found by them and handed to me for investigation as to the rightful owner; and their spontaneous liberality and hearty contributions to the Garibaldi Fund in 1859, to the New York Sanitary Fair in 1864, and to the relief of the orphans and wounded of the late war of Italy and Prussia against Austria. Suffice it to say that our aim is to render them useful, honest, industrious, and intelligent citizens. In that direction we have been laboring, and with what success has been seen."

CHAPTER XVIII.

THE "LAMBS" OF COTTAGE PLACE.

BEYOND a certain point, the history of these various schools becomes monotonous. It is simply a history of kindness, of patience, of struggles with ignorance, poverty, and intemperance; of lives poured out for the good of those who can never make a return, of steady improvement and the final elevation of great numbers of children and youth who are under these permanent and profound influences.

In no one of the many branches whose labors and results I am describing, has probably so much vitality been expended, so much human earnestness been offered with such patience, humility, and faith, as in the humble Mission of "Cottage Place."

It began with a "Boys' Meeting," under Mr. Macy, a practical philanthropist, of whom I shall speak again.

The quarter is a very notorious one, and contains numbers of idle and vagrant boys and girls. The success of Mr. Macy with the meeting, and the experience he gained there of a wild class of girls induced

him and his sisters to attempt in 1859 to found a
School for girls; to this was gradually added a "Free
Reading-room," a library, and various temperance and
other associations. Ladies of position and wealth
were attracted to it, as well as others, from seeing the
quiet and earnest nature of the work done; there was
no show or "blowing of trumpets," or any great expense, but there were two or three men and women
connected with it who evidently thought night and day
of the rough boys and miserable girls that attended
it; who felt no toil too great, if it could truly benefit
these unfortunate creatures.

The lady-volunteers seemed to catch the same
spirit of Christian sacrifice and earnestness. One
who has since become a missionary in a distant heathen land, poured out here for these American heathen
some of the best years of her youth in the most enthusiastic and constant labors.

Others visited the homes of the poor, some taught
in the classes, and all labored with their own hands to
arrange the festivals and dinners which they provided
so freely for the needy children. For twelve years
now those young ladies or their friends have wrought
unceasingly at this labor of love.

The great burden of the School, however, fell on
Miss Macy, a woman of long experience with this
class, and a profound and intense spirit of humanity.
I never shall forget the scene (as reported to me) when,

at the opening of the School, after the July riots in
1863 against the colored people, a deputation of hard-
looking, heavy-drinking Irish women, the mothers of
some twenty or thirty of the children, waited on her
to demand the exclusion of some colored children.
In the most amiable and Quaker-like manner, but
with the firmness of the old Puritan stock from which
she sprung, she assured them that, if every other
scholar left, so long as that school remained it should
never be closed to any child on account of color.
They withdrew their children, but soon after returned
them.

Like the other Schools, the Cottage Place gives a
great deal of assistance to the poor, but it does so in
connection with education, and therefore creates no
pauperism.

The same experience is passed through here as
under the other Schools. The children are nearly all
the offspring of drunkards, but they do not themselves
drink as they grow up. The slovenly learn cleanliness, the vagrant industry, the careless punctuality
and order. Thieving was very prevalent in the School
when it was founded; now it is never known. All
have been beggars; but, as they improve under teaching, and when they leave their homes, they never follow begging as a pursuit. Hardly a graduate of the
School, whether boy or girl, is known who has become
a thief, or beggar, or criminal, or prostitute. Such is

the power of daily kindness and training, of Christianity early applied.

Outside of the School, great numbers of lads are brought under the influence of the "Bands of Hope," the "Reading-room," and the lectures and amusements offered them.

The result of all this has been noticed by the neighboring manufacturers in the moral improvement of the Ward.

THE LITTLE BEGGARS OF THE FIRST WARD.

One of the eye-sores which used to trouble me was the condition of the city behind Trinity Church. Often and often have I walked through Greenwich and Washington Streets, or the narrow lanes of the quarter, watching the ragged, wild children flitting about; or have visited the damp underground basements which every high tide flooded, crowded with men, women, and children; or climbed to the old rookeries, packed to the smallest attic with a wretched population, and have wished so that something might be done for this miserable quarter, which is in a Ward where more wealth is accumulated than in any other one place in America.

First I induced our Board to send a careful agent through the district, to collect exact statistics. Then an application was made to the wealthy Corporation of Trinity Church, to assist or to found some charitable enterprise for this wretched population under the shadow of its spire. For two years we continued these applications, but without avail. Then it occurred to me that we should try the business-men who were daily passing these scenes of misery and crime.

Fortunately, I struck upon a young merchant of singular conscientiousness of purpose, who had felt for a long time the sad evils of the Ward. With him I addressed another gentleman of a well-known elevation of character, and a certain manly persistency that led him never to turn back when he had " put his hand to the plow." A few personal friends joined them, and I soon saw that we were secure of the future. Our leader had a great social influence, and he at once turned it to aid his philanthropic scheme; he himself gave freely, and called upon his friends for money. The School was founded in 1860, and at once gathered in a large number of the waifs of the First Ward, and has had a like happy influence with our other Schools.

Our treasurer and leader, Mr. J. Couper Lord— alas! too early taken from us all—sustained it himself in good part during disastrous years. Through his aid, also, a Free Reading-room was founded in the same building, which has been more uniformly successful and useful than any similar enterprise in the city. His devotion to the interests of these poor people has left an enduring harvest of good through the whole quarter.

The following extract from our Journal will give a good idea of the changes effected by this charity, now rightly called the " Lord School ":—

A STREET-SWEEPER IN THE LORD SCHOOL.

"For a number of years, the writer of this remembers a little girl in the First Ward School who was a kind of *bête noir* of the school—Ann Jane T——. Both of her parents were drunkards, and were half the time on the Island under arrest; she herself was twice found drunk in the School before she was thirteen years old; once she attacked the teacher violently. She swept crossings for a living, and ' lived about,' often sleeping in halls and stairways; for a year she occupied the same bed and living-room with eight large boys and girls from the school, and some thirteen grown people; the lower part of the house was a dance-saloon and place of bad character. Annie seemed a hopeless case; she swore and used the most vile language, and was evidently growing up to be a most abandoned woman. The teacher of the Lord Industrial School, Miss Blodgett, was a person of singular sweetness and dignity of character, as well as remarkable personal beauty. She soon acquired a great influence over the wild girl. Once little Annie was found waiting with her broom in a bitter storm of sleet and hail on a corner, and the teacher asked her why she was there? and why she did not go home? She said she only wanted just to see the teacher—and the fact was she hadn't any home—' for you know, Miss Blodgett, there is no one cares for me in all New York but you!' This touched the teacher's heart.

"At length the father died on Blackwell's Island, and the mother was in prison, and Miss B. persuaded Annie to go away to a place she had found for her in an excellent family in the West. When the mother came out she was furious, and often made Miss B. tremble for fear she would insist on having the child back; but she gradually saw her absence was for the best. Now the mother is permanently in the Alms-house.

"The following letter came recently about Annie, who has been in her place some three years. The liberal and kind

10

friends of the School will feel that one such case will repay all their sacrifices. Yet there are hundreds like them, though not so striking.

"It should be observed that nearly all the scholars live a good deal as Annie did, in crowded tenements, and more or less associated with dance-saloons and places of bad character. Yet only one has ever gone astray. Here is the letter:

"'F——, ILL., Feb. 15, 1870.

"MY DEAR MISS FLAGG—Your favor of the 25th ult. was duly received. I am very happy to be able to give you good accounts of Annie, about whom you inquire. She has been with us constantly since she left you, and is now our main dependence. We have sent her to school a considerable portion of the time, and she is now in constant attendance there. Her truthfulness and honesty are something quite remarkable. We do not think she has eaten a piece of cake or an apple, without special permission, since she has been with us. Nothing seems to give her more pleasure than to be able to do something, especially for Mrs. W. or myself. We have been inquired of about getting such girls, by other people—our friends. Have you others whom you wish to place in situations which we could assure you would be good? If so, please inform me as to the manner in which you are accustomed to do it. Do you pay their fare to their new home, and are there any other particulars about which parties would wish to be informed? Respectfully yours,

"'GEO. W. W.'"

Since Mr. Lord's death, another treasurer, Mr. D. E. Hawley, is bearing the burden of the School, and, in company with a committee of prominent businessmen of the First Ward, is making it a benefit not to be measured, to all the poor people of the quarter.

A TRULY "RAGGED SCHOOL."

It is remarkable that the School which is most of a "Ragged School," of all these, is in one of the former fashionable quarters of the city. The quaint, pleasing old square called St. John's Park is now occupied as a freight depot, and the handsome residences bordering it have become tenement-houses. Between the grand freight station and the river, overlooked by the statue of the millionaire, are divers little lanes and alleys, filled with a wretched population.

Their children are gathered into this School. An up-hill work the teachers have had of it thus far, owing to the extreme poverty and misery of the parents, and the little aid received from the fortunate classes.

FOURTEENTH WARD SCHOOL.

This is a large and useful charity, and is guided by two sisters of great elevation of purpose and earnestness of character, who are known as "Friends of the Poor" in all that quarter.

THE COLORED SCHOOL.

Here gather great numbers of destitute colored children of the city. Some are rough boys and young men, who are admirably controlled by a most gentle lady, who is Principal; her assistant was fittingly prepared for the work by teaching among the freedmen.

The colored people of the city seldom fall into such helpless poverty as the foreign whites; still there is a good deal of destitution and exposure to temptation among them. The children seem to learn as readily as whites, though they are afflicted with a more sullen temper, and require to be managed more delicately—praise and ridicule being indispensable implements for the teacher. Their singing far surpasses that of our other scholars.

Among our other schools is a most useful one for a peculiarly wild class, in the Rivington-street Lodging-house; one in West Fifty-third and in West Fifty-second Streets, and a very large and well-conducted one for the shanty population near the Park, called

THE PARK SCHOOL.

A very spirited teacher here manages numbers of wild boys and ungoverned girls. The most interesting feature is a Night-school, where pupils come, some from a mile distant, having labored in factories or street-trades all day long—sometimes even giving up their suppers for the sake of the lessons, with a hunger for knowledge which the children of the favored classes know little of. Two other Schools shall conclude our catalogue—one in the House of Industry (West Sixteenth Street), and the other in the Eighteenth-street Lodging-house. Both Schools are struggling with great obstacles and difficulties, as they are planted in the quarter which has produced the notorious " Nineteenth-street Gang." The teacher in the latter has already overcome most of them, and has tamed as wild a set of little street-barbarians as ever plagued a school-teacher.

A rigid rule has been laid down and followed out in these Schools—that is, not to admit or retain pupils who might be in the Public Schools. Our object is to supplement these useful public institutions, and we are continually sending the children forth, when they seem fit, to take places in the Free Schools. Many, however, are always too poor, ragged and necessarily irregular in attendance, to be adapted to the more systematic and respectable places of instruction. As has been already mentioned, the plan has been steadily pursued from the beginning by the writer, to make these as good Primary Schools as under the circumstances they were capable of becoming. The grade of the teachers has been constantly raised, and many of the graduates of our best training academy for teachers in New York State—the Oswego Normal School—have been secured at remunerative salaries.

Within the last four years, also, a new officer has been appointed by the Board of Trustees, to constantly examine the schools and teachers, keep them at the highest grade possible, and visit the families of the children. This place has been ably filled by an intelligent and educated gentleman, Mr. John W. Skinner, with the best effects on our system of instruction.

Our plan of visitation among the families of the poor, whereby the helping hand is held out to juvenile poverty and ignorance all the while, has been effectually carried out by a very earnest worker, Mr. M. Dupuy, in the lower wards, and by a young German-American of much judgment and zeal, Mr. Holste, in the German quarter, and by quite a number of female visitors.

"PLEASE, SIR, MAY I HAVE A BED?"

(A sketch from life.)

No. 1

CHAPTER XIX.

THE BEST REMEDY FOR JUVENILE PAUPERISM.

"Améliorer l'homme par la terre et la terre par l'homme."

DEMETZ.

AMONG the lowest poor of New York, as we stated in a previous chapter, the influence of *overcrowding* has been incredibly debasing. When we find half a dozen families—as we frequently do—occupying one room, the old and young, men and women, boys and girls of all ages sleeping near each other, the result is inevitable. The older persons commit unnatural crimes; the younger grow up with hardly a sense of personal dignity or purity; the girls are corrupted even in childhood; and the boys become naturally thieves, vagrants, and vicious characters. Such apartments are at once "fever-nests" and seminaries of vice. The inmates are weakened and diseased physically, and degraded spiritually. Where these houses abound, as formerly in the Five Points, or now in the First Ward, or near Corlear's Hook, or in the Seventeenth Ward near the Tenth Avenue, there is gradually formed a hideous society of vice and pauperism. The men are idle and drunken, the women lazy, quarrelsome, and given to begging; the children see nothing but examples of drunkenness, lust, and idleness, and they grow up inevitably as sharpers, beggars, thieves, burglars, and prostitutes. Amid such communities of outcasts the institutions of education and religion are comparatively powerless. What is done for the children on one sacred day is wiped out by the influence of the week, and even daily instruction has immense difficulty in counteracting the lessons of home and parents.

For such children of the outcast poor, a more radical cure is needed than the usual influences of school and church.

The same obstacle also appeared soon with the homeless lads and girls who were taken into the Lodging-houses. Though without a home, they were often not legally vagrant—that is, they had some ostensible occupation, some street-trade—and no judge would commit them, unless a very flagrant case of vagrancy was made out against them. They were unwilling to be sent to Asylums, and, indeed, were so numerous that all the Asylums of the State could not contain them. Moreover, their care and charge in public institutions would have entailed expenses on the city so heavy, that tax-payers would not have consented to the burden.

The workers, also, in this movement felt from the beginning that " asylum-life " is not the best training for outcast children in preparing them for practical

life. In large buildings, where a multitude of children
are gathered together, the bad corrupt the good, and
the good are not educated in the virtues of real life.
The machinery, too, which is so necessary in such
large institutions, unfits a poor boy or girl for practical
handwork.

The founders of the Children's Aid Society early
saw that the best of all Asylums for the outcast child,
is the *farmer's home.*

The United States have the enormous advantage
over all other countries, in the treatment of difficult
questions of pauperism and reform, that they possess
a practically unlimited area of arable land. The demand for labor on this land is beyond any present
supply. Moreover, the cultivators of the soil are in
America our most solid and intelligent class. From
the nature of their circumstances, their laborers,
or "help," must be members of their families, and
share in their social tone. It is, accordingly, of the
utmost importance to them to train up children who
shall aid in their work, and be associates of their
own children. A servant who is nothing but a servant, would be, with them, disagreeable and inconve-
nient. They like to educate their own "help." With
their overflowing supply of food also, each new mouth
in the household brings no drain on their means.
Children are a blessing, and the mere feeding of a
young boy or girl is not considered at all.

With this fortunate state of things, it was but a natural inference that the important movement now inaugurating for the benefit of the unfortunate children of New York should at once strike upon a plan of

EMIGRATION.

Simple and most effective as this ingenious scheme now seems—which has accomplished more in relieving New York of youthful crime and misery than all other charities together—at the outset it seemed as difficult and perplexing as does the similar cure proposed now in Great Britain for a more terrible condition of the children of the poor.

Among other objections, it was feared that the farmers would not want the children for help; that, if they took them, the latter would be liable to ill-treatment, or, if well treated, would corrupt the virtuous children around them, and thus New York would be scattering seeds of vice and corruption all over the land. Accidents might occur to the unhappy little ones thus sent, bringing odium on the benevolent persons who were dispatching them to the country. How were places to be found? How were the demand and supply for children's labor to be connected? How were the right employers to be selected? And, when the children were placed, how were their interests to be watched over, and acts of oppression or hard dealing prevented or punished? .Were they to be indentured, or not? If this was the right scheme, why had it not been tried long ago in our cities or in England? *and* ?

These and innumerable similar difficulties and objections were offered to this projected plan of relieving the city of its youthful pauperism and suffering. They all fell to the ground before the confident efforts to carry out a well-laid scheme; and practical experience has justified none of them.

To awaken the demand for these children, circulars were sent out through the city weeklies and the rural papers to the country districts. Hundreds of applications poured in at once from the farmers and mechanics all through the Union. At first, we made the effort to meet individual applications by sending just the kind of children wanted; but this soon became impracticable.

. Each applicant or employer always called for "a perfect child," without any of the taints of earthly depravity. The girls must be pretty, good-tempered, not given to purloining sweetmeats, and fond of making fires at daylight, and with a constitutional love for Sunday Schools and Bible-lessons. The boys must be well made, of good stock, never disposed to steal apples or pelt cattle, using language of perfect propriety, and delighting in family-worship and prayer-meetings more than in fishing or skating parties. These demands, of course, were not always successfully complied with. Moreover, to those who desired the children of "blue eyes, fair hair, and blond complexion," we were sure to send the dark-eyed and brunette; and the particular virtues wished for were very often precisely those that the child was deficient in. It was evidently altogether too much of a lottery for bereaved parents or benevolent employers to receive children in that way.

Yet, even under this incomplete plan, there were many cases like the following, which we extract from our Journal:—

A WAIF.

"In visiting, during May last, near the docks at the foot of Twenty-third Street, I found a boy, about twelve years of age, sitting on the wharf, very ragged and wretched-looking. I asked him where he lived, and he made the answer one hears so often from these children—'I don't live nowhere.' On further inquiry, it appeared that his parents had died a few years before—that his aunt took him for a while, but, being a drunken woman, had at length turned him away; and for some time he had slept in a box in Twenty-second Street, and the *boys fed him*, he occasionally making a sixpence with holding horses or doing an errand. He had eaten nothing that day, though it was afternoon. I gave him something to eat, and he promised to come up the next day to the office.

"He came up, and we had a long talk together. He was naturally an intelligent boy, of good temperament and organization; but in our Christian city of New York he had never heard of Jesus Christ! His mother, long ago, had taught him a prayer, and occasionally he said this in the dark nights, lying on the boards. * * * Of schools or churches, of course, he knew nothing. We sent him to a gentleman in Delaware, who had wished to make the experiment of bringing up a vagrant boy of the city. He thus writes at his arrival:—

"'The boy reached Wilmington in safety, where I found him a few hours after he arrived. Poor boy! He bears about him, or, rather, *is*, the unmistakable evidence of the life he has led—covered with vermin, almost a leper, ignorant in the extreme, and seeming wonder-struck almost at the voice of kindness and sympathy, and bewildered with the idea of possessing a wardrobe gotten for him.

"'So far as I can judge from so short an observation, I should think him an amiable boy, grateful for kindness shown him, rather timid than energetic, yet by no means deficient in intellectual capacity, and altogether such a one as, by God's help, can be made something of. Such as he is, or may turn out to be, I accept the trust conferred upon me, not insensible of the responsibility I incur in thus becoming the instructor and trainer of a being destined to an endless life, of which that which he passes under my care, while but the beginning, may determine all the rest.'

"In a letter six months later, he writes:—

"'It gives me much pleasure to be able to state that Johnny S—— continues to grow in favor with us all. Having been reclaimed from his vagrant habits, which at first clung pretty close to him, he may now be said to be a steady and industrious boy.

"'I have not had occasion, since he has been under my care, to reprove him so often as once even, having found gentle and kindly admonition quite sufficient to restrain him. He is affectionate in disposition, very truthful, and remarkably free from the use of profane or rough language. I find less occasion to look after him than is usual with children of his age, in order to ascertain that the animals intrusted to his care are well attended to, etc.

"' * * * Johnny is now a very good speller out of books, reads quite fairly, and will make a superior penman—an apt scholar, and very fond of his books. I have been his teacher thus far. He attends regularly a Sabbath School, of which I have the superintendence, and the religious services which follow.'"

The effort to place the city-children of the street in country families revealed a spirit of humanity and kindness, throughout the rural districts, which was truly delightful to see. People bore with these children of poverty, sometimes, as they did not with their own. There was—and not in one or two families alone—a sublime spirit of patience exhibited toward these unfortunate little creatures, a bearing with defects and inherited evils, a forgiving over and over again of sins and wrongs, which showed how deep a hold the spirit of Christ had taken of many of our countrywomen.

To receive such a letter as this elevated one's respect for human nature:—

"S——, OHIO, February 14, 1859.

"I wish to add a few words to Carrie's letter, to inform you of her welfare and progress. As she has said, it is now one year since she came to us; and, in looking back upon the time, I feel that, considering her mental deficiencies, she has made as much progress in learning as could be expected. Her health, which was at first and for several months the greatest source of anxiety to us, is so much improved that she is, indeed, *well*. Her eyes are better; though rather weak, they do not much interfere with her studies. She could neither sew nor knit when she came here, and she can now do plain kinds of both, if it is prepared for her. She could not tell all the alphabet, and could spell only three or four words. She now reads quite fluently, though sometimes stopping at a 'hard word,' and is as good at spelling as many Yankee children of her age. I hope she has learned some wholesome moral truths, and she has received much religious instruction. Though really quite a conscientious child when she came, she had a habit of telling lies to screen herself from *blame*, to which she is peculiarly sensitive; but I think she has been

cured of this for a long time, and I place perfect confidence in
her word and in her honesty. I succeeded in getting her fitted
to enter one of our intermediate schools by teaching her at home
until the beginning of the present winter. I am obliged, on
account of her exceeding dullness, to spend much time in teaching her out of school, in order that she may be able to keep up
with her classes. But I think this has been a work worth doing,
and I especially feel it to be so now, as I am employed in this
retrospect.

"I am often asked by my friends, who think the child is little
more than half-witted, why I do not 'send her back, and get a
brighter one.' My answer is, that she is just the one who needs
the care and kindness which Providence has put it into my power
to bestow. We love her dearly; but, if I did not, I should not
think of sending her back to such a place as your great city.
She is just one of those who could be imposed upon and abused,
and perhaps may never be able to take care of herself wholly."

Having found the defects of our first plan of emigration, we soon inaugurated another, which has since
been followed out successfully during nearly twenty
years of constant action.

We formed little companies of emigrants, and,
after thoroughly cleaning and clothing them, put them
under a competent agent, and, first selecting a village
where there was a call or opening for such a party, we
dispatched them to the place.

The farming community having been duly notified,
there was usually a dense crowd of people at the station, awaiting the arrival of the youthful travelers.
The sight of the little company of the children of misfortune always touched the hearts of a population
naturally generous. They were soon billeted around

among the citizens, and the following day a public meeting was called in the church or town-hall, and a committee appointed of leading citizens. The agent then addressed the assembly, stating the benevolent objects of the Society, and something of the history of the children. The sight of their worn faces was a most pathetic enforcement of his arguments. People who were childless came forward to adopt children; others, who had not intended to take any into their families, were induced to apply for them; and many who really wanted the children's labor pressed forward to obtain it.

In every American community, especially in a Western one, there are many spare places at the table of life. There is no harassing "struggle for existence." They have enough for themselves and the stranger too. Not, perhaps, thinking of it before, yet, the orphan being placed in their presence without friends or home, they gladly welcome and train him. The committee decide on the applications. Sometimes there is almost a case for Solomon before them. Two eager mothers without children claim some little waif thus cast on the strand before them. Sometimes the family which has taken in a fine lad for the night feels that it cannot do without him, and yet the committee prefer a better home for him. And so hours of discussion and selection pass. Those who are able, pay the fares of the children, or otherwise make some gift to the Society, until at length the business of charity is finished, and a little band of young wayfarers and homeless rovers in the world find themselves in comfortable and kind homes, with all the boundless advantages and opportunities of the Western farmer's life about them.

CHAPTER XX.

PROVIDING COUNTRY HOMES.

THE OPPOSITION TO THIS REMEDY—ITS EFFECTS.

THIS most sound and practical of charities always met with an intense opposition here from a certain class, for bigoted reasons. The poor were early taught, even from the altar, that the whole scheme of emigration was one of " proselytizing," and that every child thus taken forth was made. a "Protestant." Stories were spread, too, that these unfortunate children were re-named in the West, and that thus even brothers and sisters might meet and perhaps marry! Others scattered the pleasant information that the little ones "were sold as slaves," and that the agents enriched themselves from the transaction.

These were the obstacles and objections among the poor themselves. So powerful were these, that it would often happen that a poor woman, seeing her child becoming ruined on the streets, and soon plainly to come forth as a criminal, would prefer this to a good home in the West; and we would have the discouragement of beholding the lad a thief behind prison-bars, when a journey to the country would have saved him. Most distressing of all was, when a drunken mother or father followed a half-starved boy, already scarred and sore with their brutality, and snatched him from one of our parties of little emigrants, all joyful with their new prospects, only to beat him and leave him on the streets.

With a small number of the better classes there was also a determined opposition to this humane remedy. What may be called the "Asylum-interest" set itself in stiff repugnance to our emigration-scheme. They claimed—and I presume the most obstinate among them still claim—that we were scattering poison over the country, and that we benefited neither the farmers nor the children. They urged that a restraint of a few years in an Asylum or House of Detention rendered these children of poverty much more fit for practical life, and purified them to be good members of society.

We, on the other hand, took the ground that, as our children were not criminals, but simply destitute and homeless boys and girls, usually with some ostensible occupation, they could not easily, on any legal grounds, be inclosed within Asylums; that, if they were, the expense of their maintenance would be enormous, while the cost of a temporary care of them in our Schools and Lodging-houses, and their transference to the West, was only trifling—in the proportion of fifteen dollars to one hundred and fifty dollars, reckoning the latter as a year's cost for a child's support in an Asylum. Furthermore, we held and stoutly maintained that an asylum-life is a bad preparation for practical life. The child, most of all, needs individual care and sympathy. In an Asylum, he is "Letter B, of Class 3," or "No. 2, of Cell 426," and that is all that is known of him. As a poor boy, who must live in a small house, he ought to learn to draw his own water, to split his wood, kindle his fires, and light his candle; as an "institutional child," he is lighted, warmed, and watered by machinery. He has a child's imitation, a desire to please his superiors, and readiness to be influenced by his companions. In a great caravansary he soon learns the external virtues which secure him a good bed and meal—decorum and apparent piety and discipline—while he practices the vices and unnamable habits which masses of boys of any class nearly always teach one another. His virtue seems to have an alms-house flavor; even his vices do not present the frank character of a thorough street-boy; he is found to lie easily, and to be very weak under temptation; somewhat given to hypocrisy, and something of a sneak. And, what is very natural, *the longer he is in the Asylum, the less likely he is to do well in outside life.* I hope I do no injustice to the unfortunate graduates of our Asylums; but that was and continues to be my strong impression of the institutional effect on an ordinary street boy or girl. Of course there are numerous exceptional cases among children—of criminality and inherited habits, and perverse and low organization, and premature cunning, lust, and temper, where a half-prison life may be the very best thing for them; but the majority of criminals among children, I do not believe, are much worse than the children of the same class outside, and therefore need scarcely any different training.

One test, which I used often to administer to myself, as to our different systems, was to ask—and I request any Asylum advocate to do the same—" If your son were suddenly, by the death of his parents and relatives, to be thrown out on the streets, poor and homeless—as these children are—where would you prefer him to be placed—in an Asylum, or in a good farmer's home in the West?"

"The plainest farmer's home rather than the best Asylum—a thousand times!" was always my sincere answer.

Our discussion waxed warm, and was useful to both sides. Our weak point was that, if a single boy or girl in a village, from a large company we had sent, turned out bad, there was a cry raised that "every New-York poor child," thus sent out, became "a thief or a vagabond," and for a time people believed it.

Our antagonists seized hold of this, and we immediately dispatched careful agents to collect statistics in the Central West, and, if possible, disprove the charges. They, however, in the meantime, indiscreetly published their statistics, and from these it appeared that only too many of the Asylum graduates committed offenses, and that those of the shortest terms did the best. The latter fact somewhat confused their line of attack.

The effort of tabulating, or making statistics, in regard to the children dispatched by our society, soon appeared exceedingly difficult, mainly because these youthful wanderers shared the national characteristic of love-of-change, and, like our own servants here, they often left one place for another, merely for fancy or variety. This was especially true of the lads or girls over sixteen or seventeen. The offer of better wages, or the attraction of a new employer, or the desire of "moving," continually stirred up these latter to migrate to another village, county, or State.

In 1859 we made a comprehensive effort to collect some of these statistics in regard to our children who had begun their new life in the West. The following is an extract from our report at this time:—

"During the last spring, the secretary made an extended journey through the Western States, to see for himself the nature and results of this work, carried on for the last five years through those States, under Mr. Tracy's careful supervision. During that time we have scattered there several thousands of poor boys and girls. In this journey he visited personally, and heard directly of, many hundreds of these little creatures, and appreciated, for the first time, to the full extent, the spirit with which the West has opened its arms to them. The effort to reform and improve these young outcasts has become a mission-work there. Their labor, it is true, is needed. But many a time a bountiful and Christian home is opened to the miserable little stranger, his habits are patiently corrected, faults without number are borne with, time and money are expended on him, solely and entirely from the highest religious motive of a noble self-sacrifice for an unfortunate fellow-creature. The peculiar warm heartedness of the Western people, and the equality of all classes, give them an especial adaptation to this work, and account for their success.

" ' Wherever we went' (we quote from his account) ' we found the children sitting at the same table with the families, going to the school with the children, and every way treated as well as any other children. Some whom we had seen once in the most extreme misery, we beheld sitting, clothed and clean, at hospitable tables, calling the employer , father,' loved by the happy circle, and apparently growing up with as good hopes and prospects as any children in the country. Others who had been in the city on the very line between virtue and vice, and who at any time might have fallen into crime, we saw pursuing industrial occupations, and gaining a good name for themselves in their village. The observations on this journey alone would have rewarded years of labor for this class. The results—so far as we could ascertain them—were remarkable, and, unless we reflect on the wonderful influences possible from a Christian home upon a child unused to kindness, they would almost seem incredible.

" ' The estimate we formed from a considerable field of observation was, that, out of those sent to the West under fifteen years, not more than *two per cent.* turned out bad; and, even of those from fifteen to eighteen, not more than *four per cent.* '

" The former estimate is nearly the same as one forwarded to us since by an intelligent clergyman of Michigan (Rev. Mr. Gelston, of Albion), of the result in his State. Of course, some of the older boys disappear entirely; some few return to the city; but it may generally be assumed that we hear of the worst cases—that is, of those who commit criminal offenses, or who come under the law—and it is these whom we reckon as the failures. One or two of such cases, out of hundreds in a given district who are doing well, sometimes make a great noise, and give a momentary impression that the work is not coming out well there; and there are always a few weak-minded people who accept such rumors without examination. Were the proportion of failures far greater than it is, the work would still be of advantage to the West, and a rich blessing to the city.

"It is also remarkable, as years pass away, how few cases ever come to the knowledge of the Society, of ill-treatment of these children. The task of distributing them is carried on so publicly by Mr. Tracy, and in connection with such responsible persons, that any case of positive abuse would at once be known and corrected by the community itself.

"'On this journey,' says the secretary, 'we heard of but one instance even of neglect. We visited the lad, and discovered that he had not been schooled as he should, and had sometimes been left alone at night in the lonely log-house. Yet this had roused the feelings of the whole country-side; we removed the boy, amid the tears and protestations of the "father" and "mother," and put him in another place. As soon as we had left the village, he ran right back to his old place!'

    *   *   *   *   *   *   *

"We give our evidence below, consisting of letters from prominent gentlemen, clergymen, bankers, farmers, judges, and lawyers, through the West, where the main body of these poor children have been placed. We think these letters, coming from some hundred different towns, and the evidence on our books from the boys themselves, establish the remarkable success of the work. Some of the writers speak of the children as thriving 'as well as any other children;' and, in some cases, those who have become disobedient and troublesome are said to have been so principally through the fault of their employers; few instances, comparatively, from this four or five thousand, are known to have committed criminal offenses—in some States not more than four per cent. This is true of Michigan; and in Ohio, we do not think, from all the returns we can gather, that the proportion is even so large as that. The agent of the American and Foreign Christian Union for Indiana, a gentleman of the highest respectability, constantly traveling through the

State—a State where we have placed five hundred and fifty-seven children—testifies that 'very few have gone back to New York,' and that 'he has heard of no one who has committed criminal offenses.'

"The superintendent of the Chicago Reform School, one of the most successful and experienced men in this country in juvenile reform, states that his institution had never had but three of our children committed by the Illinois State Courts, though we have sent to. the State two hundred and sixty-five, and such an institution is, of course, the place where criminal children of this class would at once be committed.

"A prominent gentleman residing in Battle Creek, Michigan, in the neighborhood of which we have put out about one hundred and twenty, writes: 'I think it is susceptible of proof that no equal number of children raised here are superior to those you have placed out.' Two prominent gentlemen from Pennsylvania, one of them a leading judge in the State, write that they have not known an instance of one of our children being imprisoned for a criminal offense, though we have sent four hundred and sixty-nine to this State."

These important results were obtained in 1859, with but four or five thousand children settled in the West. We have now in various portions of our country try *between twenty and twenty-four thousand* who have been placed in homes or provided with work.

The general results are similar. The boys and girls who were sent out when under fourteen are often heard from, and succeed remarkably well. In hundreds of instances, they cannot be distinguished from the young men and women natives in the villages. Large numbers have farms of their own, and are prospering reasonably well in the world. Some are in the professions, some are mechanics or shop-

11

keepers; the girls are generally well married. Quite a number have sent donations to the Society, and some have again in their turn brought up poor children. It was estimated that more than a thousand were in the national army in the civil war. With them the experiment of "Emigration" has been an unmingled blessing. With the larger boys, as we stated before, exact results are more difficult to attain, as they leave their places frequently. Some few seem to drift into the Western cities, and take up street-trades again. Very few, indeed, get back to New York. The great mass become honest producers on the Western soil instead of burdens or pests here, and are absorbed into that active, busy population; not probably becoming saints-on-earth, but not certainly preying on the community, or living idlers on the alms of the public. Many we know who have also led out their whole family from the house of poverty here, and have made the last years of an old father or mother easier and more comfortable.

The immense, practically unlimited demand by Western communities for the services of these children shows that the first-comers have at least done moderately well, especially as every case of crime is bruited over a wide country-side, and stamps the whole company sent with disgrace. These cases we always hear of. The lives of poor children in these homes seem like the annals of great States in this, that,

THE STREET BOY ON A FARM.

(A year later.)

No. 2.

when they make no report and pass in silence, then
we may be sure happiness and virtue are the rule.
When they make a noise, crime and misery prevail.
Twenty years' virtuous life in a street-boy makes no
impression on the public. A single offense is heard
for hundreds of miles. A theft of one lad is imputed
to scores of others about him.

The children are not indentured, but are free to
leave, if ill-treated or dissatisfied; and the farmers
can dismiss them, if they find them useless or otherwise unsuitable.

This apparently loose arrangement has worked
well, and put both sides on their good behavior. We
have seldom had any cases brought to our attention
of ill-treatment. The main complaint is, that the
older lads change places often. This is an unavoidable result of a prosperous condition of the laboring
classes. The employers, however, are ingenious, and
succeed often, by little presents of a calf, or pony, or
lamb, or a small piece of land, in giving the child a
permanent interest in the family and the farm.

On the whole, if the warm discussion between the
"Asylum-interest" and the "Emigration-party" were
ever renewed, probably both would agree (if they
were candid) that their opponents' plan had virtues
which they did not then see. There are some children
so perverse, and inheriting such bad tendencies, and
so stamped with the traits of a vagabond life, that a

Reformatory is the best place for them. On the other hand, the majority of orphan, deserted, and neglected boys and girls are far better in a country home. The Asylum has its great dangers, and is very expensive. The Emigration-plan must be conducted with careful judgment, and applied, so far as is practicable, to children under, say, the age of fourteen years. Both plans have defects, but, of the two, the latter seems to us still to do the most good at the least cost.

A great obstacle in our own particular experience was, as was stated before, the superstitious opposition of the poor. This is undoubtedly cultivated by the priests, who seem seldom gifted with the broad spirit of humanity of their brethren in Europe. They apparently desire to keep the miserable masses here under their personal influence.

Our action, however, in regard to these waifs, has always been fair and open. We know no sect or race. Both Catholic and Protestant homes were offered freely to the children. No child's creed was interfered with. On the committees themselves in the Western villages have frequently been Roman Catholics. Notwithstanding this, the cry of "proselytizing" is still kept up among the guides of the poor against this most humane scheme, and continually checks our influence for good with the younger children, and ultimately will probably diminish to a great degree the useful results we might accomplish in this direction.

The experience we have thus had for twenty years in transferring such masses of poor children to rural districts is very instructive on the general subject of "Emigration as a cure for Pauperism."

CHAPTER XXI.

RESULTS AND FACTS OF EMIGRATION TO THE WEST.

OUR FIRST EMIGRANT PARTY. (FROM OUR JOURNAL.)

BY A VISITOR.

"On Wednesday evening, with emigrant* tickets to Detroit, we started on the *Isaac Newton* for Albany. Nine of our company, who missed the boat, were sent up by the morning cars, and joined us in Albany, making forty-six boys and girls from New York, bound westward, and, to them, homeward. They were between the ages of seven and fifteen—most of them from ten to twelve. The majority of them orphans, dressed in uniform —as bright, sharp, bold, racy a crowd of little fellows as can be grown nowhere out of the streets of New York. The other ten were from New York at large—no number or street in particular. Two of these had slept in nearly all the station-houses in the city. One, a keen-eyed American boy, was born in Chicago —an orphan now, and abandoned in New York by an intemperate brother. Another, a little German Jew, who had been entirely friendless for four years, and had finally found his way into the Newsboys' Lodging-house. Dick and Jack were brothers of Sarah O——, whom we sent to Connecticut. Their father is intemperate; mother died at Bellevue Hospital three weeks since; and an older brother has just been sentenced to Sing Sing Prison. Their father, a very sensible man when sober, begged me to take the boys along, 'for I am sure, sir, if left in New York, they will come to the same bad end as their brother.' We took them to a shoe-shop. Little Jack made awkward work in trying on a pair. 'He don't know them, sir; there's not been a cover to his feet for three winters.'

---

* Since this first experience, we have always sent our children by regular trains, in decent style.

"Another of the ten, whom the boys call 'Liverpool,' defies description. Mr. Gerry found him in the Fourth Ward, a few hours before we left. Really only twelve years old, but in dress a seedy loafer of forty. His boots, and coat, and pants would have held two such boys easily—filthy and ragged to the last thread. Under Mr. Tracy's hands, at the Lodging-house, 'Liverpool' was soon remodeled into a boy again; and when he came on board the boat with his new suit, I did not know him. His story interested us all, and was told with a quiet, sad reserve, that made us believe him truthful. A friendless orphan in the streets of Liverpool, he heard of America, and determined to come, and after long search found a captain who shipped him as cabin-boy. Landed in New York, 'Liverpool' found his street condition somewhat bettered. Here he got occasional odd jobs about the docks, found a pretty tight box to sleep in, and now and then the sailors gave him a cast-off garment, which he wrapped and tied about him, till he looked like a walking rag-bundle when Mr. G. found him.

"As we steamed off from the wharf, the boys gave three cheers for New York, and three more for 'Michigan.' All seemed as careless at leaving home forever, as if they were on a target excursion to Hoboken.

"We had a steerage passage, and after the cracker-box and ginger-bread had passed around, the boys sat down in the gang-way and began to sing. Their full chorus attracted the attention of the passengers, who gathered about, and soon the captain sent for us to come to the upper saloon. There the boys sang and talked, each one telling his own story separately, as he was taken aside, till ten o'clock, when Captain S. gave them all berths in the cabin; meanwhile, a lady from Rochester had selected a little boy for her sister, and Mr. B., a merchant from Illinois, had made arrangements to take 'Liverpool' for his store. I afterwards met Mr. B. in Buffalo, and he said he would not part with the boy for any consideration; and I thought then that to take such a boy from such a condition, and put him into such hands, was worth the whole trip.

"At Albany we found the emigrant train did not go out till noon, and it became a question what to do with the children for the intervening six hours. There was danger that Albany street-boys might entice them off, or that some might be tired of the journey, and hide away, in order to return. When they were gathered on the wharf, we told them that we were going to Michigan, and if any of them would like to go along, they must be on hand for the cars. This was enough. They hardly ventured out of sight. The Albany boys tried hard to coax some of them away; but ours turned the tables upon them, told them of Michigan, and when we were about ready to start, several of them came up bringing a stranger with them. There was no mistaking the long, thick, matted hair, unwashed face, the badger coat, and double pants flowing in the wind—a regular 'snoozer.'

"'Here's a boy what wants to go to Michigan, sir; can't you take him with us?'

"'But, do you know him? Can you recommend him as a suitable boy to belong to our company?' No; they didn't know his name even. 'Only he's as hard-up as any of us. He's no father or mother, and nobody to live with, and he sleeps out o' nights.' The boy pleads for himself. He would like to go and be a farmer—and to live in the country—will go anywhere I send him—and do well if he can have the chance.

"Our number is full—purse scant—it may be difficult to find him a home. But there is no resisting the appeal of the boys, and the importunate face of the young vagrant. Perhaps he will do well; at any rate, we must try him. If left to float here a few months longer, his end is certain. 'Do you think I can go, sir?' 'Yes, John, if you will have your face washed and hair combed within half an hour.' Under a brisk scrubbing, his face lights up several shades; but the twisted, tangled hair, matted for years, will not yield to any amount of washing and pulling—barbers' shears are the only remedy.

"So a new volunteer is added to our regiment. Here is his enrollment:—

"'John ——, American—Protestant—18 years—Orphan—Parents died in R——, Maine—A "snoozer" for four years—Most of the time in New York, with an occasional visit to Albany and Troy, "when times go hard"—Intelligent—Black, sharp eye—Hopeful.'

"As we marched, two deep, round the State House to the depot, John received many a recognition from the 'outsiders,' among whom he seems to be a general favorite, and they call out after him, 'Good-by, Smack,' with a half-sad, half-sly nod, as if in doubt whether he was playing some new game, or were really going to leave them and try an honest life.

"At the depot we worked our way through the Babel of at least one thousand Germans, Irish, Italians, and Norwegians, with whom nothing goes right; every one insists that he is in the wrong car—that his baggage has received the wrong mark—that Chicago is in this direction, and the cars are on the wrong track; in short, they are agreed upon nothing except in the opinion that this is a 'bad counthry, and it's good luck to the soul who sees the end on't.' The conductor, a red-faced, middle-aged man, promises to give us a separate car; but, while he whispers and negotiates with two Dutch girls, who are traveling without a protector, the motley mass rush into the cars, and we are finally pushed into one already full—some standing, a part sitting in laps, and some on the floor under the benches—crowded to suffocation, in a freight-car without windows—rough benches for seats, and no back—no ventilation except through the sliding-doors, where the little chaps are in constant danger of falling through. There were scenes that afternoon and night which it would not do to reveal. Irishmen passed around bad whisky and sang bawdy songs; Dutch men and women smoked and sang, and grunted and cursed; babies squalled and nursed, and left no baby duties undone.

"Night came on, and we were told that 'passengers furnish their own lights!' For this we were unprepared, and so we tried to endure darkness, which never before seemed half so thick as in that stifled car, though it was relieved here and and there for a few minutes by a lighted pipe. One Dutchman in the corner kept up a constant fire; and when we told him we were choking with smoke, he only answered with a complacent grunt and a fresh supply of the weed. The fellow seemed to puff when he was fairly asleep, and the curls were lifting beautifully above the bowl, when smash against the car went the pipe in a dozen pieces! No one knew the cause, except, perhaps, the boy behind me, who had begged an apple a few minutes before.

"At Utica we dropped our fellow-passengers from Germany,

and, thus partially relieved, spent the rest of the night in tolerable comfort.

"In the morning, we were in the vicinity of Rochester, and you can hardly imagine the delight of the children as they looked, many of them for the first time, upon country scenery. Each one must see everything we passed, find its name, and make his own comments. 'What's that, mister?' 'A cornfield.' 'Oh, yes; them's what makes buckwheaters.' 'Look at them cows (oxen plowing); my mother used to milk cows.' As we whirled through orchards loaded with large, red apples, their enthusiasm rose to the highest pitch. It was difficult to keep them within doors. Arms stretched out, hats swinging, eyes swimming, mouths watering, and all screaming—'Oh! oh! just look at 'em! Mister, be they any sich in Michigan? Then I'm in for *that* place—three cheers for Michigan!' We had been riding in comparative quiet for nearly an hour, when all at once the greatest excitement broke out. We were passing a cornfield spread over with ripe yellow pumpkins. 'Oh! yonder! look! Just *look* at 'em!' and in an instant the same exclamation was echoed from forty-seven mouths. 'Jist *look* at 'em! What a heap of *mushmillons*!' 'Mister, do they make mushmillons in Michigan?' 'Ah, fellers, *aint* that the country tho'—won't we have nice things to eat?' 'Yes, and won't we *sell* some, too?' 'Hip! hip! boys; three cheers for Michigan!'

"At Buffalo we received great kindness from Mr. Harrison, the freight-agent · and this was by no means his first service to the Children's Aid Society. Several boys and girls whom we have sent West have received the kindest attention at his hands. I am sure Mr. H.'s fireside must be a happy spot. Also Mr. Noble, agent for the Mich. C. R. R., gave me a letter of introduction, which was of great service on the way.

"We were in Buffalo nine hours, and the boys had the liberty of the town, but were all on board the boat in season. We went down to our place, the steerage cabin, and no one but an emigrant on a lake-boat can understand the night we spent. The berths are covered with a coarse mattress, used by a thousand different passengers, and never changed till they are filled with stench and vermin. The emigrants spend the night in washing, smoking, drinking, singing, sleep, and licentiousness. It was

the last night in the freight-car repeated, with the addition of a
touch of sea-sickness, and of the stamping, neighing, and bleat-
ing of a hundred horses and sheep over our heads, and the
effluvia of their filth pouring through the open gangway. But
we survived the night; *how* had better not be detailed. In the
morning we got outside upon the boxes, and enjoyed the beautiful
day. The boys were in good spirits, sung songs, told New York
yarns, and made friends generally among the passengers. Occasionally, some one more knowing than wise would attempt to
poke fun at them, whereupon the boys would 'pitch in,' and
open such a sluice of Bowery slang as made Mr. Would-be-funny
beat a retreat in double-quick time. No one attempted that
game twice. During the day the clerk discovered that three
baskets of peaches were missing, all except the baskets. None
of the boys had been detected with the fruit, but I afterwards
found they had eaten it.

"Landed in Detroit at ten o'clock, Saturday night, and took a
first-class passenger-car on Mich. C. R. R., and reached D——c,
a 'smart little town,' in S. W. Michigan, three o'clock Sunday
morning. The depot-master, who seldom receives more than
three passengers from a train, was utterly confounded at the crowd
of little ones poured out upon the platform, and at first refused
to let us stay till morning; but, after a deal of explanation, he
consented, with apparent misgiving, and the boys spread themselves on the floor to sleep. At day-break they began to
inquire, 'Where be we?' and, finding that they were really
in Michigan, scattered in all directions, each one for himself, and
in less than five minutes there was not a boy in sight of the
depot. When I had negotiated for our stay at the American
House (!) and had breakfast nearly ready, they began to straggle
back from every quarter, each boy loaded down—caps, shoes,
coat-sleeves, and shirts full of every green thing they could lay
hands upon—apples, ears of corn, peaches, pieces of pumpkins,
etc. 'Look at the Michigan filberts!' cried a little fellow, running up, holding with both hands upon his shirt bosom, which
was bursting out with *acorns*. Little Mag (and she is one of the
prettiest, sweetest little things you ever set eyes upon), brought
in a 'nosegay,' which she insisted upon sticking in my coat—a
mullen-stock and corn-leaf, twisted with grass!

"Several of the boys had had a swim in the creek, though it was a pretty cold morning. At the breakfast-table the question was discussed, how we should spend the Sabbath. The boys evidently wanted to continue their explorations; but when asked if it would not be best to go to church, there were no hands down, and some proposed to go to Sunday School, and 'boys' meeting, too.'

"The children had clean and happy faces, but no change of clothes, and those they wore were badly soiled and torn by the emigrant passage. You can imagine the appearance of our 'ragged regiment,' as we filed into the Presbyterian church (which, by the way, was a school-house), and appropriated our full share of the seats. The 'natives' could not be satisfied with staring, as they came to the door and filled up the vacant part of the house. The pastor was late, and we 'occupied the time' in singing. Those sweet Sabbath School songs never sounded so sweetly before. Their favorite hymn was, 'Come, ye sinners, poor and needy,' and they rolled it out with a relish. It was a touching sight, and pocket-handkerchiefs were used quite freely among the audience.

"At the close of the sermon the people were informed of the object of the Children's Aid Society. It met with the cordial approbation of all present, and several promised to take children. I was announced to preach in the afternoon; but, on returning to the tavern, I found that my smallest boy had been missing since day-break, and that he was last seen upon the high bridge over the creek, a little out of the village. So we spent the afternoon in hunting, instead of going to church. (Not an uncommon practice here, by the way.)

"We dove in the creek and searched through the woods, but little George (six years old) was not to be found; and when the boys came home to supper there was a shade of sadness on their faces, and they spoke in softer tones of the lost playmate. But the saddest was George's brother, one year older. They were two orphans—all alone in the world. Peter stood up at the table, but when he saw his brother's place at his side vacant, he burst out in uncontrollable sobbing. After supper he seemed to forget his loss, till he lay down on the floor at night, and there was the vacant spot again, and his little heart flowed over with grief. Just so again when he awoke in the morning, and at breakfast and dinner.

"Monday morning the boys held themselves in readiness to receive applications from the farmers. They would watch at all directions, scanning closely every wagon that came in sight, and deciding from the appearance of the driver and the horses, more often from the latter, whether they ' would go in for *that* farmer.'

"There seems to be a general dearth of boys, and still greater of girls, in all this section, and before night I had applications for fifteen of my children, the applicants bringing recommendations from their pastor and the justice of peace.

"There was a rivalry among the boys to see which first could get a home in the country, and before Saturday they were all gone. Rev. Mr. O. took several home with him; and nine of the smallest I accompanied to Chicago, and sent to Mr. Townsend, Iowa City. Nearly all the others found homes in Cass County, and I had a dozen applications for more. A few of the boys are bound to trades, but the most insisted upon being farmers, and learning to drive horses. They are to receive a good common-school education, and one hundred dollars when twenty-one. I have great hopes for the majority of them. 'Mag' is *adopted* by a wealthy Christian farmer. 'Smack,' the privateer from Albany, has a good home in a Quaker settlement. The two brothers, Dick and Jack, were taken by an excellent man and his son, living on adjacent farms. The German boy from the 'Lodging-house' lives with a physician in D——.

"Several of the boys came in to see me, and tell their experience in learning to farm. One of them was sure he knew how to milk, and being furnished with a pail, was told to take his choice of the cows in the yard. He sprang for a two-year-old steer, caught him by the horns, and called for a ' line to make him fast.' None seemed discontented but one, who ran away from a tinner, because he wanted to be a farmer.

"But I must tell you of the lost boy. No tidings were heard of him up to Monday noon, when the citizens rallied and scoured the woods for miles around; but the search was fruitless, and Peter lay down that night sobbing, and with his arms stretched out, just as he used to throw them round his brother.

"About ten o'clock a man knocked at the door, and cried out, 'Here is the lost boy!' Peter heard him, and the two brothers met on the stairs, and before we could ask where he had been, Peter had George in his place by his side on the floor. They have gone to live together in Iowa.

"On the whole, the first experiment of sending children West is a very happy one, and I am sure there are places enough with good families in Michigan, Illinois, Iowa, and Wisconsin, to give every poor boy and girl in New York a permanent home. The only difficulty is to bring the children *to* the homes.

"E. P. SMITH."

A LATER PARTY TO THE WEST.

"'JANUARY, 1868.

"'DEAR SIR—It will, perhaps, be interesting for you to know some facts connected with the disposal of my party at the West. We numbered thirty-two in all: two babies—one a fine little fellow one year old, and the other twenty-one years old, but, nevertheless, the greatest babe in the company. Just before I reached Chicago, I was surprised to find that my party numbered only about twenty, instead of thirty-two. I went into the forward car. You may imagine my surprise to find my large babe, W—— D——, playing upon a concertina, and M—— H——, alias M—— B——, footing it down as only a clog-dancer, and one well acquainted with his business at that, could do, while eight or ten boys, and perhaps as many brakesmen and baggagemen, stood looking on, evidently greatly amused. It was plain to see that I was an unwelcome visitor. Order was at once restored, and the boys went back and took their seats. As we neared A——, a gentleman by the name of L—— came to me, and, after making some inquiries, said: "I wish you would let me take that boy," pointing to G—— A——, a little fellow about eight years old. I told him we never allowed a child to go to a home from the train, as we had a committee appointed in A——, to whom application must be made. I promised, however, that I would keep the boy for him until Monday and if he came, bringing satisfactory recommendations, he should have him. He said if money was any inducement, he would give me

thousand dollars would not be an inducement without the recommendation. The little fellow was really the most remarkble child I ever saw, so amiable and intelligent, and yet so good-looking. When I reached A——, I had not been out of the cars five minutes when a gentleman went to G——, and placing his hand on his shoulder, said, " This is the little man I want." I told him he had been engaged already. We passed through the crowd at the depot, and finally reached the hotel. We had been there but a short time when I had another application for G——. The first applicant came up also, and asserted his claim ; said that, if L—— did not come and get the boy, he had the first right to him. L—— did not come, and I had some difficulty to settle the matter between the two applicants. Didn't know but I should have to resort to Solomon's plan, and divide the boy, but determined to let him go to the best home.

" ' Matters went off very pleasantly the first day. I found *good* homes for some ten or twelve boys ; but, in the evening, I missed the boys from the hotel, and, in looking for them, was attracted to a saloon by the dulcet tones of my babe's concertina, and entered. D—— was playing, and two of the boys were delighting the audience with a comic Irish song. All the rowdies and rum-drinkers in the town seemed to have turned out to meet them. I stepped inside of the door, and, with arms folded, stood looking very intently at them, without uttering a word. First the music ceased, then the singing, and one by one the boys slunk out of the room, until I was left alone with the rabble. It was rather amusing to hear their exclamations of surprise. "Halloo! what's up ?" "What's broke loose now ?" I went to the hotel, found the boys there, and a more humble set I never saw. I gave them a lecture about a yard long, and professed to feel very much hurt at the idea of finding a boy who came out with me, in a rum-shop. I gave them to understand what I should expect of them in future, and ended by having the door opened and extending an invitation to leave to those boys who thought they could do better for themselves than I should do for them. As no disposition to leave manifested itself, I then put the question to vote whether they would remain with me and do just as I wished, or go and look out for themselves. Every hand went up, and some of the boys ex-

twenty-five dollars if I would let him have the boy. I said five pressed themselves very sorry for what they had done. W—— D—— left a day or two after, taking the concertina with him, which I afterward learned belonged to another boy. The most of my trouble seemed to take wing and fly away with him. He was the scapegoat of the party.

"'Illinois is a beautiful farming country. All the farmers seem to be wealthy. The large boys, with two exceptions, were placed upon farms. Quite a number of boys came back to the hotel to say good-by, and thank me for bringing them out. I will note a few of the most interesting cases: John Mahoney, age 16, with Mr. J—— T—— (farmer); came in town Sunday to show me a fine mule his employer had given him. J—— C——, age 14, went with Mrs. D——, who has a farm; came in to tell me how well pleased he is with his place; says he will work the farm as soon as he is able, and get half the profits. D—— M——, age 17, went with A—— H. B—— (farmer); came back to tell me his employer had given him a pig, and a small plot of ground to work for himself. J—— S——, age 17, went with J—— B——; saw him after the boy had been with him three or four days; he likes him very much, and has given him a Canadian pony, with saddle and bridle. I might mention other cases, but I know the above to be facts.

"'The boys met with a great deal of sympathy. One old gentleman came in just for the purpose of seeing a little boy who had lost an eye, and was a brother to a boy his son had taken. When I told the little fellow that the gentleman lived near the man who had taken his brother, he climbed up on his knee, and putting his arms around his neck, said: "I want to go home with you, and be your boy; I want to see my brother." The old gentleman wept, and wiping the tears from his eyes, said: "This is more than I can stand; I will take this boy home with me." He is a wealthy farmer and a good man, and I am sure will love the little fellow very much, for he is a very interesting child. Yours,

"'C. R. FRY.'"

———

"This letter is from a farmer—a deaf-mute—who has a destitute deaf-mute lad placed with him :—

"'C—— H——, IND., March 5, 1860.

"'MY DEAR SIR—I received your kind letter some days ago. It has given me great pleasure to hear that you had arrived at your home. I got a report from you. The first of the time when you left D——, he cried and stamped on the floor by the door, but I took him to show him the horses; I told him when he will be a big man I would give him a horse. Then he quit crying, and he began to learn A, B, C, on that day when you left here. Now D—— is doing very well, and plays the most of anything; he likes to stay here very well; he can learn about dog and cat. I am willing to take care of him over twenty-one years old, if he stays here as long as he ever gets to be twenty-one years old; then I will give him a horse, money, clothes, school, etc. Last Saturday, D—— rode on my colt himself; the colt is very gentle; on advice, he got off the colt; he petted the colt the most of time; he likes to play with the young colt. He likes to stay with me, and he said he don't like to go back where you are. He gathers chips and fetches wood in the stove, and is willing to do all his work directly. I wonder that he bold boy and mock some neighbors.

"'Yours truly, friend,

"'L. F. W.

"'Write a letter to me immediately and let me know. He likes to go about with me, but not when it is very cold; I send him to stay in the house, out of the cold. When it is warm day, he likes to go about with me. Sometimes he goes to town. He pets the colt every day; sometimes he waters the colt and feed some corn himself.'"

THE HUNGRY BOY IN A HOME.

"In our first Report there was an account of a little boy, whom our visitor, Rev. Mr. Smith, found under a cart in the street, gnawing a bone which he had picked up for his breakfast. He had a good-natured little face, and a fine, dark eye. Mr. S. felt for him, and said, 'Where do you live, my boy?'

'*Don't live nowhere.*' 'But, where do you stay?' He said a woman had taken him in, in Thirteenth Street, and that he slept in one corner of her room. His mother had left him, and 'lived all about, doin' washin'.' Mr. Smith went around with him to the place, and found a poor, kind woman, who had only a bare room and just enough to live, and yet had sheltered and fed the wretched little creature. 'She was the poorest creature in New York,' she said, 'but somehow everything that was poor always came to her. and while God gave her anything, she meant to share it with those who were poorer than she.' The boy was sent to Pennsylvania, and the following is the letter from his mistress, or rather friend, to the poor mother here. It speaks for itself. May God bless the kind mother's heart, which has taken in thus the outcast child!

"'H——, PENN., Dec. 8, 1855.

"'Mr. Q——: I have but a moment to write this morning. You wish to know how Johnny, as you call him, gets along. We do not know him by that name. Having a William and a John before he came here, we have given him the name of Frederick; he is generally called Freddy. He is well, and has been, since I last wrote to you. He is a very healthy boy, not having been sick a day since he came here. His feet trouble him at times very much; they are so tender that he is obliged to wear stockings and shoes all the year. We do not expect his feet will ever bear the cold, as they were so badly frozen while on the way from the city here. But do not imagine that he suffers much, for he does not. When his boots or shoes are new, he complains a good deal; but after a little he gets along without scarcely noticing it. To-day our winter's school commences. Samuel, Freddy, and Emily will attend; and I hope Freddy will be able to write to you when the school closes. He learns to write very easy, and will, with little pains, make a good penman. He is an excellent speller—scarcely ever spells a word wrong—but he is not a good reader; but we think he will be, as we call him ambitious and persevering, and he is unwilling to be behind boys of his age. Do you ask if he is a good boy? I can assure you he has the name of a good boy throughout the neighborhood; and wherever he is known, his kind, obliging manners..

make him many friends. Again, do you inquire if he is beloved at home? I will unhesitatingly say that we surely love him as our own; and we have had visitors here for a number of days without once thinking that he was not our own child.

"'I wish you could see the children as they start for school this morning. Fred, with his black plush cap, green tunic black vest, gray pants, striped mittens, and his new comforter, which he bought with his own money. Samuel carries the dinner-pail this morning; it is filled with bread and butter, apple pie, and gingerbread; and Fred has his slate, reader, spelling-book, and Testament—and he has not forgotten to go down to the cellar and fill his pockets with apples.

"'I am not very well, and I make bad work of writing. I am afraid you will not find out what I have written.

"'Fred often speaks of you, and of his dear sister Jane. He wants you to tell Mr. Brace how you get along, and get him to write to us all about it.

"'With desire for your welfare,

"'I subscribe myself your friend,

"'SALLY L——.'"

THE PRISON-BOY.

"The boy of whom this is written was taken from one of the City Prisons:—

"'H——, Oct. 12, 1855.

"'DEAR SIR—Yours, making inquiries about F. C., was duly received. His health has been generally good and so far as his behavior is concerned, it has been as good as could have been expected from the history he has given us of himself, previous to his coming to live with us. We soon learned that very little dependence could be placed on his truthfulness or honesty; in fact, he was a fair specimen of New York juvenile vagrancy. He has wanted a close supervision, and we have endeavored to correct what was wrong, and to inculcate better things, and, we think, with some success. He has learned to read and spell very well; besides these, he has attended to writing and arithmetic, and has made some improvement in them. The first winter that he came to live with us, we did not think it best to send him to our Public School, but kept him under our own personal instruction. The last winter he attended our Public School five and a half months. He has been in our Sabbath School from the time he first came, and has usually had his lessons well. He has, from the first, been glad to attend all religious meetings, and we think that his moral perception of things has much improved, and we can but hope that, with proper attention, he may grow up to be a useful and respectable man. He seemed quite satisfied with his home.

"'Yours, most respectfully,

"'C. S. B.'"

"This, again, is about a poor friendless little girl, sent to a good family in old Connecticut:—

"'N——, CT., Oct. 11, 1855.

"'MR. MACY:

"'*Dear Sir*—With regard to Sarah, I would say that she is a very good girl, and is also useful to us, and, I think, fitting herself to be useful to herself at a future day.

"'She has now been with us about two and a half years, and has become a part of our family; and we should feel very sorry to part with her. She attended school last winter at the N. Union High School, which affords advantages equal to any school in the country. She made much improvement in her studies, and at the end of the winter term a public examination was held at the school, and Mr. B., the Principal, stated, in presence of more than three hundred persons, that Sarah G. lived in my family, and was taken by me from the "Children's Aid Society," of New York; and stated, also, that when she commenced to go to school, she was unable to read a word, and wished them to notice the improvement that had been made in her case. The audience seemed to be surprised that she had been able to accomplish so much in so short a time.

"'She also attends Sabbath School very regularly, and gets her lessons very perfectly, and appears to take great delight in doing so. I think she has improved in many respects. She speaks, occasionally of the way in which she used to live in

New York, and of the manner in which she was treated by her parents, when they were alive, and says she can never be thankful enough to the kind friends, who, being connected with the Children's Aid Society, sought her out, and provided her with a comfortable home in the country, far removed from the temptations, and vices, and miseries of a city like New York. I would say that she has not been to school the past summer, and tha. she had made little progress in penmanship during her attendance last winter, and that she is not now able to write you her self, but I think will be able to do so when you wish to hear from her again.

"'Respectfully yours,

"'WM. K. L.'"

FROM THE GUTTER TO THE COLLEGE.

"YALE COLLEGE, NEW HAVEN, Oct. 11, 1871.
"Rev. C. L. BRACE, Secretary Children's Aid Society:

"*Dear Sir*—I shall endeavor in this letter to give you a brief sketch of my life, as it is your request that I should.

"I cannot speak of my parents with any certainty at all. I recollect having an aunt by the name of Julia B——. She had me in charge for some time, and made known some things to me of which I have a faint remembrance. She married a gentleman in Boston, and left me to shift for myself in the streets of your city. I could not have been more than seven or eight years of age at this time. She is greatly to be excused for this act, since I was a very bad boy, having an abundance of self-will.

"At this period I became a vagrant, roaming over all parts of the city. I would often pick up a meal at the markets or at the docks, where they were unloading fruit. At a late hour in the night I would find a resting-place in some box or hogshead, or in some dark hole under a staircase.

"The boys that I fell in company with would steal and swear, and of course I contracted those habits too. I have a distinct recollection of stealing up upon houses to tear the lead from around the chimneys, and then take it privily away to some junk-shop, as they call it; with the proceeds I would buy a ticket for the pit in the Chatham-street Theatre, and something to eat with the remainder. This is the manner in which I was drifting out in the stream of life, when some kind person from your Society persuaded me to go to Randall's Island. I remained at this place two years. Sometime in July, 1859, one of your agents came there and asked how many boys who had no parents would love to have nice homes in the West, where they could drive horses and oxen, and have as many apples and melons as they should wish. I happened to be one of the many who responded in the affirmative.

"On the 4th of August twenty-one of us had homes procured for us at N——, Ind. A lawyer from T——, who chanced to be engaged in court matters, was at N—— at the time. He desired to take a boy home with him, and I was the one assigned him. He owns a farm of two hundred acres lying close to town. Care was taken that I should be occupied there and not in town. I was always treated as one of the family. In sickness I was ever cared for by prompt attention. In winter I was sent to the Public School. The family room was a good school to me, for there I found the daily papers and a fair library.

"After a period of several years I taught a Public School in a little log cabin about nine miles from T——. There I felt that every man ought to be a good man, especially if he is to instruct little children.

"Though I had my pupils read the Bible, yet I could not openly ask God's blessing on the efforts of the day. Shortly after I united myself with the Church. I always had attended Sabbath School at T——. Mr. G—— placed me in one the first Sabbath. I never doubted the teachings of the Scriptures. Soon my pastor presented the claims of the ministry. I thought about it for some time, for my ambition was tending strongly toward the legal profession. The more I reflected the more I felt how good God had been to me all my life, and that if I had any ability for laboring in His harvest, He was surely entitled to it.

"I had accumulated some property on the farm in the shape of a horse a yoke of oxen, etc., amounting in all to some $300. These I turned into cash, and left for a preparatory school. This

course that I had entered upon did not meet with Mr. G——'s
hearty approbation. At the academy I found kind instructors
and sympathizing friends. I remained there three years, relying
greatly on my own efforts for support. After entering the class
of '74' last year, I was enabled to go through with it by the
kindness of a few citizens here.

"I have now resumed my duties as a Sophomore, in faith in
Him who has ever been my best friend. If I can prepare myself
for acting well my part in life by going through the college cur-
riculum, I shall be satisfied.

"I shall ever acknowledge with gratitude that the Children's
Aid Society has been the instrument of my elevation.

"To be taken from the gutters of New York city and placed
in a college is almost a miracle.

"I am not an exception either. Wm. F——, who was taken
West during the war, in a letter received from W—— College,
dated Oct. 7, writes thus: 'I have heard that you were studying
for the ministry, so am I. I have a long time yet before I enter
the field, but I am young and at the right age to begin.' My
prayer is that the Society may be amplified to greater usefulness.   Yours very truly,

"JOHN G. B."

———

ONCE A NEW YORK PAUPER, NOW A WESTERN FARMER

"C——, MICH., Oct. 26, 1871.

"Mr. J. MACY:

"*Dear Sir*—I received your very kind and welcome letter a
few days since, and I assure you that I felt very much rejoiced
to know that you felt that same interest in hearing and knowing
how your Western boys and girls get along, as you have expressed
in former times.

"In your letter you spoke of the time you accompanied our
company of boys to the West as not seeming so long to you as it
really was. For my own part, if I could not look to the very
many pleasant scenes that it has been my privilege to enjoy
while I have been in the West, I do not think it would seem so
long to me since we all marched two and two for the boat up the

Hudson River on our route for Michigan. There were some among us who shed a few tears as we were leaving the city, as we all expected, for the last time. But as we sped on and saw new sights, we very willingly forgot the city with all its dusty atmosphere and temptations and wickedness, for the country all around us was clothed in its richest foliage; the birds were singing their sweetest songs, and all nature seemed praising our Heavenly Father in high notes of joy.

"In the midst of this enchantment we were introduced to the farmers in the vicinity of A——, and then and there we many of us separated to go home with those kind friends, and mould the character of our future life.

"For my own part, I was more than fortunate, for I secured a home with a *good* man and every comfort of life I enjoyed. I had the benefit of good schools until I was nearly of age, and when I became of age a substantial present of eighty acres of good farming land, worth fifty dollars per acre, was given me, and thus I commenced life. Once a New York pauper, now a Western farmer. If these lines should chance to meet the eyes of any boy or girl in your Society, I would say to them, don't delay, but go to the West and there seek your home and fortune. You may have some trials and temptations to overcome, but our lives seem happier when we know that we have done our duties and have done the will of our Heavenly Father, who has kindly cared for us all through our lives.

"Last winter it was my privilege to be with you all through the Christmas festivities, and it did my soul good to return and enjoy Christmas with you after an absence of nearly fifteen years. I met you there as I also did at the Newsboys' Lodging-house. Those were times of rejoicing to me to see the wickedness we escaped by not staying at large in your city. When I returned home I brought with me a girl of eleven years of age, and intend to do as well by her as my circumstances will allow. I have been married nearly three years, and by God's grace assisting us we intend to meet you all on the other shore. I have written you a very long letter, but I will now close. I shall be pleased to hear from you again at any time when you feel at liberty to write. Hoping to hear from you soon again, I remain truly your friend,   C. H. J——."

EMIGRATION.

With reference to the cost of this method of
charity, we have usually estimated the net expenses
of the agent, his salary, the railroad fares, food and
clothing for the child, as averaging fifteen dollars
per head for each child sent. Whenever practicable,
the agent collects from the employers the railroad
expenses, and otherwise obtains gifts from benevolent
persons; so that, frequently, our collections and "returned fares" in this way have amounted to $6,000
or $8,000 per annum. These gifts, however, are be-
coming less and less, and will probably eventually
cease altogether; the farmer feeling that he has
done his fair share in receiving and training the child.

We are continually forced, also, towards the
newer and more distant States, where labor is more
in demand, and the temper of the population is more
generous, so that the average expense of the aid thus
given will in the future be greater for each boy or girl
relieved.

The opposition, too, of the bigoted poor increases,
undoubtedly under the influence of some of the more
prejudiced priests, who suppose that the poor are
thus removed from ecclesiastical influences. A
class of children, whom we used thus to benefit,
are now sent to the Catholic Protectory, or are
retained in the City Alms-house on Randall's Island.

12

Were our movement allowed its full scope, we could take the place of every Orphan Asylum and Alms-house for pauper children in and around New York, and thus save the public hundreds of thousands of dollars, and immensely benefit the children. We could easily "locate" 5,000 children per annum, from the ages of two years to fifteen, in good homes in the West, at an average net cost of fifteen dollars per head.

If Professor Fawcett's objection* be urged, that we are thus doing for the children of the Alms-house poor, what the industrious and self-supporting poor cannot get done for their own children, we answer that we are perfectly ready to do the same for the outside hard-working poor; but their attachment to the city, their ignorance or bigotry, and their affection for their children, will always prevent them from making use of such a benefaction to any large degree. The poor, living in their own homes, seldom wish to send out their children in this way. We do "place out" a certain number of such children; but the great majority of our little emigrants are the "waifs and strays" of the streets in a large city.

OUR AGENTS.

The Charity I am describing has been singularly fortunate in its agents; but in none more so than

---

* See Fawcett on " Pauperism."

in those who performed its responsible work in the West.

Mr. E. P. Smith, who writes the interesting description above, of the first expedition we sent to the West, has since become honorably distinguished by labors among the freedmen as agent of the Christian Commission.

Our most successful agent, however, was Mr. C. C. Tracy, who had a certain quaintness of conversation and anecdote, and a solid kindness and benevolence, which won his way with the Western farmers, as well as the little flocks he conducted to their new fold.

One of his favorite apothegms became almost a proverb.

"Won't the boy run away?" was the frequent anxious inquiry from the farmers.

"Did ye ever see a cow run away from a hay-stack?" was Mr. Tracy's rejoinder. "Treat him well, and he'll be sure to stay."

And the bland and benevolent manner in which ne would reply to an irritated employer, who came back to report that the "New-York boy" had knocked over the milk-pail, and pelted the best cow, and let the cattle in the corn, and left the young turkeys in the rain, etc., etc., was delightful to behold.

"My dear friend, can you expect boys to be perfect at once? Didn't you ever pelt the cattle when you were a boy?"

Mr. T. testified before the Senate Committee in 1871, that he had transplanted to the West some four or five thousand children, and, to the best of his knowledge and belief, very few ever turned out bad.

Whenever any of these children chanced to be defective in mind or body, or, from any other cause, became chargeable on the rural authorities, we made ourselves responsible for their support, during any reasonable time after their settlement in the West.

Our present agents, Mr. E. Trott and Mr. J. P. Brace, are exceedingly able and judicious agents, so that we transported, in 1871, to the country, some three thousand children, at an expense, including all salaries and costs, of $31,638.

We have also a resident Western agent, Mr. C. R. Fry, who looks after the interests of those previously sent, and prepares for future parties, traveling from village to village. The duties of all these agents are very severe and onerous.

It is a matter of devout thankfulness that no accident has ever happened to any one of the many parties of children we have sent out, or to the agents.

The following testimony was given by Mr. J. Macy, Assistant Secretary of the Children's Aid Society, before the Senate Committee, in 1871 :—

"Mr. J. Macy testified that he corresponds annually with from eight thousand to ten thousand persons, and, on an average, receives about two thousand letters from children and their employers. He has personal knowledge of a great many boys growing up to be respectable citizens, others having married well, others graduating in Western colleges. Out of twenty-one thousand, not over twelve children have turned out criminals. The percentage of boys returning to the city from the West is too small to be computed, not more than six annually. From correspondence and personal knowledge, he is thoroughly satisfied that but very few turned out bad, and that the only way of saving large boys from falling into criminal practices is to send them into good country-homes. He regarded, the system of sending families to the West as one of the best features of the work of the Society. Not a family has been sent West which has not improved by the removal. The Society had never changed the name of a child, and Catholic children had often been intrusted to Catholic families." ＊ ＊ ＊ ＊ ＊

——————

"Letter from a newsboy to the Superintendent of the Lodging-house:—

"'M——, IND., Nov. 24, 1859.

"'TO MY FRIEND AND BENEFACTOR.—So I take my pen in my hand to let you know how I am, and how I am getting along. As far as I see, I am well satisfied with my place; but I took a general look around, and, as far as I see, all the boys left in M—— are doing well, especially myself, and I think there is as much fun as in New York, for nuts and apples are all free. I am much obliged to you, Mr. O'Connor, for the paper you sent me. I received it last night; I read it last night—something about the Newsboys' Lodging-house.

"'All the newsboys of New York have a bad name; but we should show ourselves, and show them, that we are no fools; that we can become as respectable as any of their countrymen, for some of you poor boys can do something for your country— for Franklin, Webster, Clay, were poor boys once, and even Commodore V. C. Perry or Math. C. Perry. But even George Law, and Vanderbilt, and Astor—some of the richest men of New York—and Math. and V. C. Perry were nothing but printers, and in the navy on Lake Erie. And look at Winfield Scott. So now, boys, stand up and let them see you have got the real stuff in you. Come out here and make respectable and honorable men, so they can say, there, that boy was once a newsboy.

"'Now, boys, you all know I have tried everything. I have been a newsboy and when that got slack, you know I have smashed baggage. I have sold nuts, I have peddled, I have worked on the rolling billows up the canal. I was a boot-black; and you know when I sold papers I was at the top of our profession. I had a good stand of my own, but I found that all would not do. I could not get along, but I am now going ahead. I have a first-rate home, ten dollars a month, and my board; and I tell you, fellows, that is a great deal more than I could scrape up my best times in New York. We are all on an equality, my boys, out here, so long as we keep yourselves respectable.

"'Mr. O'Connor, tell Fatty or F. John Pettibone, to send me a Christmas number of *Frank Leslie's* and *Harper's Weekly* a *Weekly News* or some other pictorials to read, especially the *Newsboys' Pictorial*, if it comes out. No old papers, or else none. If they would get some other boys to get me some books. I want something to read.

"'I hope this letter will find you in good health, as it leaves me. Mr. O'Connor, I expect an answer before two weeks—a letter and a paper. Write to me all about the Lodging-house. With this I close my letter, with much respect to all.

"'I remain your truly obedient friend,

"'J. K.'"

CHAPTER XXII.

A PRACTICAL PHILANTHROPIST AMONG THE YOUNG "ROUGHS."

A SKETCH of the long and successful efforts for the improvement of the dangerous classes we have been describing would be imperfect without an account of

THE OFFICE OF THE CHILDREN'S AID SOCIETY.

This has become a kind of eddying-point, where the two streams of the fortunate and the unfortunate classes seem to meet. Such a varying procession of humanity as passes through these plain rooms, from one year's end to the other, can nowhere else be seen. If photographs could be taken of the human life revealed there, they would form a volume of pictures of the various fortunes of large classes in a great city. On one day, there will be several mothers with babes. They wish them adopted, or taken by any one. They relate sad stories of desertion and poverty; they are strangers or immigrants. When the request is declined, they beseech, and say that the child must die, for they cannot support both. It is but too plain that they are illegitimate children. As they depart, the horrible feeling presses on one, that the child will soon follow the fate of so many thousands born out of wedlock. Again, a pretty young woman comes to beg a home for the child of some friend, who cannot support it. Her story need not be told; the child is hers, and is the offspring of shame. Or some person from the higher classes enters, to inquire for the traces of some boy, long disappeared—the child of passion and sin.

But the ordinary frequenters are the children of the street—the Arabs and gypsies of our city.

Here enters a little flower-seller, her shawl drawn over her head, barefooted and ragged—she begs for a home and bread; here a newsboy, wide-awake and impudent, but softened by his desire to "get West;" here "a bummer," ragged, frouzy, with tangled hair and dirty face, who has slept for years in boxes and privies; here a "canawl-boy," who cannot steer his little craft in the city as well as he could his boat; or a petty thief who wishes to reform his ways, or a bootblack who has conceived the ambition of owning land, or a little "revolver" who hopes to get quarters for nothing in a Lodging-house and "pitch pennies" in the interval. Sometimes some yellow-haired German boy, stranded by fortune in the city, will apply, with such honest blue eyes, that the first employer that enters will carry him off; or a sharp, intelligent Yankee lad, left adrift by sudden misfortune, comes in to do what he has never done before—ask for assistance. Then

an orphan-girl will appear, floating on the waves of
the city, having come here no one knows why, and
going no one can tell whither.

Employers call to obtain "perfect children;"
drunken mothers rush in to bring back their children
they have already consented should be sent far from
poverty and temptation; ladies enter to find the best
object of their charities, and the proper field for their
benevolent labors; liberal donors; "intelligent foreigners," inquiring into our institutions, applicants for
teachers' places, agents, and all the miscellaneous
crowd who support and visit agencies of charity.

A PRACTICAL PHILANTHROPIST.

The central figure in this office, disentangling all
the complicated threads in these various applications,
and holding himself perfectly cool and bland in this
turmoil, is "a character"—Mr. J. Macy.

He was employed first as a visitor for the Society;
but, soon betraying a kind of bottled-up "enthusiasm
of humanity" under a very modest exterior, he was
put in his present position, where he has become a
sort of embodied Children's Aid Society in his own
person. Most men take their charities as adjuncts to
life, or as duties enjoined by religion or humanity.
Mr. Macy lives in his. He is never so truly happy as
when he is sitting calmly amid a band of his "lambs,"
as he sardonically calls the heavy-fisted, murderous-

looking young vagabonds who frequent the Cottage-place Reading-room, and seeing them all happily engaged in reading or quiet amusements. Then the look of beatific satisfaction that settles over his face, as, in the midst of a loving passage of his religious address to them, he takes one of the obstreperous lambs by the collar, and sets him down very hard on another bench—never for a moment breaking the thread or sweet tone of his bland remarks—is a sight to behold; you know that he is happier there than he would be in a palace.

His labors with these youthful scapegraces around Cottage Place, during the last fifteen years, would form one of the most instructive chapters in the history of philanthropy. I have beheld him discoursing sweetly on the truths of Christianity while a storm of missiles was coming through the windows; in fact, during the early days of the meeting, the windows were always barricaded with boards. The more violent the intruders were, the more amiable, and at the same time, the more firm he became.

In fact, he never seemed so well satisfied as when the roughest little "bummers" of the ward entered his Boys' Meeting. The virtuous and well-behaved children did not interest him half so much. By a patience which is almost incredible, and a steady kindness of years, he finally succeeded in subduing these wild young vagrants, frequently being among them

every night of the week, holding magic-lantern exhibitions, temperance meetings, social gatherings, and
the like, till he really knew them and attracted their
sympathies. His cheerfulness was high when the
meeting grew into an Industrial School, where the
little girls, who perplexed him so, could be trained by
female hands, and his happiness was at its acme when
the liberality of one or two gentlemen enabled him to
open a Reading-room for " the lambs." The enterprise was always an humble one in appearance; but
such were the genuineness and spirit of humanity in
it—the product of his sisters as well as himself—that
it soon met with kind support from various ladies and
gentlemen, and now is one of those lights in dark
places which must gladden any observer of the misery
and crime of this city.

Mr. Macy's salvation in these exhausting and
nerve-wearing efforts, and divers others which I have
not detailed, is his humor. I have seen him take two
lazy-looking young men, who had applied most pite-
ously for help, conduct them very politely to the door,
and, pointing amiably to the Third Avenue, say,
"Now, my boys, just be kind enough to walk right
north up that avenue for one hundred miles into the
country, and you will find plenty of work and food.
Good-by! good-by!" The boys depart, mystified.

Or a dirty little fellow presents himself in the
office. " Please, sir, I am an orphant, and I want a

home!" Mr. Macy eyes him carefully; his knowledge
of "*paidology*" has had many years to ripen in; he sees,
perhaps, amid his rags, a neatly-sewed patch, or notes
that his naked feet are too white for a "bummer."
He takes him to the inner office. "My boy! Where
do you live? Where's your father?"

"Please, sir, I don't live nowhere, and I hain't got
no father, and me mither is dead!" Then follows a
long and touching story of his orphanage, the tears
flowing down his cheeks. The bystanders are almost
melted themselves. Not so Mr. Macy. Grasping the
boy by the shoulder, "Where's your mother, I say?"
"Oh, dear, I'm a poor orphant, and I hain't got no
mither!" "Where is your *mother*, I say? Where do
you live? I give you just three minutes to tell, and
then, if you do not, I shall hand you over to that
officer!" The lad yields; his true story is told, and
a runaway restored to his family.

In the midst of his highest discouragements at
Cottage Place, Mr. Macy frequently had some characteristic story of his "lambs" to refresh him in his
intervals of rest. And some peculiar exhibition of
mischief or wickedness always seemed to act as a kind
of tonic on him and restore his spirits.

I shall not forget the cheerfulness with which he
related one day that, after having preached with great
unction the Sunday previous on "stealing," he came
back the next and discovered that a private room in

the building, which he only occasionally used, had been employed by the boys for some time as a receptacle for stolen goods !

On another occasion, he had held forth with peculiar "liberty" on the sin of thieving, and, when he sat down almost exhausted, discovered, to his dismay, that his hat had been stolen! But, knowing that mischief was at the bottom, and that a crowd of young "roughs" were outside waiting to see him go home bareheaded, he said nothing of his loss, but procured a cap and quietly walked away.

I think the contest of wits among them—they for mischief and disturbance, and he to establish order and get control over them—gave a peculiar zest to his religious labors, which he would not have had in calmer scenes and more regular services. If they put pepper on the stove, he endured it much longer than they could, and kept them until they were half suffocated ; and when they barricaded the door outside, he protracted the devotional exercises or varied them with a "magic lantern," to give time for forcing the door, and an orderly exit.*

The girls, however, were his great torment, especially when they stoned their spiritual guides; these,

---

* Mr. Macy, on one occasion, on a bitter winter day, found the lock of the room picked and the boys within. He accused some of the larger boys. They denied, "No sir—no: it couldn't be us; because we was in the liquor-shop on the corner; we ain't got nowheres else to go to !"

however, he eventually forwarded into the Cottage-place Industrial School, which sprang from the Meeting, and there they were gradually civilized.

For real suffering and honest effort at self-help, he had a boundless sympathy; but the paupers and professional beggars were the terror of his life. He dreaded nothing so much as a boy or girl falling into habits of dependence. Where he was compelled to give assistance in money, he has been known to set one boy to throw wood down and the other to pile it up, before he would aid.

His more stormy philanthropic labors have been succeeded by calmer efforts among a delightful congregation of poor German children in Second Street, who love and revere him. When he needs, however, a little refreshment and intoning, he goes over to his Cottage-place Reading-room, and sits with or instructs his "lambs!"

His main work, however, is in the "office" of the Children's Aid Society, which I have described above. Though a plain half-Quaker himself, he has all the tact of a *diplomat*, and manages the complicated affairs of poverty and crime that come before him with a wonderful skill, getting on as well with the lady as the street-vagrant, and seldom ever making a blunder in the thousand delicate matters which pass through his hands. When it is remembered that some seventeen thousand street-children have passed through that

office to homes in the country, and that but one law-
suit has ever occurred about them (and that through
no mistake of the Society), while numbers of bitter
enemies watch every movement of this charity, it will
be seen with what consummate judgment these delicate
matters have been managed. Besides all this, he is
the guide, philosopher, and friend of hundreds of these
young wayfarers in every part of the country, sustaining with them an enormous correspondence; but, as
sympathy, and advice, and religious instruction on
such a gigantic scale would soon weary out even his
vitality, he stereotypes his letters, and, by a sort of
pious fraud, says to each what is written for all. It is
very interesting to come across the quaint, affectionate
words and characteristic expressions of this devoted
philanthropist addressed to "his boys," but put up in
packages of a thousand copies, and to think to how
many little rovers over the land they bring sympathy
and encouragement.

CHAPTER XXIII.

RAISING MONEY FOR A CHARITY.

ONE of the trials of a young Charity is raising money. I was determined to put this on as sound and rational a basis as possible. It seemed to me, that, if the facts were well known in regard to the great suffering and poverty among the children in New York, and the principles of our operations were well understood, we could more safely depend on this enlightened public opinion and sympathy than on any sudden "sensation" or gush of feeling.

Our Board fully concurred in these views, and we resolutely eschewed all "raffles" and pathetic exhibitions of abandoned children, and "pedestrian" or other exhibitions offered us for the benefit of humanity, and never even enjoyed the perfectly legitimate benefit of a "fair." Once, in a moment of enthusiasm I was led into arranging a concert, for the benefit of a School; but that experience was enough. Our effort at musical benevolence became a series of most inharmonious squabbles. The leading soprano singer had a quarrel with the bass; the instrumental split with the vocal performers; our best solo went off in a huff,

and, at last, by superhuman exertions, we reconciled
the discordant elements and got our concert fairly
before the public, and retired with a few hundred
dollars.

Whatever gave the public a sensation, always had
a reaction. The solid ground for us was evidently
the most rational one. I accordingly made the most
incessant exertions to enlighten and stir up the public.
In this labor the most disagreeable part was presenting our "cause" to individuals. I seldom solicited
money directly, but sought rather to lay the wants
and methods before them. Yet, even here, some
received it as if it were some new move of charlatanry,
or some new device for extracting money from full
purses. Evidently, to many minds, the fact of a man
of education devoting himself to such pursuits was
in itself an enigma or an eccentricity. Fortunately, I
was able early to make use of the pulpits of the city
and country, and sometimes was accustomed to spend
every night in the week and the Sunday in delivering
sermons and addresses throughout the Eastern States.
As a general thing, I did not urge a collection, though
occasionally having one, but chose rather to convince
the understanding, and leave the matter before the
people for consideration. No public duties of mine
were ever more agreeable than these; and the results
proved afterwards most happy, in securing a large
rural "constituency," who steadily supported our

movements in good times and bad; so quietly devoted, and in earnest, that death did not diminish their interest—some of our best bequests having come from the country.

The next great implement was that profession which has done more for this Charity than any other instrumentality. Having, fortunately, an early connection with the press, I made it a point, from the beginning, to keep our movements, and the evils we sought to cure, continually before the public in the columns of the daily journals. Articles describing the habits and trials of the poor; editorials urging the community to work in these directions; essays discussing the science of charity and reform; continual paragraphs about special charities, were poured forth incessantly for years through the daily and weekly press of New York, until the public became thoroughly imbued with our ideas and a sense of the evils which we sought to reform. To accomplish this, I had to keep up a constant connection with the press, and was, in fact, often daily editor, in addition to my other avocations.

As a result of this incessant publicity, and of the work already done, a very superior class of young men consented to serve in our Board of Trustees; men who, in their high principles of duty, and in the obligations which they feel are imposed by wealth and position, bid fair hereafter to make the name of New

York merchants respected as it never was before throughout the country. With these as backers and supervisors, we were enabled to approach the Legislature for aid, on the ground that we were doing a humane work which lightened the taxes and burdens of the whole community and was in the interest of all. Year after year our application was rejected, but finally we succeeded, and laid a solid and permanent basis thus for our future work.

SOURCES OF INCOME.

Our first important acquisition of property was a bequest from a much-esteemed pupil of mine, J. B. Barnard, of New Haven, Conn., of $15,000, in 1856. We determined to use this at once in the work. For many years, finding the needs of the city so enormous, and believing that our best capital was in the results of our efforts, and not in funds, we spent every dollar we could obtain at once upon our labors of charity.

At length, in 1863, a very fortunate event occurred for us: a gentleman had died in New York, named John Rose, who left a large property which he willed should be appropriated to forming some charitable institution for neglected children, and, under certain conditions, to the Colonization Society. The will was so vaguely worded, that the brother, Mr. Chauncey Rose, felt it necessary to attempt to break it. This, after long litigation, he succeeded in doing, and the property—now swollen to the amount of nearly a million dollars—reverted mainly to him. With a rare conscience and generosity, he felt it his duty not to use any of this large estate for himself, but to distribute it among various charities in New York, relating to poor children, according to what appeared to be the intention of his brother. To our Society he gave, at different times, something like $200,000. Of this, we made $150,000 an invested fund; and henceforth we sought gradually to increase our permanent and assured income, so that the Association might continue its benevolent work after the present managers had departed.

And yet we were glad that a good proportion of our necessary expenses should be met by current contributions, so that the Society might have the vitality arising from constant contact with the public, as well as the permanency from invested property.

If we take a single year, 1870, as showing the sources of our income, we shall find that out of nearly $200,000 received that year, including $32,000 for the purchase of two Lodging-houses, and $7,000 raised by the local committees of the Schools, $60,000 came by tax from the county, $20,000 from the "Excise Fund" (now abolished), nearly $20,000 from the Board of Education, being a *pro rata* allotment on the average number of pupils, and about $9,000 from the

Comptroller of the State; making about $109,000, or a little over one-half of our income, received from the public authorities. Of the ninety-odd thousand received from private sources, about eleven thousand came from our investments, leaving some $80,000 as individual contributions during one year—a remarkable fact, both as showing the generosity of the public and their confidence in the work.

This liberal outlay, both by the city and private individuals, has been and is being constantly repaid, in the lessening of the expenses and loss from crime and pauperism, and the increasing of the number of honest and industrious producers.

CHAPTER XXIV.

AT first sight, it would seem very obvious that a place of mental improvement and social resort, with agreeable surroundings, offered gratuitously to the laboring-people, would be eagerly frequented. On its face, the "FREE READING-ROOM" appears a most natural, feasible method of applying the great lever of sociality (without temptations) to lifting up the poorer classes. The working-man and the street-boy get here what they so much desire, a pleasant place, warmed and lighted, for meeting their companions, for talking, playing innocent games, or reading the papers; they get it, too, for nothing. When we remember how these people live, in what crowded and slatternly rooms, or damp cellars, or close attics, some even having no home at all, and that their only social resort is the grog-shop, we might suppose that they would jump at the chance of a pleasant and Free Saloon and Reading-room. But this is by no means the case. This instrument of improvement requires peculiar management to be successful. Our own experience is instructive.

The writer of this had had the Reading-room "on the brain" for many years, when, at length, on talking over the subject with a gentleman in the eastern part of the city—one whose name has since been a tower of strength to this whole movement—he consented to father the enterprise, and be the treasurer—an office in young charities, be it remembered, no sinecure.

We opened, accordingly, near the Novelty Iron-Works, under the best auspices,

THE ELEVENTH WARD FREE READING-ROOM.

The rooms were spacious and pleasant, furnished with a plenty of papers and pamphlets, and, to add to the attractions and help pay expenses, the superintendent was to sell coffee and simple refreshments. Our theory was, that coffee would compete with liquor as a stimulus, and that the profits of the sale would pay most of the running cost. We were right among a crowded working population, and everything promised success.

At first there were considerable numbers of laboring-men present every day and evening; but, to our dismay, they began to fall off. We tried another superintendent; still the working-man preferred his "dreary rooms," or the ruinous liquor-shops, to our pleasant Reading-room. The coffee did not suit him; the refreshments were not to his taste; he would not read, because he thought he ought to call for something to eat or drink if he did; and so at length he dropped off. Finally, the attendance became so thin and the expenses were accumulating to such a degree, that we closed the room, and our magnanimous treasurer footed the bills. This failure discouraged us for some years, but the idea seemed to me sound, and I was resolved to try it once more under better circumstances.

In looking about for some specially-adapted instrument for influencing "the dangerous classes," I chanced, just after the remarkable religious "Revival" of 1858, on a singular character,

A REFORMED PUGILIST.

This was a reformed or converted prize-fighter, named Orville (and nicknamed "Awful") Gardner. He was a broad-shouldered, burly individual, with a tremendous neck, and an arm as thick as a moderate-sized man's leg. His career had been notorious and infamous in the extreme, he having been one of the roughs employed by politicians, and engaged in rows and fights without number, figuring several times in the prize-ring, and once having bitten off a man's nose!

Yet the man must have been less brutal than his life would show. He was a person evidently of volcanic emotions and great capacity of affection. I was curious about his case, and watched it closely for some

years, as showing what is so often disputed in modern
times—the reforming power of Christianity on the
most abandoned characters.

The point through which his brutalized nature had
been touched, had been evidently his affection for an
only child—a little boy. He described to me once, in
very simple, touching language, his affection and love
for this child; how he dressed him in the best, and
did all he could for him, but always keeping him away
from all knowledge of his own dissipation. One day
he was off on some devilish errand among the immigrants on Staten Island, when he saw a boat approaching quickly with one of his "pals." The man rowed
up near him, and stopped and looked at him "very
queer," and didn't say anything.

"What the devil are you looking at me in that
way for?" said Gardner.

"Your boy is drownded!" replied the other.

Gardner says he fell back in the boat, as if you'd
hit him right straight from the shoulder behind the
ear, and did not know anything for a long time. When
he recovered, he kept himself drunk for three weeks,
and smashed a number of policemen, and was "put
up," just so as to forget the bright little fellow who
had been the pride of his heart.

This great loss, however, must have opened his
nature to other influences. When the deep religious
sympathy pervaded the community, there came over

13

him suddenly one of those Revelations which, in some form or other, visit most human beings at least once in their lives. They are almost too deep and intricate to be described in these pages. The human soul sees itself, for the first time, as reflected in the mirror of divine purity. It has for the moment a conception of what CHRIST is, and what Love means. Singularly enough, the thought and sentiment which took possession of this ruffian and debauchee and prize-fighter, and made him as one just cured of leprosy, was the Platonic conception of Love, and that embodied in the ideal form of Christianity. Under it he became as a little child; he abandoned his vices, gave up his associates, and resolved to consecrate his life to humanity and the service of Him to whom he owed so much. The spirit, when I first met him, with which he used to encounter his old companions must have been something like that of the early Christian converts.

Thus, an old boon companion meets him in the street: "Why, Orful, what the h——ll's this about your bein' converted?"

And the other turns to him with such pent-up feeling bursting forth, telling him of the new things that have come to him, that the "rough" is quite melted, and begins a better course of life.

Again, he is going down a narrow street, when he suddenly sees coming up a bitter enemy. His old fire flames up, but he quenches it, walks to the other, and, with the tears streaming down his cheeks, he takes him by the hand and tells him "the old story" which is always new, and the two ruffians forget their feuds and are friends.

Could the old Greek philosopher have seen this imbruted athlete, so mysteriously and suddenly fired with the ideal of Love till his past crimes seemed melted in the heat of this great sentiment, and his rough nature appeared transformed, he would have rejoiced in beholding at length the living embodiment of an ideal theory for so many ages held but as the dream of a poetic philosopher.

Gardner was only a modern and striking instance of the natural and eternal power of Christianity.

We resolved to put him where he could reach the classes from which he had come. With considerable exertion the necessary sums were raised to open a "Coffee and Reading Room" in the worst district of the city—the Fourth Ward. Great numbers of papers and publications were furnished gratuitously by that body who have always been so generous to this enterprise—the conductors of the press of the city. A bar for coffee and cheap refreshments was established, and Gardner was put at the head of the whole as superintendent.

THE DRUNKARDS' CLUB

The opening is thus described in our Journal :—

"We must confess, as one of the managers of that institution, we felt particularly nervous about that opening meeting.

"Messrs Beecher and Cochrane and other eminent speakers had been invited to speak, and the Mayor was to preside. It was certainly an act of some self-denial to leave their country-seats or cool rooms, and spend a hot summer evening in talking to Fourth-ward rowdies. To requite this with any sort of 'accident' would have been very awkward. Where would we of the committee have hid our heads if our friends the 'roughs' had thought best to have a little bit of a shindy, and had knocked Brother Beecher's hat in, and had tossed the Hon. John Cochrane out of the window, or rolled the Mayor down-stairs? We confess all such possible eventualities did present themselves, and we imagined the sturdy form of our eminent clerical friend breasting the opposing waves of rowdies, and showing himself as skillful in demolishing corporeal enemies as he is in overthrowing spiritual. We were comforted in spirit, however, by remembering that the saint at the head of our establishment—the renowned Gardner—would now easily take a place in the church militant, and perhaps not object to a new exercise of muscle in a good cause."

   *   *   *   *   *   *   *   *

"After other addresses, Gardner—'Awful Gardner'—was called for. He came forward—and a great trial it must have been to have faced that crowd, where there were hundreds who had once been with him in all kinds of debaucheries and deviltries—men who had drunk and fought and gambled and acted the rowdy with him—men very quick to detect any trace of vanity or cant in him. He spoke very simply and humbly; said that he had more solid peace and comfort in one month now than he had in years once; spoke of his 'black life,' his sins and disgrace, and then of his most cordial desire to welcome all his old companions there. In the midst of these remarks there seemed to come up before him suddenly a memory of Him who had saved him, his eyes filled with tears, and, with a manly and deep feeling that swept right through the wild audience, he made his acknowledgment to 'Him who sticketh closer than a brother—even the Lord Jesus Christ.'

" No sermon could have been half so effective as these stammering ungrammatical, but manly remarks."

Our Reading-room under this guidance became soon a very popular resort; in fact, it deserved the nickname one gentleman gave it, "The Drunkards' Club." The marked, simple, and genuine reform in a man of such habits as this pugilist, attracted numbers of that large class of young men who are always trying to break from the tyranny of evil habits and vices. The rooms used to be thronged with reformed or reforming young men. The great difficulty with a man under vices is to make him believe that change for him is possible. The sight of Gardner always demonstrated this possibility. Those men who are sunk in such courses cannot get rid of them gradually, and nothing can arouse them and break the iron rule of habits but the most tremendous truths.

"Awful Gardner" had but one theory of reform—absolute and immediate change, in view of the love of Christ, and of a deserved and certain damnation.

The men to whom he spoke needed no soft words; they knew they were "in hell" now; some of them could sometimes for a moment realize what such a character as Christ was, and bow before it in unspeakable humility. No one whom I have ever seen could so influence the "roughs" of this city. He ought to have been kept as a missionary to the rowdies.

I extract from our Journal:—

"The moral success of the room has been all that we could have desired. Hundreds of young men have come there continually to read or chat with their friends—many of them even who had habitually frequented the liquor-saloons, and many persons with literally no homes. The place, too, has become a kind of central point for all these who have become more or less addicted to excessive drinking, and who are desirous of escaping from the habit.

"There are days when the spectacle presented there is a most affecting one; the room filled with young men, each of whom has a history of sorrow or degradation—broken-down gentlemen, ruined merchants, penniless clerks, homeless laboring-men and printers (for somehow this most intelligent profession seems to contain a large number of cases who have been ruined by drunkenness), and outcast men of no assignable occupation. These have been attracted in part by the cheerfulness of the room and the chances for reading, and in part by Gardner's influence, who has labored indefatigably in behalf of these poor wretches. Under the influences of the Room, incredible as it may seem, over *seven hundred* of these men have been started in sober courses and provided with honest employments, and many of them have become hopefully religious. It is believed that the whole quarter has been improved by the opening of this agreeable and temperate place of resort."

But, alas! even with a man so truly repentant and reformed, Nature does not let him off so easily. He had to bear in his body the fruits of his vices. His hervous system began to give way under the fearful strain both of his sins and his reform. He found it necessary to leave this post of work and retire to a quiet place in New Jersey, where he has since passed a calm and virtuous life, working, I suppose, at his trade, and, so far as I know, he has never been false to the great truths which once inspired him. With his departure, however, we thought it best to close the Reading-room, especially as we could not realize our hope of making it self-supporting. So ended the second of our experiments at " virtuous amusements."

I now resolved to try the experiment, without any expectation of sustaining the room with sales of refreshments. The working classes seem to be utterly indifferent to such attractions. They probably cannot compete a moment with those of the liquor-shops. With the aid of friends, who are always ready in this city to liberally support rational experiments of philanthropy, we have since then opened various Free Reading-rooms in different quarters of the city.

One of the most successful was carried on by Mr. Macy at Cottage Place, for his " lambs."

Here sufficient books and papers were supplied by friends, little temperance and other societies were formed, the room was pleasant and cozy, and, above all, Mr. Macy presided or infused into it his spirit. The " lambs " were occasionally obstreperous and given to smashing windows, but to this Mr. M. was sufficiently accustomed, and in time the wild young barbarians began to feel the influences thrown around the place, until now one may see of a winter evening

eighty or a hundred lads and young men quietly reading, or playing backgammon or checkers.

The room answers exactly its object as a place of
innocent amusement and improvement, competing
with the liquor-saloons. The citizens of the neighborhood have testified to its excellent moral influences on
the young men.

A similar room was opened in the First Ward by
the kind aid of the late Mr. J. Couper Lord, and
the good influences of the place have been much
increased by the exertions of Mr. D. E. Hawley and
a committee of gentlemen.

There are other Reading-rooms connected with the
Boys' Lodging-houses. Most of them are doing an
invaluable work; the First ward room especially
being a centre for cricket-clubs and various social re-
unions of the laboring classes, and undoubtedly saving great numbers of young men from the most dangerous temptations. Mr. Hawley has inaugurated
here also a very useful course of popular lectures to
the laboring people.

This Reading-room is crowded with young men
every night, of the class who should be reached, and
who would otherwise spend their leisure hours at the
liquor-saloons. Many of them have spoken with much
gratitude of the benefit the place has been to them.

The Reading-rooms connected with Boys' Lodging-
houses, though sometimes doing well, are not uni-

formly successful, perhaps from the fact that working-men do not like to be associated with homeless boys.

Besides those connected with the Children's Aid Society, the City Mission and various churches have founded others, so that now the Free Reading-room is recognized as one of the means for improving the "dangerous classes," as much as the Sunday School, Chapel, or Mission.

The true theory of the formation of the Reading-room is undoubtedly the inducing the laboring class to engage in the matter themselves, and then to assist them in meeting the expenses. But the lowest poor and the young men who frequent the grog-shops are so indifferent to mental improvement, and so seldom associate themselves for any virtuous object, that it is extremely difficult to induce them to combine for this. Moreover, as they rise in the social scale, they find organizations ready to hand, like the " Cooper Union," where Reading-rooms and Libraries are provided gratuitously. For the present, the Reading-room may be looked upon, like the Public School, as a means of improvement offered by society, in its own interest, to all.

CHAPTER XXV.

HOMELESS GIRLS.

It was a fortunate event for our charity which led, in 1861, a certain New York merchant to accept the position of President of our Society.

Mr. William A. Booth had the rare combination of qualities which form a thorough presiding officer, and at the same time he was inspired by a spirit of consecration to what he believed his Master's service, rarely seen among men. His faculty of "rolling off" business, of keeping his assembly or board on the points before them—for even business men have sometimes the female tendency of rather wide-reaching discussions and conversations—his wonderful clearness of comprehension, and a judicial faculty which nearly always enabled him to balance with remarkable fairness both sides of a question, made him beyond comparison the best presiding officer for a business-board I have ever seen. With him, we always had short and very full sessions, and reached our points rapidly and efficiently. He had, too, the capacity, rare among men of organizing brains, of accepting a rejection or rebuff to any proposition he may have made (though this happened seldom) with perfect good humor. Perhaps more than with his public services in our Board, I was struck with his private career. Hour after hour in his little office, I have seen different committees and officials of numerous societies, charities, and financial associations come to him with their knotty points, and watched with admiration as he disentangled each question, seeming always to strike upon the course at once wise and just. A very small portion of his busy time was then given to his own interests, though he had been singularly successful in his private affairs. He seemed to me to carry out wonderfully the Christian ideal in practical life in a busy city; living day after day "for others," and to do the will of Him whom he followed.

In our first labors together, I feared that, owing to his stricter school of Presbyterian theology, we might not agree in some of our aims and plans; but the practical test of true benefit to these unfortunate children soon brought our theoretic views to a harmony in religious practice; and as we both held that the first and best of all truths to an outcast boy is the belief and love of Christ as a friend and Saviour, we agreed on the substantial matter. I came, year by year, greatly to value his judgment and his clear insight as to the *via media*.

Both with him and our Treasurer, Mr. Williams, the services of love rendered so many years to this cause of humanity, could not, as mere labor, have been purchased with very lucrative salaries.

Mr. Booth's wise policy with the Society was to encourage whatever would give it a more permanent foot-hold in the city, and, in this view, to stimulate especially the founding of our Lodging-houses by means of "funds," or by purchasing buildings.

How this plan succeeded, I shall detail hereafter.

At this present stage in our history, his attention was especially fixed on the miserable condition of the young street-girls, and he suggested to me what I had long been hoping for, the formation of a Lodging-house for them, corresponding to that which had been so successful with the newsboys.

As a preparatory step, I consulted carefully the police. They were sufficiently definite as to the evil, but not very hopeful as to the cure.

THE STREET-GIRLS.

I can truly say that no class we have ever labored for seemed to combine so many elements of human misfortune and to present so many discouraging features as this. They form, indeed, a class by themselves.

Their histories are as various as are the different lots of the inhabitants of a populous town. Some have come from the country, from kind and respecta-

THE HOMELESS.

ble homes, to seek work in the city; here they gradually consume their scanty means, and are driven from one refuge to another, till they stand on the street, with the gayly-lighted house of vice and the gloomy police-station to choose between. Others have sought amusement in the town, and have been finally induced to enter some house of bad character as a boarding-house, and have been thus entrapped; and finally, in despair, and cursed with disease, they break loose, and take shelter even in the prison-cell, if necessary. Others still have abandoned an ill-tempered step-mother or father, and rushed out on the streets to find a refuge, or get employment anywhere.

Drunkenness has darkened the childhood of some, and made home a hideous place, till they have been glad to sleep in the crowded cellar or the bare attic of some thronged "tenement," and then go forth to pick up a living as they could in the great metropolis. Some are orphans, some have parents whom they detest, some are children of misfortune, and others of vice; some are foreigners, some native. They come from the north and the south, the east and the west; all races and countries are represented among them. They are not habitually vicious, or they would not be on the streets. They are unlucky, unfortunate, getting a situation only to lose it, and finding a home, to be soon driven from it. Their habits are irregular, they do not like steady labor, they have learned nothing well, they have no discipline, their clothes are neglected, they have no appreciation of what neatness is, yet if they earn a few shillings extra, they are sure to spend them on some foolish gewgaw. Many of them are pretty and bright, with apparently fine capacities, but inheriting an unusual quantity of the human tendencies to evil. They are incessantly deceived and betrayed, and they as constantly deceive others. Their cunning in concealing their indulgences or vices surpasses all conception. Untruth seems often more familiar to them than truth. Their worst quality is their superficiality. There is no depth either to their virtues or vices. They sin, and immediately repent with alacrity; they live virtuously for years, and a straw seems suddenly to turn them. They weep at the presentation of the divine character in Christ, and pray with fervency; and, the very next day, may ruin their virtue or steal their neighbor's garment, or take to drinking, or set a whole block in ferment with some biting scandal. They seem to be children, but with woman's passion, and woman's jealousy and scathing tongue. They trust a superior as a child; they neglect themselves, and injure body and mind as a child might; they have a child's generosity, and occasional freshness of impulse and desire of purity; but their passions sweep over them with the force of maturity, and their temper, and power of setting persons by the ears, and backbiting, and occasional intensity of hate, belong to a later period of life. Not unfrequently, when real danger or severe sickness arouses them, they show the wonderful qualities of womanhood in a power of sacrifice which utterly forgets self, and a love which shines brightly, even through the shadow of death.

But their combination of childishness and undisciplined maturity is an extremely difficult one to manage practically, and exposes them to endless sufferings and dangers. Their condition fifteen years ago seemed a thoroughly hopeless one.

There was then, if we mistake not, but a single refuge in the whole city, where these unfortunate creatures could take shelter, and that was Mr. Pease's Five Points Mission, which contained so many women who had been long in vicious courses, as to make it unsuitable for those who were just on the dividing line.

Our plan for their relief took the shape of

THE GIRLS' LODGING-HOUSE.

It is no exaggeration to say that this instrument of charity and reform has cost us more trouble than all our enterprises together.

The simple purpose and plan of it was, like that of our other efforts, to reform habits and character through material and moral appliances, and subsequently through an entire change of circumstances, and at the same time to relieve suffering and misfortune.

We opened first a shelter, where any drifting, friendless girl could go for a night's lodging. If she had means, she was to pay a trifling sum—five or six cents; if not, she aided in the labor of the house, and thus in part defrayed the expense of her board. Agents were sent out on the docks and among the slums of the city to pick up the wayfarers; notices were posted in the station-houses, and near the ferries and railroads depots, and even advertisements put into the cheap papers. We made a business of scattering the news of this charity wherever there were forlorn girls seeking for home or protection, or street-wandering young women who had no place to lay their heads.

We hoped to reach down the hand of welcome to the darkest dens of the city, and call back to virtue some poor, unbefriended creature, who was trembling on the very line between purity and vice. Our charity seemed to stand by the ferries, the docks, the police-stations, and prisons, and open a door of kindness and virtue to these hard-driven, tired wanderers on the ways of life. Our design was that no young girl, suddenly cast out on the streets of a great city, should be without a shelter and a place where good influences could surround her. We opened a House for the houseless; an abode of Christian sympathy for the utterly un-

befriended and misguided; a place of work for the idle
and unthrifty.

The plan seemed at once to reach its object:
the doors opened on a forlorn procession of unfortunates. Girls broke out of houses of vice, where
they had been entrapped, leaving every article of
dress, except what they wore, behind them; the
police brought wretched young wanderers, who had
slept on the station-floors; the daughters of decent
country-people, who had come to the town for amusement or employment, and, losing or wasting their
means, had walked the streets all the night long,
applied for shelter; orphans selling flowers, or peddling about the theatres; the children of drunkards;
the unhappy daughters of families where quarreling
and abuse were the rule; girls who had run away;
girls who had been driven away; girls who sought a
respite in intervals of vice,—all this most unfortunate
throng began to beset the doors of the "Girls' Lodging-house."

We had indeed reached the class intended, but
now our difficulties only began

It would not do to turn our Lodging-house into a
Reformatory for Magdalens, nor to make it into a convenient resting-place for those who lived on the wages
of lust. To keep a house for reforming young women of
bad character would only pervert those of good, and
shut out the decent and honest poor. We must draw a

line; but where? We attempted to receive only those of apparent honesty and virtue, and to exclude those who were too mature; keeping, if possible, below the age of eighteen years. We sought to shut out the professional "street-walkers." This at once involved us in endless difficulties. Sweet young maidens, whom we guilelessly admitted, and who gave most touching stories of early bereavement and present loneliness, and whose voices arose in moving hymns of penitence, and whose bright eyes filled with tears under the Sunday exhortation, turned out perhaps the most skillful and thorough-going deceivers, plying their bad trade in the day, and filling the minds of their comrades with all sorts of wickedness in the evening. We came to the conviction that these girls would deceive the very elect. Then some "erring child of poverty," as the reporters called her, would apply at a late hour at the door, after an unsuccessful evening, her breath showing her habit, and be refused, and go to the station-house, and in the morning a fearful narrative would appear in some paper, of the shameful hypocrisy and cruel machinery of charitable institutions.

Or, perhaps, she would be admitted, and cover the house with disgrace by her conduct in the night. One wayfarer, thus received, scattered a contagious disease, which emptied the whole house, and carried off the housekeeper and several lodgers. Another, in the night dropped her newly-born dead babe into the vault.

The rule, too, of excluding all over eighteen years of age caused great discontent with the poor, and with certain portions of the public. And yet, as rigidly as humanity would allow, we must follow our plan of benefiting children and youth.

It soon turned out, however, that the young street-children who were engaged in street-trades, had some relative to whom their labor was of profit, so that they gradually drifted back to their cellars and attics, and only occasionally took a night's lodging when out late near the theatre. Those who were the greatest frequenters of the House proved to be the young girls between fourteen and eighteen.

And a more difficult class than these to manage, no philanthropic mortal ever came in contact with. The most had a constitutional objection to work; they had learned to do nothing well, and therefore got but little wages anywhere; they were shockingly care-less, both of their persons and their clothing; and, worse than all, they showed a cunning and skill of deceit and a capacity of scandal, and of setting the family by the ears in petty quarrels and jealous-ies, which might have discouraged the most sanguine reformer.

The matron, Mrs. Trott, who had especially to struggle with these evils, had received a fitting pre-paratory training: she had taught in the "Five

Points." She was a thorough disciplinarian; believed in work, and was animated by the highest Christian earnestness.

As years passed by, the only defect that appeared in her was, perhaps, what was perfectly natural in such circumstances. The sins of the world, and the calamities of the poor, began to weigh on her mind, until its spring was fairly bent. Society seemed to her diseased with the sin against purity. The outcast daughters of the poor had no chance in this hard world. All the circumstances of life were against the friendless girl. Often, after most self-denying, and, to other minds, successful efforts to benefit these poor creatures, some enthusiastic spectator would say, "How much good you are doing!" "Well," she would say, with a sigh, "I sometimes hope so!"

Once, I asked her if she could not write a cheerful report for our trustees, giving some of the many encouraging facts she knew.

To my dismay, when the document appeared, the first two pages were devoted to a melancholy recollection of the horrible typhus which had once desolated the household! I think, finally, her mind took almost a sad pleasure in dwelling on the woes and miseries of humanity. Still, even with this constitutional weight on her, she did her work for those unfortunate girls faithfully and devotedly.

The great danger and temptation of such establishments, as I have always found, are in the desire of keeping the inmates, and showing to the public your "reforms." My instruction always was, that the "Girls' Lodging-house" was not to be a "Home." We did not want to make an asylum of it. We hoped to begin the work of improvement with these young girls, and then leave them to the natural agencies of society. To teach them to work, to be clean, and to understand the virtues of order and punctuality; to lay the foundations of a housekeeper or servant; to bring the influences of discipline, of kindness, and religion to bear on these wild and un-governed creatures—these were to be the great objects of the "Lodging-house;" then some good home or respectable family were to do the rest. We were to keep lodgers a little while only, and then to pass them along to situations or places of work.

The struggles of Mr. and Mrs. Trott, the superin-tendent and matron, against these discouraging evils in the condition and character of this class, would make a history in itself. They set themselves to work upon details, with an abounding patience, and with a humanity which was not to be wearied.

The first effort was to teach the girls something like a habit of personal cleanliness; then, to enforce order and punctuality, of which they knew nothing; next, to require early rising, and going to bed at a reasonable hour. The lessons of housekeeping were begun at the foundation, being tasks in scrubbing and cleaning; then, bed-making, and finally plain cooking, sewing, and machine-work. Some of the inmates went out for their daily labor in shops or factories; but the most had to be employed in house-work, and thus paid for their support. They soon carried on the work of a large establishment, and at the same time made thousands of articles of clothing for the poor children elsewhere under the charge of the Society.

A great deal of stress, of course, was laid on religious and moral instruction. The girls always "listened gladly," and were easily moved by earnest and sympathetic teaching and oratory.

Fortunately for the success of this Charity, one of our trustees, a man filled with "the milk of human kindness," Mr. B. J. Howland, took part in it, as if it were his main occupation in life. Twice in the week, he was present with these poor girls for many years, teaching them the principles of morality and religion, training them in singing, contriving amusements and festivals for them, sympathizing in their sorrows and troubles, until he became like a father and counselor to these wild, heedless young creatures.

When, at length, the good old man departs— *et serus in cœlum redeat!*—the tears of the friendless and forgotten will fall on his grave,

> " And the blessings of the poor
> Shall waft him to the other shore."

Of the effects of the patient labors of years, we will quote a few instances from Mrs. Trott's journal. She is writing, in the first extract, of a journey at the West:—

"Several stations were pointed out, where our Lodging house girls are located; and we envied them their quiet, rural homes, wishing that others might follow their example. Maggie M., a bright American girl, who left us last spring, was fresh in our memory, as we almost passed her door. The friendless child bids fair to make an educated, respectable woman. She writes of her advantages and privileges, and says she intends to improve them, and make the very best use of her time.

"Our old friend, Mary F., is still contented and happy; she shows no inclination to return, and remains in the place procured for her two years ago. She often expresses a great anxiety for several of the girls whom she left here, and have turned out very bad. We were rather doubtful of Mary's intentions when she left us, but have reason for thankfulness that thus far she tries to do right, and leads a Christian life. She was a girl well informed, of good common-sense, rather attractive, and, we doubt not, is ' a brand plucked from the burning.'

"Emma H., a very interesting, amiable young girl, who spent several months at the Lodge, while waiting for a good opening, has just been to visit us. She is living with Mrs. H., Judge B——'s daughter, on the Hudson. They are mutually pleased with each other; and Mrs. B. says that 'Emma takes an adopted daughter's place, and nothing would tempt me to part with her.' Emma was well dressed, and as comfortably situated as one could wish. There is no reason why she should not educate herself, and fill a higher position in the future.

"S. A. was a cigar-girl when she came to the Lodging-house six years ago. An orphan, friendless and homeless—we all knew her desire to obtain an education, her willingness to make any sacrifice, and put up with the humblest fare, that she might accomplish this end; and then her earnest desire to do good, and her consistent Christian character, since she united with the Church, and the real missionary she proved among the girls, when death was in the house, leaving her school, and assisting night and day among the sick. She is now completing her education, and will soon graduate with honors. Her teacher speaks of her in the highest terms.

"There was another, J. L., a very pretty little girl, who was with us at the same time, who was guilty of the most aggravating petty thefts. She was so modest and pleasing in her demeanor, so sincere in her attachments, that it was difficult to believe, until she acknowledged her guilt, that she had picked the pockets of the very persons to whom she had made showy presents. Vanity was her ruling motive—a desire to appear smart and generous, and to show that she had rich friends, who supplied her with money. She was expostulated with long and tenderly, promised to reform, and has lately united with a church where she is an active and zealous member. We have never heard a word respecting her dishonesty since she left us, and she now occupies a responsible position as forewoman in a Broadway store.

"P. E. was also a Lodging-house girl, a year or more, at the same time. She came to us in a very friendless, destitute condition. She was one of the unfortunates with the usual story of shame and desertion—she had just buried her child, and needed an asylum. We have every reason to believe her repentance sincere, and that she made no false pretensions to piety when her name was added to the list of professing Christians. The church took an unusual interest in her, and have paid her school expenses several years. She is now teaching.

"Our next is Mary M. Here is a bit of romance. When she first entered our home, she was reduced to the very lowest extremity of poverty and wretchedness. She remained with us some time, and then went to a situation in Connecticut, where she married a young Southern gentleman, who fell desperately in love with her (because she cared for him when ill), returned to New York, and, when she called upon us, was boarding at the Fifth-avenue Hotel. This was noticed at the time in several Eastern and New York papers. She showed her gratitude to us by calling and making presents to members of the House—looking up an associate, whom she found in a miserable garret clothing her, and returning her to her friends. She greatly surprised us in the exhibition of the true womanly traits which she always manifested. This is a true instance of the saying that a resident of the Five Points to-day may be found in her home in Fifth Avenue to-morrow.

"Without going into details, we could also mention S. H., who has often been in our reports as unmanageable; the two D—— girls, who came from Miss Tracy's school; the two M—— sisters, who had a fierce drunken mother, that pawned their shoes for rum one cold winter's morn, before they had arisen from their wretched bed; two R—— sisters, turned into the streets by drunken parents, brought to our house by a kind-hearted expressman, dripping with rain; and little May, received, cold and hungry, one winter's day—all comfortably settled in country homes; most of them married, and living out West--not forgetting Maggie, the Irish girl who wrote us, soon after she went West, that her husband had his little farm, pigs, cow, etc.; requesting us to send them a little girl for adoption. Her prospect here never would have been above a garret or cellar.

"We have L. M. in New York, married to a mechanic. Every few months she brings a bundle of clothing for those who were once her companions. She is very energetic and industrious, and highly respected.

"M. E., another excellent Christian girl. She has been greatly tried in trying to save a reckless sister from destruction; once she took her West; then she returned with her when she found her sister's condition made it necessary. Such sisterly affection is seldom manifested as this girl has shown. She bought her clothing out of her own earnings, when she had scarcely a change for herself; and, after the erring sister's death, paid her child's board, working night and day to do so.

"These cases are true in every particular, and none of recent date. There are many more hopeful ones among our young girls, who have not been away from us long, and of whom we hear excellent reports."

One of the best features of this most practical "institution" for poor girls is a Sewing-machine

14

School, where lessons are given gratuitously. In three weeks, a girl who had previously depended wholly on her needle, and could hardly earn her three dollars a week, will learn the use of the machine, and earn from one dollar to two dollars per day.

During one year this Sewing-machine School sent forth some one thousand two hundred poor girls, who earned a good living through their instruction there. The expense was trifling, as the machines were all given or loaned by the manufacturers, and for the room, we employed the parlor of the Lodging-house.

During the winter of 1870–71, the trustees determined to try to secure a permanent and convenient house for these girls.

Two well-known gentlemen of our city headed the subscription with $1,000 each; the trustees came forward liberally, and the two or three who have done so much for this charity took on themselves the disagreeable task of soliciting funds, so that in two months we had some $27,000 subscribed, with which we both secured an excellent building in St. Mark's Place, and adapted it for our purposes. Our effort is in this to make the house more attractive and tasteful than such places usually are; and various ladies have co-operated with us, to exert a more profound and renovating influence on these girls.

We have already engrafted on this Lodging-house a School to train ordinary house-servants; to teach plain cooking, waiting, the care of bedrooms, and good laundry-work. Nothing is more needed among this class, or by the public generally, than such a "Training-school."

Of the statistics of the Lodging-house, Mrs. Trott writes as follows :—

"Ten thousand two hundred and twenty-five lodgers. What an army would the registered names make, since a forlorn, wretched child of thirteen years, from the old Trinity station-house, headed the lists in 1861 !

"Among this number there are many cosily sitting by their own hearth-stones; others are filling positions of usefulness and trust in families and stores; some have been adopted in distant towns, where they fill a daughter's place; and some have gone to return no more. A large number we cannot trace.

"During this period, three thousand one hundred and one have found employment, and gone to situations, or returned to friends.

"Fifteen thousand four hundred and twenty-nine garments have been cut and made, and distributed among the poor, or used as outfits in sending companies West."

CHAPTER XXVI.

THE NINETEENTH-STREET GANG OF RUFFIANS.

A MORAL "DISINFECTANT."

DURING the summer of 1865, I was present in London as a delegate to the International Reformatory Convention, and had the opportunity, for the second or third time, to investigate thoroughly the preventive and reformatory institutions of Great Britain.

On my return I found that the President of our Board, of whom I have already spoken, had taken a lease of a building in a notorious quarter.

His idea was that some of my observations in England might be utilized here and tested in a preventive institution. The quarter was well known to me. It had been the home and school of the murderous gang of boys and young men known as

"THE NINETEENTH-STREET GANG."

It happens that the beginnings and the process of growth of this society of young criminals were thoroughly known by me at the time, and, as one case of this kind illustrates hundreds going on now, I will describe it in detail:—

Seventeen years ago, my attention had been called to the extraordinarily degraded condition of the children in a district lying on the west side of the city, between Seventeenth and Nineteenth Streets, and the Seventh and Tenth Avenues. A certain block, called "Misery Row," in Tenth Avenue, was the main seed-bed of crime and poverty in the quarter, and was also invariably a "fever-nest." Here the poor obtained wretched rooms at a comparatively low rent; these they sub-let, and thus, in little, crowded, close tenements, were herded men, women, and children of all ages. The parents were invariably given to hard drinking, and the children were sent out to beg or to steal. Besides them, other children, who were orphans, or who had run away from drunkards' homes, or had been working on the canal-boats that discharged on the docks near by, drifted into the quarter, as if attracted by the atmosphere of crime and laziness that prevailed in the neighborhood. These slept around the breweries of the ward, or on the hay-barges, or in the old sheds of Eighteenth and Nineteenth Streets. They were mere children, and kept life together by all sorts of street-jobs—helping the brewery laborers, blackening boots, sweeping sidewalks, "smashing baggages" (as they called it), and the like. Herding together, they soon began to form an unconscious society for vagrancy and idleness. Finding that work brought but poor pay, they tried shorter roads to getting money by pettey thefts, in which they were very adroit. Even if they earned a considerable sum by a lucky day's job, they quickly spent it in gambling, or for some folly.

The police soon knew them as "street-rats;" but, like the rats, they were too quick and cunning to be often caught in their petty plunderings, so they gnawed away at the foundations of society undisturbed. As to the "popular education" of which we boast, and the elevating and inspiring faith of Christianity which had reared its temples all around them, they might almost as well have been the children of the Makololos in Central Africa. They had never been in school or church, and knew of God and Christ only in street-oaths, or as something of which people far above them spoke sometimes.

I determined to inaugurate here a regular series of the "moral disinfectants," if I may so call them, for this "crime-nest," which act almost as surely, though not as rapidly, as do the physical disinfectants—the sulphate of iron, the chloride of lime, and the various deodorizers of the Board of Health—in breaking up the "fever-nests" of the city.

These measures, though imitated in some respects from England, were novel in their combination.

The first step in the treatment is to appoint a kind-hearted agent or "Visitor," who shall go around

the infected quarter, and win the confidence of, and
otherwise befriend the homeless and needy children
of the neighborhood. Then we open an informal, simple, religious meeting—the Boys' Meeting which I
have described; next we add to it a free Reading-
room, then an Industrial School, afterwards a Lodging-house; and, after months or years of the patient
application of these remedies, our final and most
successful treatment is, as I have often said, the
forwarding of the more hopeful cases to farms in
the West.

While seeking to apply these long-tried remedies
to the wretched young population in the Sixteenth
Ward, I chanced on a most earnest Christian man, a
resident of the quarter, whose name I take the liberty
of mentioning—Mr. D. Slater, a manufacturer.

He went around himself through the rookeries of
the district, and gathered the poor lads even in his
own parlor; he fed and clothed them; he advised and
prayed with them. We opened together a religious
meeting for them. Nothing could exceed their wild
and rowdy conduct in the first gatherings. On one or
two occasions some of the little ruffians absolutely
drew knives on our assistants, and had to be handed
over to the police. But our usual experience was repeated even there. Week by week patient kindness
and the truths of Christianity began to have their
effect on these wild little heathen of the street. We

find, in our Journal of 1856, the following entries (p. 11):—

"The other meeting has been opened in the hall, at the corner of Sixteenth Street and Eighth Avenue, by Mr. D. Slater. It had, in the beginning, a rather stormy time, being frequented by the rowdy and thieving boys of the quarter. Mr. S. has once or twice been obliged to call in the help of the police, and to arrest the ringleaders. Now, however, by his patient kindness and anxiety for the welfare of the lads, he has gained a permanent influence. The police have remarked how much less the streets, on a Sunday, have been infested, since he opened the meeting, with vagabond boys. Several notorious street-boys have abandoned their bad habits, and now go regularly to the Public Schools, or are in steady business. The average attendance the first month was 88; it is now 162. The average evening attendance is 104.

"There is a family of four boys, all orphans, whom their friends could do nothing with, and turned into the streets. They lived by petty stealing, and slept in hay-lofts in winter, and on stoops or in coal-boxes in summer. Since they came to the meeting they have all gone to work; they attend Public School, and come regularly to evening meeting. They used to be in rags and filth, but now are clean and well dressed. Their uncle came to me and said the meeting had done them more good than all their friends together."—(*Mr. Slater's Report.*)

"Yesterday, Mr. Slater brought a thin, sad boy to us—had found him in the streets and heard his story, and then gave him a breakfast, and led him up to our office. The lad seemed like one weary almost of living. 'Where are your father and mother, my boy?' 'Both dead, sir.' 'Where are your other relatives or friends?' 'Haint got no friends, sir; I've lived by myself on the street.' 'Where did you stay?' 'I slept *in the privy* sometime, sir; and then in the stables in Sixteenth Street.' 'Poor fellow,' said some one, 'how did you get your living?' 'Begged it—and then, them stable-men, they give me bread sometimes.' 'Have you ever been to school, or Sunday School?' 'No, sir.' So the sad story went on. Within two blocks of our richest houses, a desolate boy grows up, not merely out of Christianity and out of

education, but out of a common human shelter, and of means of
livelihood.

"The vermin were creeping over him as he spoke. A few
days before this, Mr. S. had brought up three thorough-going
street-boys—active, bold, impudent, smart fellows—a great deal
more wicked and much less miserable than this poor fellow.
Those three were sent to Ohio together, and this last boy, after
a thorough washing and cleansing, was to be dispatched to Illinois. A later note adds: 'The lad was taken by an old gentleman of property, who, being childless, has since adopted the boy
as his own, and will make him heir to a property.'"

Several other lads were helped to an honest livelihood. A Visitor was then appointed, who lived and
worked in the quarter. But our moral treatment for
this nest of crime had only commenced.

We appealed to the public for aid to establish the
reforming agencies which alone can cure these evils,
and whose foundation depends mainly on the liberality, in money, of our citizens. We warned them that
these children, if not instructed, would inevitably
grow up as ruffians. We said often that they would
not be like the stupid foreign criminal class, but that
their crimes, when they came to maturity, would show
the recklessness, daring, and intensity of the American character. In our very first report (for 1854) we
said:—

"It should be remembered that there are no dangers to the
value of property, or to the permanency of our institutions, so
great as those from the existence of such a class of vagabond,
ignorant, ungoverned children. This 'dangerous class' has not
begun to show itself, as it will in eight or ten years, when these
boys and girls are matured. Those who were too negligent, or

too selfish to notice them as children, will be fully aware of them as men. They will vote—they will have the same rights as we ourselves, though they have grown up ignorant of moral principle, as any savage or Indian. They will poison society. They will perhaps be embittered at the wealth and the luxuries they never share. Then let society beware, when the outcast, vicious, reckless multitude of New York boys, swarming now in every foul alley and low street, come to know their power and use it!"

Again, in 1857, we said:—

"Why should the 'street-rat,' as the police call him—the boy whose home in sweet childhood was a box or a deserted cellar; whose food was crumbs begged or bread stolen; whose influences of education were kicks and cuffs, curses, neglect, destitution and cold; who never had a friend, who never heard of duty either to society or God—why should he feel himself under any of the restraints of civilization or of Christianity? Why should he be anything but a garroter and thief?"

*   *   *   *   *   *   *   *

"Is not this crop of thieves and burglars, of shoulder-hitters and short-boys, of prostitutes and vagrants, of garroters and murderers, the very fruit to be expected from this seed, so long being sown? What else was to be looked for? Society hurried on selfishly for its wealth, and left this vast class in its misery and temptation. Now these children arise and wrest back, with bloody and criminal hands, what the world were too careless or too selfish to give. The worldliness of the rich, the indifference of all classes to the poor, will always be avenged. Society must act on the highest principles, or its punishment incessantly comes within itself. The neglect of the poor, and tempted, and criminal, is fearfully repaid." (Pp. 5, 6.)

But the words fell on inattentive ears.

We found ourselves unable to continue our reforming agencies in the Sixteenth Ward; no means were supplied; our Visitor was dismissed, the meeting

closed; Mr. Slater moved away, heavily out of pocket
with his humane efforts, and much discouraged
with the indifference of the Christian community to
these tremendous evils; and the "Nineteenth-street
Gang" grew up undisturbed in its evil courses, taking
new lessons in villainy and crime, and graduating in
the manner the community has felt the past few
years. Both the police and the public have noted the
extraordinary recklessness and ferocity of their crimes.
One, a mere lad, named Rogers, committed a murder,
a few years ago, on a respectable gentleman, Mr.
Swanton, accompanied by his wife, in the open street,
on the west side of the city. He was subsequently
executed. Some have been notorious thieves and burglars.

Another murdered an unoffending old man, Mr.
Rogers, in open day, before his own door, and near
the main thoroughfare of the city. The whole community was deeply thrilled by this horrible murder,
and, though three of the "Gang" were arrested, the
offender was never discovered. Subsequently, one of
the suspected young men was murdered by one of his
own "pals."

The amount of property they have destroyed would
have paid the expense of an Industrial School, Reading-room, Lodging-house and our other agencies for
them, ten times over.

Now and then we have rescued two or three brothers of them, and have seen them become honest and industrious farmers in the West, while one of the same family, remaining here, would soon be heard of in Sing Sing or the city prisons.

The history of the growth of the "Nineteenth-street Gang" is only one example of the histories of scores of similar bands of ruffians now in process of formation in the low quarters of the city.

Our preventive agency was now placed, through the especial assistance of one of our trustees, in a better building, in Eighteenth Street. Here we had all our moral "disinfectants" under one roof, in the best possible efficiency.

The person to be appointed Superintendent, whom I had accidentally encountered, was a "canny Scotch-man," and proved singularly adapted to the work. I feared at first that he was "too pious" for his place; as experience shows that a little leaven of carnal habits, and the jolly good nature which Relig-ion ought only to increase, but which, when mis-applied, it does sometimes somewhat contract, is use-ful in influencing these young heathen of the street. Perhaps they are so far down in the moral scale, that too strict a standard, when first applied to them, tends to repel or discourage them.

I particularly dreaded our friend's devotional exercises. But time and experience soon wore off the Scotch Presbyterian starch, and showed that the "root of the matter" was in him. The first quality needed in such a position is patience—a spirit which is never discouraged by ingratitude or wearied out by ill conduct. This our apparently somewhat sternly-righteous superintendent could attempt to show.

Then, next, the guide of such lads must be just—inflexibly just—and exact in the smallest particulars; for, of all things which a street-boy feels, is first any neglect of obligations.

This virtue was easy to the superintendent. He had, too, in him a deep well of kindness for the forlorn and unfortunate, which the lads soon appreciated. To my great satisfaction, at this time a gentleman threw himself into the movement, who possessed those qualities which always command success, and especially the peculiarities with which boys instinctively sympathize.

He was gifted with a certain vitality of temperament and rich power of enjoyment of everything human, which the rough lads felt immediately. He evidently liked horses and dogs; a drive four-in-hand, and a gallop "to hounds," were plainly things not opposed to his taste. He appreciated a good dinner (as the boys happily discovered), and had no moral scruples at a cigar, or an occasional glass of wine.

All this physical energy and richness of tempera-

ment seemed to accompany him in his religious and
philanthropical life. He was indefatigable in his
efforts for the good of the lads; he conducted their
religious meeting every Sunday evening; he advised and guided, he offered prizes, gave festivals
and dinners, supplied reasonable wants, and corre-
sponded with them. And, at length, to crown his
efforts, he proposed to a few friends to purchase
the house, and make it a home for the homeless
boys forever.

This benevolent measure was carried through with
the same energy with which he manages his business,
and the street-boys of the west side of New York will
long feel the fruits of it.

For our own and the public benefit, our worthy
superintendent had, among his other qualities, what
was of immense importance for his work—the true
Scotch economy.

No manufacturer ever managed his factory, no
hotel-keeper ever carried on his establishment with
such an eye for every penny of useless expenditure, as
this faithful manager of trust-funds looked after every
item of cost in this School and Lodging-house. Thus,
for instance, during the month of May last, he lodged
eighty boys every night, and fed them with two meals,
at a cost to each lodger of five cents for a meal and five
cents for lodging, at the same time feeding and lodg-

ing some gratuitously. The boys were kept clean, had enough to eat, and were brought under all the good moral and mental influences of the House; and, at the end of the month, the institution had not only cost nothing to the public, but Mr. Gourley absolutely turned over eleven dollars and sixty-five cents to the Society. That is, his rent being paid, he had managed to keep his boys, pay the wages and food of three servants, a night-watchman, and errand-boy, and the salaries and table expenses of the superintendent, matron, and their family of four children. If this is not "economical charity," it would be difficult to find it.

On one occasion the patience of our worthy superintendent was put to a severe test.

For two years he fed and lodged two youthful "vessels of wrath." They were taught in the Night-school, they were preached to, and prayed with in the Sunday meeting, they were generously feasted in the Thanksgiving and Christmas festivals. At last, as the crowning work of benevolence, he clothed and cleaned them, and took them with him to find them a home in the Far West.

Here, when they had reached the land of independence, they began to develop "the natural man" in a most unpleasant form.

They would not go to the places selected; their language was so bad that the farmers would not take them; finally, after their refusing to take places where they were wanted, and making themselves generally disagreeable, Mr. Gourley had to inform the lads that they must shift for themselves! Hereupon they turned upon their benefactor with the vilest language. Subsequently they met him in the streets of the Western town, and were about to show themselves—what a Western paper calls—"muscular orphans," by a vigorous assault on their benevolent protector; but finding, from the bearing of our excellent brother, that he had something of the old Covenanter's muscle in him, and could show himself, if necessary, a worthy member of the old Scotch "Church militant," they wisely avoided the combat.

Mr. Gourley returned home down-hearted, his high Calvinistic views of the original condition of the human heart not being weakened by his experience. We all felt somewhat discouraged; but, as if to show us that human nature is never to be despaired of, Mr. Gourley afterwards received the following *amende* from the two ingrates :—

HOPEFUL NEWS FROM HARD CASES.

"P——, MICH., June 6, 1870.

" Mr. J. GOURLEY :

" *Dear Sir*—Knowing that you are one of those who can forget and forgive, I take the liberty of writing these few lines to you, hoping that I will not offend you by so doing. W—— and I both wish to return our thanks to the Society for giving us the aid they have. We are now both in a fair way of making men of ourselves. We are happy to think that we are free from the evil temptations that the poor boys of New York are exposed to. We are respected by all who know us here. Boys of New York little know of the pleasure there is to be found in a home in the 'Far West.' We expect to stay here for two years yet, and then make a short visit to New York. We would like to visit the 'Old Hotel,' if you have no objection. We would like to have you write and let us know how the boys are getting along, and if little Skid and Dutchy are still in the hotel. I would advise all boys who have no home to go West, and they will be sure to find one. W—— is foreman on the largest farm in the town, and has hired for three years at one hundred dollars per year, and found in everything. I am working in a saw-mill this summer. I worked on a farm the first winter and summer. Last winter I worked in the lumber-wood, and this summer I will try the mill. I get twenty dollars a month, and have since I left you at the depot. We both went to work the next day. I wish you would be so kind as to answer this, and oblige your obedient servants,

"B. T.
"M. W."

TABULAR STATEMENT SINCE ORGANIZATION.

Year.	No. of Boys.	No. of Lodgings.	No. of Meals.	No. Provided for.	Expenses.	Receipts.
1866 to 1867..... ...	847	15,380	48,511	272	$6,205 48	$3,053 40
1867 to 1868........	952	23,933	39,401	159	5,141 08	4,065 25
1868 to 1869........	890	22,921	25,345	127	7,923 58	3,068 83
1869, 9 months.....	563	15,506	15,429	37	3,832 04	1,995 21
1869 to 1870........	919	25,516	27,932	86	4,766 55	3,510 84
1870 to 1871........	750	28,302	30,693	69	4,294 51	3,586 67
Totals.......	4,921	131,467	187,311	751	$32,093 24	$19,279 90

The Eighteenth-street Lodging-house has been gradually and surely preventing the growth of a fresh "gang" of youthful ruffians; and has already saved great numbers of neglected boys.

CHAPTER XXVII.

THE MINISTRY OF FLOWERS.

THE LITTLE VAGABONDS OF CORLEAR'S HOOK.

IF any of my readers should ever be inclined to investigate a very miserable quarter of the city, let them go down to our "Corlear's Hook," so infamous twenty years ago for murders and terrible crimes, and then wind about among the lanes and narrow streets of the district. Here they will find every available inch of the ground made use of for residences, so that each lot has that poisonous arrangement, a "double house," whereby the air is more effectually vitiated, and a greater number of human beings are crowded together. From this massing-together of families, and the drunken habits prevailing, it results very naturally that the children prefer outdoor life to their wretched tenements, and, in the milder months, boys and girls live a *dolce far niente* life on the docks and wood-piles, enjoying the sun and the swimming, and picking up a livelihood by petty thieving and peddling.

Sometimes they all huddle together in some cellar, boys and girls, and there sleep. In winter they creep back to the tenement-houses, or hire a bed in the vile

lodgings which are found in the Ward. They grow
up, naturally, the wildest little "Topseys" and "Ga-
vroches"'that can be found. Ragged, impudent, sharp,
able "to paddle their canoe" through all the rapids of
the great city—the most volatile and uncertain of
children; to day in school, to-morrow miles away;
many of them the most skillful of petty thieves, and
all growing up to prey on the city.

· In the midst of this quarter we found an old Public School building—a dilapidated old shell—which
we hired and refitted. It had the especial advantage
of being open to air and light on four sides. We soon
transformed it into one of the most complete and
attractive little agencies of instruction and charity
which ever arose in the dark places of a crowded
metropolis. We struck upon a superintendent—Mr.
G. Calder—who, with other good qualities, had the
artistic gift—who, by a few flowers, or leaves, or old
engravings, could make any room look pleasing. He
exerted his talent in embellishing this building, and
in making a cheerful spot in the midst of a ward filled
with rookeries and broken-down tenements. In the
bit of a back yard he created a beautiful garden, with
shrubbery and flowers, with vases and a cool shaded
seat—and these in a place of the size of a respectable
closet. There a poor child could stand and fancy
herself, for a moment, far away in the country.
Thence, on a spring morning, drowning the prevalent

smells of bilge-water and sewers, ascended the sweet odors of hyacinth and heliotrope, sweet-william and violet. Above, in the school-rooms and the lodging-rooms, these sweet flowers were scattered about, taming and refining, for the time, the rough little subjects who frequented them. Soon a novel reward was proposed, and the best children in the School were allowed to take a plant home with them, and, if they brought it back improved in a few months, to receive others as a premium; so that the School not merely distributed its light of morality and intelligence in the dreary dens of the Ward, but was represented by cheerful and fragrant flowers in the windows of poor men's homes.

In the School-room, too, was placed a little aquarium, which became an increasing source of delight to the young vagabonds. Our diligent superintendent was not content. He now built a green-house, and, though no gardener, soon learned to care for and raise quantities of exquisite flowers, which should brighten the building in the gloomy winter.

For the Industrial School we procured a teacher who taught as if life and death depended on the issues of each lesson. She seemed to pour out her life on " Enumeration," and gave an Object-lesson on an orange as if all the future prospects of the children depended on it. Such a teacher could not fail to interest the lively little vagrants of Rivington Street.

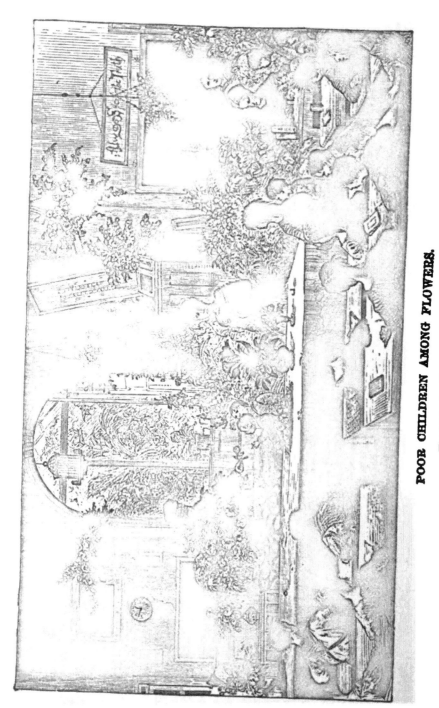

POOR CHILDREN AMONG FLOWERS.

(The Rivington Street Lodging-House.)

Her sweet assistant was as effective in her own way; so it came that a hundred and fifty of the young flibbertigibbets of the ward were soon gathered and attempted to be brought under the discipline of an Industrial School. But it was like schooling little Indians. A bright day scattered them as a splash scatters a school of fish, and they disappeared among the docks and boats of the neighborhood. No intellectual attraction could compete with a " target company," and the sound of the fire-bell drove all lessons out of their heads. Still, patience and ingenuity and devotion accomplished here, as in all our schools, their work—which, if not "perfect," has been satisfactory and encouraging.

But this was only a part of our efforts. Besides the school of a hundred and fifty children in the day from the neighborhood, might be found a hundred boys gathered from boxes, and barges, and all conceivable haunts, who came in for school and supper and bed.

Here, for some inscrutable reason, the considerable class of "canawl-boys," or lads who work on the canal-boats of the interior, came for harbor. Besides our Day and Night Schools, we opened here also a Free Reading-room for boys and young men in the neighborhood, and we held our usual Sunday-evening Meeting. In this meeting, fortunately for its good effects, various gentlemen took part, with much experience in practical life and of earnest characters.   One, a young officer in the army, whose service for his country fitted him for the service of humanity; another, an enthusiastic and active young business man; and still another—one of those men of calm judgment, profound earnestness of character, and an almost princely generosity, who, in a foreign country, would be at the head of affairs, but here throw their moral and mental weight into enterprises of religion and philanthropy.

The effects of these Meetings were exemplified by many striking changes of character, and instances of resistance to temptation among the lads, which greatly encouraged us.

The building seemed so admirably adapted to our work, that, emboldened by our success with the Eighteenth-street House, we determined to try to purchase it.   Two of our Trustees took the matter in hand. One had already, in the most generous manner, given one-third of the amount required for the purchase of that building; but now he offered what was still more —his personal efforts towards raising the amount needed here, $18,000.

No such disagreeable and self-denying work is ever done, as begging money.   The feeling that you are boring others, and getting from their personal regard, what ought to be given solely for public motives, and the certainty that others will apply to you as you apply to them, and expect a subscription as a personal return, are all great "crosses." The cold rebuff, too; the suspicious negative, as if you were engaged in rather doubtful business, are other unpleasant accompaniments of this business. And yet it ought to be regarded simply and solely as an unpleasant public duty. Money must be given, or refused, merely from public considerations. The giving to one charity should never leave an obligation that your petitioner must give to another. These few gentlemen in the city, of means and position, who do this unpleasant work, deserve the gratitude of the community.

No other city in the world, we believe, makes such liberal gifts from its means, as does New York towards all kinds of charitable and religious objects. There is a certain band of wealthy men who give in a proportion almost never known in the history of benefactions. We know one gentleman of large income who habitually, as we understand from good authority, bestows, in every kind of charitable and religious donations, $300,000 a year! As a general rule, however, the very rich in New York give very little. Our own charity has been mainly supported by the gifts of the middle and poorer classes.

In this particular case, the trustee of whom we have spoken threw that enormous energy which has already made him, though a young man, one of the

foremost business men of the city, into this labor.
With him was associated a refined gentleman, who
could reach many with invested wealth. Under this
combination we soon raised the required sum, and
all had the profound satisfaction of seeing a temporary "Home for Homeless Boys" placed in one of
the worst quarters of the city, to scatter its benefactions for future years, when we are all gone.

During the past year, a still more beautiful feature
has been added to this Lodging-house. We had occasion to put up in the rear a little building for bath-
rooms. It occurred to some gentlemen who are always
devising pleasant things for these poor children, that
a green-house upon this, opening into the school-room,
would be a very agreeable feature, and that our superintendent's love for flowers could thus be used in
the most practical way for giving pleasure to great
numbers of poor children. A pretty conservatory,
accordingly, was erected on the top of the bath-room,
opening into the audience-room, so that the little
street-waifs, as they looked up from their desks, had
a vista of flowers before them. Hither, also, were
invited the mothers of the children in the Day-school
to occasional parties or exhibitions; and here the
plants were shown which had been intrusted to them.

The room is one of the most attractive school-
rooms in the city, and I have no doubt its beautiful
flowers are one cause of the great numbers of poor

children which flock to it, while the influence of its
earnest teachers, and of the whole instrumentality,
has been to improve the character of the neighboring
quarter.

FOUR YEARS' WORK AT THE RIVINGTON-STREET LODGING-
HOUSE. (1868, 1869, 1870, 1871.)

Number of different boys provided for.............. 2,659
Number of lodgings furnished................ 80,344
Number of meals furnished... 78,756
Number of boys sent West........................... 161
Number of boys provided with employment.......... 105
Number of boys restored to friends............... . 126
Number of boys patronizing the savings-bank.... . 310
Amount saved by the boys............. ....$2,873 00
Total expenses.......................................26,018 10
Amount paid by the boys............................ 8,614 68

THE LITTLE COPPER-STEALERS.

THE ELEVENTH-WARD LODGING-HOUSE.

The history of this useful charity would be only a
repetition of that of the others. It is placed among
the haunts which are a favorite of the little dock-
thieves, and iron and copper-stealers, and of all the
ragged crowd who live by peddling wood near the
East River wharves. It has had a checkered career.
One superintendent was "cleaned out" twice on successive nights, and had his till robbed almost under
his nose. Another was almost hustled out of the
dormitory by the youthful vagabonds; but order has
at length been gained; considerable numbers of the
15

gamins have been turned into honest farmers, and others are pursuing regular occupations.

The Night-school is busily attended; the Day-school is a model of industry; the "Bank" is used, and the Sunday-evening Meeting is one of the most interesting and impressive which we have.

Its recent success and improvement are due to the personal interest and exertions of one of our trustees, who has thrown into this labor of charity a characteristic energy, as well as the earnestness of a profound religious nature.

We have in this building, also, a great variety of charitable work crowded; but we hope, through the liberality which has founded our other Lodging-houses, to secure a more suitable building, which shall be a permanent blessing to that quarter.

STATISTICS FROM ORIGIN TO 1872.

Number of lodgings	67,196
Number of meals	65,757
Sent West	278
Restored to friends	188
Number of different boys	3,036
Amount paid by boys	$6,539 29

CHAPTER XXVIII.

THE CHILD-VAGRANT.

THERE is without doubt in the blood of most children—as an inheritance, perhaps, from some remote barbarian ancestor—a passion for roving. There are few of us who cannot recall the delicious pleasure of wandering at free will in childhood, far from schools, houses, and the tasks laid upon us, and leading in the fields or woods a semi-savage existence. In fact, to some of us, now in manhood, there is scarcely a greater pleasure of the senses than to gratify "the savage in one's blood," and lead a wild life in the woods. The boys among the poor feel this passion often almost irresistibly. Nothing will keep them in school or at home. Having perhaps kind parents, and not a peculiarly disagreeable home, they will yet rove off night and day, enjoying the idle, lazzaroni life on the docks, living in the summer almost in the water, and curling down at night, as the animals do, in any corner they can find—hungry and ragged, but light-hearted, and enjoying immensely their vagabond life. Probably as a sensation, not one that the street lad will ever have in after-life will equal the delicious feeling of carelessness and independence with which he lies on his back in the spring sunlight on a pile of dock lumber, and watches the moving life on the river, and munches his crust of bread. It frequently happens that no restraint or punishment can check this Indian-like propensity.

A ROVER REFORMED.

We recall one fine little fellow who was honest, and truthful, and kind-hearted, but who, when the roving passion in the blood came up, left everything and spent his days and nights on the wharves, and rambling about the streets. His mother, a widow, knew only too well what this habit was bringing him to, for, unfortunately, the life of a young barbarian in New York has little poetry in it. The youthful vagrant soon becomes idle and unfit to work; he is hungry, and cannot win his food from the waters and the woods, like his savage prototype; therefore, he must steal. He makes the acquaintance of the petty thieves, pickpockets, and young sharpers of the city. He learns to lie and swear; to pick pockets, rifle street-stands, and break open shop-windows or doors; so that this barbarian habit is the universal stepping-stone to children's crimes. In this case, the worthy woman locked the boy up in her room, and sent down word to us that her son would like a place in the country, if the employer would come up and take him.

We dispatched an excellent gentleman to her from

the interior, who desired a "model boy;" but, when
he arrived, he found, to his dismay, the lad kicking
through the panels of the door, and declaring he
would die sooner than go. The boy then disappeared
for a few days, when his mother discovered him
ragged and half-starved about the docks, and brought
him home and whipped him severely. The next
morning he was off again, and was gone a week,
until the police brought him back in a wretched
condition. The mother now tried the "Christian
Brothers," who had a fence ten feet high about their
premises, and kept the lad, it was said, part of the
time chained. But the fence was mere sport to the
little vagrant, and he was soon off. She then tried the
"Half-Orphan Asylum," but this succeeded no better.
Then the "Juvenile Asylum" was applied to, and the
lad was admitted; but here he spent but a short pro-
bation, and was soon beyond their reach. The mother,
now in desperation, resolved to send him to the Far
West, under the charge of the Children's Aid Society.
Knowing his habits, she led him down by the collar to
the office, sat by him there, and accompanied him to
the railroad depot with the party of children. He
was placed on a farm in Northern Michigan, where,
fortunately, there was considerable game in the neighborhood. To the surprise of us all, he did not at once
run away, being perhaps attracted by the shooting he
could indulge in, when not at work.

At length a chance was offered him of being a trapper, and he began his rovings in good earnest. From the Northern Peninsula of Michigan to the Rocky Mountains, he wandered over the woods and wilds for years, making a very good living by his sales of skins, and saving considerable money. All accounts showed him to be a very honest, decent, industrious lad—a city vagrant about to be a thief transformed into a country vagrant making an honest living.

Our books give hundreds of similar stories, where a free country-life and the amusements and sports of the farmers, when work is slack, have gratified healthfully the vagrant appetite. The mere riding a horse, or owning a calf or a lamb, or trapping an animal in winter, seems to have an astonishing effect in cooling the fire in the blood in the city rover. and making him contented.

The social habits of the army of little street-vagrants who rove through our city have something unaccountable and mysterious in them. We have, as I have described, in various parts of the city little "Stations," as it were, in their weary journey of life, where we ostensibly try to refresh them, but where we really hope to break up their service in the army of vagrancy, and make honest lads of them. These "Lodging-houses" are contrived, after much experience, so ingeniously that they inevitably attract in

the young vagabonds, and drain the quarter where
they are placed of this class. We give the boys, in
point of fact, more for their money than they can get.
anywhere else, and the whole house is made attractive
and comfortable for them. But the reasons of their
coming to a given place seem unaccountable.

Thus there will be a "Lodge" in some out-of-the-
way quarter, with no special attractions, which for
years will drag along with a comparatively small number of lodgers, when suddenly, without any change
being made, there will come a rush of street-rovers to
it, and scores will have to be sent away, and the house
be crowded for months after. Perhaps these denizens
of boxes and hay-barges have their own fashions, like
their elders, and a "Boys' Hotel" becomes popular,
and has a run of custom like the larger houses of
entertainment. The numbers too, at different seasons, vary singularly. Thus, in the coldest nights of
winter, when few boys could venture to sleep out, and
one would suppose there would be a rush to these
warmed and comfortable "Lodges," the attendance in
some houses falls off. And in all, the best months are
the spring and autumn rather than the winter or summer. Sometimes a single night of the week will show
a remarkable increase of lodgers, though for what
reason no one can divine.

The lodgers in the different houses are singularly
different. Those in the parent Lodging-house—the

Newsboys'—seem more of the true *gamin* order.: sharp, ready, light-hearted, quick to understand and quick to act, generous and impulsive, and with an air of being well used "to steer their own canoe" through whatever rapids and whirlpools. These lads seem to include more, also, of that chance medley of little wanderers who drift into the city from the country, and other large towns—boys floating on the current, no one knows whence or whither. They are, as a rule, younger than in the other "Lodges," and many of them are induced to take places on farms, or with mechanics in the country.

One of the mysterious things about this Boys' Hotel is, what becomes of the large numbers that enter it? In the course of the twelve months there passes through its hospitable doors a procession of more than *eight thousand* different youthful rovers of the streets—boys without homes or friends; yet, on any one night, there is not an average of more than two hundred. Each separate boy accordingly averages but nine days in his stay. We can trace during the year the course of, perhaps, a thousand of these young vagrants, for most of whom we provide ourselves. What becomes of the other seven thousand? Many, no doubt, find occupation in the city or country; some in the pleasant seasons take their pleasure and business at the watering-places and other large towns; some return to relatives or friends;

many are arrested and imprisoned, and the rest
of the ragged throng drift away, no one knows
whither.

The up-town Lodging-houses seem often to gather
in a more permanent class of lodgers; they become
frequently genuine boarding-houses for children. The
lads seem to be, too, a more destitute and perhaps
lower class than "the down-town boys." Possibly by
a process of "Natural Selection," only the sharpest
and brightest lads get through the intense "struggle
for existence" which belongs to the most crowded
portions of the city, while the duller are driven to
the up-town wards. We throw out the hypothesis
for some future investigator.

The great amusement of this multitude of street
vagabonds is the cheap theatre. Like most boys,
they have a passion for the drama. But to them the
pictures of kings and queens, the processions of court-
iers and soldiers on the stage, and the wealthy gentlemen aiding and rescuing distressed peasant-girls, are
the only glimpses they ever get of the great world of
history and society above them, and they are naturally
entranced by them. Many a lad will pass a night in
a box, and spend his last sixpence, rather than lose
this show. Unfortunately, these low theatres seem
the rendezvous for all disreputable characters; and
here the "bummers" make the acquaintance of the

higher class whom they so much admire, of "flash-men," thieves, pickpockets, and rogues.

. We have taken the pains at different times to see some of the pieces represented in these places, and have never witnessed anything improper or immoral. On the contrary, the popular plays were always of a heroic and moral cast. "Uncle Tom," when it was played in the Bowery, undoubtedly had a good moral and political effect, in the years before the war, on these ragamuffins.

The salvation of New York, as regards this army of young vagabonds, is, without doubt, its climate. There can be no permanent class of lazzaroni under our winters. The cold compels work. The snow drives "the street-rats," as the police call them, from their holes. Then the homeless boys seek employment and a shelter. And when they are once brought under the series of moral and physical instrumentalities contrived for their benefit, they cease soon to be vagrants, and join the great class of workers and honest producers.

A CORRECTIVE.

One of the best practical methods of correcting vagrancy among city boys would be the adoption, by every large town, of an "ordinance" similar to that passed by the Common Council of Boston.

By this Act, every child who pursues any kind of

street-trade for an occupation—such as news-vending, peddling, blackening of boots, and the like—is obliged to procure a license, which must be renewed every three months. If he is found at any time without this license, he is liable to summary arrest as a vagrant. To procure the license, each child must show a certificate that he has been, or is, attending some school, whether public, or industrial, or parish, during three hours each day.

The great advantage of a law of this nature, is, that it can be executed. Any ordinary legislation against youthful vagrants—such as arresting any child found in the streets during school-hours, or without occupation—is sure to become ineffectual through the humanity and good-nature of officials and judges. Moreover, every young rover of the streets can easily trump up some occupation, which he professes to follow.

Thus, now, as is well known, most of the begging children in New York are apparently engaged in selling "black-headed pins," or some other cheap trifle.

They can almost always pretend some occupation—if it be only sweeping sidewalks—which enables them to elude the law. Nor can we reasonably expect a judge to sentence a child for vagrancy, when it claims to be supporting a destitute parent by earnings in a street-trade, though the occupation may be a semi-vagrant one, and may lead inevitably to idleness and crime. Nor does the action of a truant-officer prevent the necessity of such a law, because this official only acts on the truant class of children, not on those who attend no school whatever. By an ordinance like this of Boston, every child can be forced to at least three hours' schooling each day; and, as any school is permitted, no sectarian or bigoted feeling is aroused by this injunction.

The police would be more ready to arrest, and the judges to sentence, the violators of so simple and rational a law. The wanderers of the street would then be brought under legal supervision, which would not be too harsh or severe. Education may not, in all cases, prevent crime; yet we well know that, on a broad scale, it has a wonderful effect in checking it.

The steady labor, punctuality, and order of a good school, the high tone in many of our Free Schools, the self-respect cultivated, the emulation aroused, the love of industry thus planted, are just the influences to break up a vagabond, roving, and dependent habit of mind and life. The School, with the Lodging-house, is the best preventive institution for vagrancy.

The Massachusetts system of "Truant-schools" —that is, Schools to which truant officers could send children habitually truant—does not seem so applicable to New York. The number of "truants" in the city is not very large; they are in exceedingly remote quarters, and it would be very difficult to collect them in any single School.

Our "Industrial Schools" seem to take their place very efficiently. The present truant-officers of the city are active and judicious, and return many children to the Schools.

COMPULSORY EDUCATION.

The best general law on this subject, both for country and city, would undoubtedly be, a law for compulsory education, allowing "Half-time Schools" to children requiring to be employed a part of the day.

There is no doubt that the time has arrived for the introduction of such laws throughout the country. During the first years of the national existence, and especially in New England and the States peopled from that region, there was so strong an impression among the common people, of the immense importance of a system of free instruction for all, that no laws or regulations were necessary to enforce it. Our ancestors were only too eager to secure mental training for themselves, and opportunities of education for their children. The public property in lands was, in many States, early set aside for purposes of school and college education; and the poorest farmers and laboring people often succeeded in obtaining for their families and descendants the best intellectual training which the country could then bestow.

But all this, in New England and other portions of the country, has greatly changed. Owing to foreign immigration and to unequal distribution of wealth, large numbers of people have grown up without the rudiments even of common-school education. Thus, according to the report of 1871, of the National Commissioners of Education, there are in the New England States 195,963 persons over ten years of age who cannot write, and, therefore, are classed as "illiterates." In New York State the number reaches the astounding height of 241,152, of whom 10,639 are of the colored race. In Pennsylvania the number is 222,356; in Ohio, 173,172, and throughout the Union the population of the illiterates sums up the fearful amount of 5,660,074. In New York State the number of illiterate minors between ten and twenty-one years amounts to 42,405. In this city there are 62,238 persons over ten who cannot write, of whom 53,791 are of foreign birth. Of minors between ten and twenty-one, there are here 8,017 illiterates.

Now, it must be manifest to the dullest mind, that a republic like ours, resting on universal suffrage, is in the utmost danger from such a mass of ignorance at its foundation. That nearly six persons (5.7) in every one hundred in the Northern States should be uneducated, and thirty out of the hundred in the Southern, is certainly an alarming fact. From this dense ignorant multitude of human beings proceed

most of the crimes of the community; these are the
tools of unprincipled politicians; these form "the
dangerous classes" of the city.   So strongly has this
danger been felt, especially from the ignorant masses
of the Southern States, both black and white, that
Congress has organized a National Bureau of Education, and, for the first time in our history, is taking
upon itself, to a limited degree, the care of education
in the States.   The law making appropriations of
public lands for purposes of education, in proportion
to the illiteracy of each State, will undoubtedly at
some period be passed, and then encouragement will
be given by the Federal Government to universal
popular education.   As long as five millions of our
people cannot write, there is no wisdom in arguing
against interference of the General Government in so
vital a matter.

During the past two years all intelligent Americans
have been struck by the excellent discipline and immense well-directed energy shown by the Prussian
nation—plainly the results of the universal and en-
forced education of the people.   The leading Power
of Europe evidently bases its strength on the law of
Compulsory Education.   Very earnest attention has
been given in this country to the subject.   Several
States are approaching the adoption of such a law.
California is reported to favor it, as well as Illinois.
Massachusetts, Rhode Island, and Connecticut have

begun compulsory education by their legislation on factory children, compelling parents to educate their children a certain number of hours each day. Even Great Britain is drawing near it by her late School acts, and must eventually pass such laws. In our own State, where, of all the free States, the greatest illiteracy exists, there has been much backwardness in this matter. But, under the new movements for reform, our citizens must see where the root of all their troubles lies. The demagogues of this city would never have won their amazing power but for those sixty thousand persons who never read or write. It is this class and their associates who made these politicians what they were.

We need, in the interests of public order, of liberty, of property, for the sake of our own safety and the endurance of free institutions here, a strict and careful law, which shall compel every minor to learn to read and write, under severe penalties in case of disobedience.

CHAPTER XXIX.

FACTORY CHILDREN.

IN our educational movements, we early opened Night-schools for the poor children. During the winter of 1870–71, we had some eleven in operation, reaching a most interesting class of children—those working hard from eight to ten hours a day, and then coming with passionate eagerness for schooling in the evening.

The experience gained in these schools still further developed the fact, already known to us, of the great numbers of children of tender years in New York employed in factories, shops, trades, and other regular occupations. A child put at hard work in this way, is, as is well known, stunted in growth or enfeebled in health. He fails also to get what is considered as indispensable in this country for the safety of the State, a common-school education. He grows up weak in body and ignorant or untrained in mind. The parent or relative wants his wages, and insists on his laboring in a factory when he ought to be in an infant-school. The employer is in the habit of getting labor where he can find it, and does not much consider whether he is allowing his little *employés* the time and leisure sufficient for preparing themselves for life. He excuses himself, too, by the plea that the child would be half-starved or thrown on the Poor-house but for this employment.

The universal experience is, that neither the benevolence of the manufacturer nor the conscience of the parent will prevent the steady employment of children of tender years in factory work, provided sufficient wages be offered. Probably, if the employer were approached by a reasonable person, and it was represented what a wrong he was doing to so young a laborer, or the parent were warned of his responsibility to educate a child he had brought into the world, they would both agree to the reasonableness of the position, and attempt to reform their ways. But the necessities of capital on the one side, and the wants of poverty on the other, soon put the children again at the loom, the machine, and the bench, and the result is—masses of little ones, bent and wan with early trial, and growing up mere machines of labor. England has found the evil terrible, and, during the past ten or fifteen years, has been legislating incessantly against it; protecting helpless infancy from the tyranny of capital and the greed of poverty, and securing a fair growth of body and mind for the children of the laboring poor.

There is something extremely touching in these Night-schools, in the eagerness of the needy boys and

girls who have been toiling all day, to pick up a mor-
sel of knowledge or gain a practical mental accom-
plishment. Their occupations are legion. The following are extracts from a recent report of one of our
visitors on this subject. At the Crosby-street School,
he says :—

"There were some hundred children ; their occupations were
as follows: They put up insect-powder drive wagons, tend oys-
ter-saloons ; are tinsmiths, engravers, office-boys, in type-found-
eries, at screws, in blacksmith-shops ; make cigars, polish, work
at packing tobacco, in barber-shops, at paper-stands ; are cash-
boys, light porters, make artificial flowers, work at hair; are
errand-boys, make ink, are in Singer's sewing-machine factory,
and printing-offices; some post bills, some are paint-scrapers,
some peddlers; they pack snuff, attend poultry-stands at market,
in shoe-stores and hat-stores, tend stands, and help painters and
carpenters.

"At the Fifth-ward School (No. 141 Hudson Street), were
fifty boys and girls. One of them, speaking of her occupation,
said : ' I work at feathers, cutting the feathers from cock's tails.
It is a very busy time now. They took in forty new hands to-
day. I get three dollars and fifty cents a week : next week I'll
get more. I go to work at eight o'clock and leave off at six.
The feathers are cut from the stem, then steamed, and curled,
and packed. They are sent then to Paris, but more South and
West.' One boy said he worked at twisting twine; another
drove a ' hoisting-horse,' another blacked boots, etc.

"At the Eleventh-ward School, foot of East Eleventh Street,
there was an interesting class of boys and girls under thirteen
years of age. One boy said he was employed during the day in
making chains of beads, and says that a number of the boys
and girls present are in the same business. Another said he
worked at coloring maps. Another blows an organ for a music-
teacher.

"At the Lord School, No. 207 Greenwich Street, the occupations of the girls were working in hair, stripping tobacco, crochet,

folding paper collars, house-work, tending baby, putting up papers in drug-store, etc., etc."

In making but a brief survey of the employment of children outside of our schools, we discover that there are from one thousand five hundred to two thousand children, under fifteen years of age, employed in a single branch—the manufacture of paper collars— while of those between fifteen and twenty years, the number reaches some eight thousand. In tobacco-factories in New York, Brooklyn, and the neighborhood, our agents found children *only four years of age*— sometimes half a dozen in a single room. Others were eight years of age, and ranged from that age up to fifteen years. Girls and boys of twelve to fourteen years earn from four dollars to five dollars a week. One little girl they saw, tending a machine, so small that she had to stand upon a box eighteen inches high to enable her to reach her work. In one room they found fifty children; some little girls, only eight years of age, earning three dollars per week. In another, there were children of eight and old women of sixty, working together. In the "unbinding cellar" they found fifteen boys under fifteen years. Twine-factories, ink-factories, feather, pocket-book, and artificial-flower manufacture, and hundreds of other occupations, reveal the same state of things.

It will be remembered that when Mr. Mundella, the English member of Parliament, who has accomplished

so much in educational and other reforms in Great
Britain, was here, he stated in a public address that
the evils of children's overwork seemed as great here
as in England. Our investigations confirm this opinion. The evil is already vast in New York, and must
be checked. It can only be restrained by legislation.
What have other States done in the matter?

MASSACHUSETTS LEGISLATION.

The great manufacturing State of New England
has long felt the evil from children's overwork, but
has only in recent years attempted to check it by
strict legislation. In 1866, the Legislature of Massachusetts passed an act restraining "the employment
of children of tender years in manufacturing establishments," which was subsequently repealed and replaced by a more complete and stringent law in 1867
(chapter 285). By this act, no child under ten years
of age is permitted to be employed in any manufacturing or mechanical establishment in the State. And
no child between ten and fifteen years can be so employed, unless he has attended some Day-school for at
least three months of the year preceding, or a "half-
time school" during the six months. Nor shall the
employment continue, if this amount of education is
not secured. The school also must be approved by
the School Committee of the town where the child
resides.

It is further provided, that no child under fifteen shall be so employed more than sixty hours per week. The penalty for the violation of the act is fifty dollars, both to employer and parent. The execution of the law is made the duty of the State Constable.

The report of the Deputy State Comptroller, Gen. Oliver, shows certain defects in the phraseology of the act, and various difficulties in its execution, but no more than might naturally be expected in such legislation. Thus, there is not sufficient power conferred on the executive officer to enter manufacturing establishments, or to secure satisfactory evidence of the law having been violated; and no sufficient certificates or forms of registration of the age and school attendance of factory children are provided for. The act, too, it is claimed, is not sufficiently yielding, and therefore may bear severely in certain cases on the poor.

The reports, however, from this officer, and from the Boston "Bureau of Labor," show how much is already being accomplished in Massachusetts to bring public attention to bear on the subject. Laws often act as favorably by indirect means as by direct. They arouse conscience and awaken consideration, even if they cannot be fully executed. As a class, New England manufacturers are exceedingly intelligent and public-spirited, and when their attention was called to this growing evil by the law, they at once set about efforts to remedy it. Many of them have established "half-time schools," which they require their young *employés* to attend; and they find their own interests advanced by this, as they get a better class of laborers. Others arrange "double gangs" of young workers, so that one-half may take the place of the other in the mill, while the former are in school. Others have founded "Night-schools." There is no question that the law, with all its defects, has already served to lessen the evil.

RHODE ISLAND LEGISLATION.

The Rhode Island act (chapter 139) does not differ materially from that of Massachusetts, except that twelve years is made the minimum age at which a child can be employed in factories; and children, even during the nine months of factory work every year, are not allowed to be employed more than eleven hours per day. The penalty is made but twenty dollars, which can be recovered before any Justice of the Peace, and one-half is to go to the complainant and the other to the District or Public School.

CONNECTICUT LEGISLATION.

In matters of educational reform Connecticut is always the leading State of the Union. On this subject of children's overwork, and consequent want of education, she has legislated since 1842.

The original act, however, was strengthened and, in part, repealed by another law passed in July, 1869 (chapter 115), which is the most stringent act on this subject in the American code. In all the other legislation the law is made to apply solely to manufacturers and mechanics; in this it includes all employment of children, the State rightly concluding that it is as much against the public weal to have a child grow up ignorant and overworked with a farmer as with a manufacturer. The Connecticut act, too, leaves out the word "knowingly," with regard to the employer's action in working the child at too tender years, or beyond the legal time. It throws on the employer the responsibility of ascertaining whether the children employed have attended school the required time, or whether they are too young for his labor. Nor is it enough that the child should have been a member of a school for three months; his name must appear on the register for sixty days of actual attendance.

The age under which three months' school-time is required is fourteen. The penalty for each offense is made one hundred dollars to the Treasurer of the State. Four different classes of officers are instructed and authorized to co-operate with the State in securing every child under fourteen three months of education, and in protecting him from overwork, namely, School-Visitors, the Board of Education, State Attorneys, and Grand Jurors. The State

Board of Education is "authorized to take such action as may be deemed necessary to secure the enforcement of this act, and may appoint an agent for that purpose."

The defects of the law seem to be that it provides for no minimum of age in which a child may be employed in a factory, and does not limit the number of hours of labor per week for children in manufacturing establishments. Neither of these limitations is necessary in regard to farm-labor.

The agent for executing the law in Connecticut, Mr. H. M. Cleaveland, seems to have acted with great wisdom, and to have secured the hearty co-operation of the manufacturers. "Three-fourths of the manufacturers of the State," he says, " of almost everything, from a needle up to a locomotive, were visited, and pledged themselves to a written agreement," that they would employ no children under fourteen years of age, except those with certificates from the local school-officers of actual school attendance for at least three months.

This fact alone reflects the greatest credit on this intelligent class. And we are not surprised that they are quoted as saying, " We do not dare to permit the children within and around our mills to grow up without some education. Better for us to pay the school expenses ourselves than have the children in ignorance."

16

Many of the Connecticut manufacturers have already, at their own expense, provided means of education for the children they are employing; and large numbers have agreed to a division of the children in their employ into alternate gangs—of whom one is in school while the other is in the factory.

The following act was drawn up by Mr. C. E. Whitehead, counsel and trustee of the Children's Aid Society, and presented to the New York Legislature of 1872. It has not yet passed:—

AN ACT FOR THE PROTECTION OF FACTORY CHILDREN.

SECTION 1.—No child under the age of ten years shall be employed for hire in any manufactory or mechanical shop, or at any manufacturing work within this State; and no child under the age of twelve years shall be so employed unless such child can intelligibly read, under a penalty of five dollars for every day during any part of which any such child shall be so employed, to be paid by the employer. Any parent, guardian, or other person authorizing such employment, or making a false return of the age of a child, with a view to such employment, shall be liable to a penalty of twenty dollars.

SEC. 2.—No child under the age of sixteen years shall be employed in any manufactory, or in any mechanical or manufacturing shop, or at any manufacturing work within the State, for more than sixty hours in one week, or after four o'clock on Saturday afternoon, or on New-year's-day, or on Christmas-day, or on the Fourth of July, or on the Twenty-second of February, or on Thanksgiving-day, under a penalty of ten dollars for each offense.

SEC. 3.—No child between the ages of ten and sixteen years shall be employed in any manufactory or workshop, or at any manufacturing work within this State, during more than nine months in any one year, unless during such year he shall have attended school as in this section hereinafter provided, nor shall such child be employed at all unless such child shall have attended a public day-school during three full months of the twelve months next preceding such employment, and shall deliver to its employer a written certificate of such attendance, signed by the teacher; the certificate to be kept by the employer as hereinafter provided, under a penalty of fifty dollars. *Provided* that regular tuition of three hours per day in a private day-school or public night-school, during a term of six months, shall be deemed equivalent to three months' attendance at a public day-school, kept in accordance with the customary hours of tuition. And provided that the child shall have lived within the State during the preceding six months. And provided that where there are more than one child between the ages of twelve and sixteen years in one family, and the commissioners or overseers of the poor shall certify in writing that the labor of such children is essential to the maintenance of the family, such schooling may be substituted during the first year of their employment by having the children attend the public schools during alternate months of such current year, until the full three months' schooling for each child shall have been had, or by having the children attend continuously a private day-school or public night-school three hours a day until the full six months' schooling for each child shall have been had.

SEC. 4.—Every manufacturer, owner of mills, agent, overseer, contractor, or other person, who shall employ operatives under sixteen years of age, or on whose premises such operatives shall be employed, shall cause to be kept on the premises a register, which shall contain, in consecutive columns: (1st), the date when each operative commenced his or her engagement; (2d), the name and surname of the operative; (3d), his or her place of nativity; (4th), his or her residence by street and number; (5th), his or her age; (6th), the name of his or her father, if living; if not, that of the mother, if living; (7th), the number of his or her school certificate, or the reason of its absence; and (8th), the date of his or her leaving the factory. Such register shall be kept open to the inspection of all public authorities, and extracts therefrom shall be furnished on the requisition of the Inspector, the School Commissioners, or other public authority. Any violation of this section shall subject the offender to a penalty of one hundred dollars.

SEC. 5.—Every such employer mentioned in the last section shall keep a register, in which shall be entered the certificates of schooling produced by children in his employ ; such certificate shall be signed by the teacher, and shall be dated, and shall certify the dates between which such scholar has attended school, and shall mention any absences made therefrom during such term, and such certificates shall be numbered in consecutive order, and such register shall also be kept open to inspection of all public authorities, as provided in the last section ; and all violations of this section shall subject the offender to a penalty of one hundred dollars.

SEC. 6.—Any teacher or other person giving a false certificate, for the purpose of being used under the provisions of this act, shall be liable to a penalty of one hundred dollars, and be deemed guilty of misdemeanor.

SEC. 7.—The parent or guardian of every child released from work under the provisions of this act shall cause the said child to attend school when so released, for three months, in accordance with the provisions of section three of this act, under a penalty of five dollars for each week of non-attendance.

SEC. 8.—All public officers and persons charged with the enforcement of this law can, at all working-hours, enter upon any factory premises, and any person refusing them admittance or hindering them shall be liable to a penalty of one hundred dollars.

SEC. 9.—Every room in any factory in which operatives are employed shall be thoroughly painted or whitewashed or cleaned at least once a year, and shall be kept as well ventilated, lighted, and cleaned as the character of the business will permit, under a penalty of ten dollars for each week of neglect.

SEC. 10.—All trap-doors or elevators, and all shafting, belting, wheels, and machinery running by steam, water, or other motive power, in rooms or places in a factory in which operatives are employed, or through which they have to pass, shall be protected by iron screens, or by suitable partitions during all the time when such doors are open, and while such machinery is in motion, under a penalty of fifty dollars, to be paid by the owner of such machinery, or the employer of such operatives, for each day during which the same shall be so unprotected.

SEC. 11.—This act shall be printed and kept hung in a conspicuous place in every factory, by the owner, agent, overseer, or person occupying such factory, under a penalty of ten dollars for each day's neglect.

SEC. 12.—All suits for penalties under this act shall be brought within ninety days after commission of the offense, and may be brought by the Inspector of Factory Children, by the District-Attorney of the county, by the School Commissioners, by the Trustees of Public Schools, or the Commissioners of Charities, before any Justice of the Peace, or in any Justice's Court, or any Court of Record; and one-half of all penalties recovered shall be paid to the school fund of the county, and one-half to the informer.

SEC. 13.—The Governor of this State shall hereafter appoint a State officer, to be known as the Inspector of Factory Children, to hold office for four years, unless sooner removed for neglect of duty, who shall receive a salary of two thousand dollars a year and traveling expenses, not exceeding one thousand dollars, whose duty it shall be to examine the different factories in this State, and to aid in the enforcement of this law, and to report annually to the Legislature the number, the ages, character of occupation, and educational privileges of children engaged in manufacturing labor in the different counties of the State, with suggestions as to the improvement of their condition.

CHAPTER XXX.

THE ORGANIZATION OF CHARITIES.

THE power of every charity and effort at moral reform is in the spirit of the man directing or founding it. If he enter it mechanically, as he would take a trade or profession, simply because it falls in his way, or because of its salary or position, he cannot possibly succeed in it. There are some things which the laws of trade do not touch. There are services of love which seek no pecuniary reward, and whose virtue, when first entered upon, is that the soul is poured out in them without reference to money-return.

In the initiation of all great and good causes there is a time of pure enthusiasm, when life and thought and labor are given freely, and hardly a care enters the mind as to the prizes of honor or wealth which are struggled for so keenly in the world. No reformer or friend of humanity, worthy of the name, has not some time in his life felt this high enthusiasm. If it has been his duty to struggle with such an evil as Slavery, the wrongs of the slave have been burned into his soul until he has felt them more even than if they were his own, and no reward of riches or fame that life could offer him would be half so sweet as the consciousness that he had broken these fetters of injustice.

If he has been inspired by Christ with a love of humanity, there have been times when the evils that afflict it clouded his daily happiness; when the thought of the tears shed that no one could wipe away; of the nameless wrongs suffered; of the ignorance which imbruted the young, and the sins that stained the conscience; of the loneliness, privation, and pain of vast masses of human beings; of the necessary degradation of great multitudes;—when the picture of all these, and other wounds and woes of mankind, rose like a dark cloud between him and the light, and even the face of GOD was obscured.

At such times it has seemed sweeter to bring smiles back to sad faces, and to raise up the neglected and forgotten, than to win the highest prize of earth; and the thought of HIM who hath ennobled man, and whose life was especially given for the poor and outcast, made all labors and sacrifices seem as nothing compared with the joy of following in His footsteps.

At such rare moments the ordinary prizes of life are forgotten or not valued. The man is inspired with "the enthusiasm of humanity." He maps out a city with his plans and aspirations for the removal of the various evils which he sees. His life flows out for those who can never reward him, and who hardly know of his labors.

But, in process of time, the first fervor of this ardent enthusiasm must cool away. The worker himself is forced to think of his own interests and those of his family. His plan, whatever it may be,—for removing the evils which have pained him, demands practical means,—men, money, and "machinery." Hence arises the great subject of "*Organization.*" The strong under-running current which carries his enterprise along is still the old faith or enthusiasm; but the question of means demands new thought and the exercise of different faculties.

There are many radical difficulties, in organizing practical charities, which are exceedingly hard to overcome.

Charities, to be permanent and efficient, must be organized with as much exactness and order as business associations, and carry with them something of the same energy and motives of action. But the tendency, as is well known from European experience, of all old charities, is to sluggishness, want of enterprise, and careless business arrangement, as well as to mechanical routine in the treatment of their subjects. The reason of this is to be found in the somewhat exceptional abnormal position—economically considered—of the worker in fields of benevolence. All laborers in the intellectual and moral field are exposed to the dangers of routine. But in education, for instance, and the offices of the Church, there is a constant and healthy competition going on, and certain prizes are held out to the successful worker, which tend continually to arouse his faculties, and lead him to invent new methods of attaining his ends. The relative want of this among the Catholic clergy may be the cause of their lack of intellectual activity, as compared with the Protestant.

In the management of charities there is a prevailing impression that what may be called "interested motives" should be entirely excluded. The worker, having entered the work under the enthusiasm of humanity, should continue buoyed up by that enthusiasm. His salary may be seldom changed. It will be ordinarily beneath that which is earned by corresponding ability outside. No rewards of rank or fame are held out to him. He is expected to find his pay in his labor.

Now there are certain individuals so filled with compassion for human sufferings, or so inspired by Religion, or who so much value the offering of respect returned by mankind for their sacrifices, that they do not need the impulse of ordinary motives to make their work as energetic and inventive and faithful as any labor under the motives of competition and gain.

But the great majority of the instruments and agents of a charity are not of this kind. They must

have something of the common inducements of mankind held out before them. If these be withdrawn,
they become gradually sluggish, uninventive, inexact,
and lacking in the necessary enterprise and ardor.

The agents of the old endowed charities of England
are said often to become as lazy and mechanical as
monks in monasteries.

To remedy such evils, the trustees of all charities
should hold out a regular scale of salaries, which different agents could attain to if they were successful.
The principle, too, which should govern the amounts
paid to each agent, should be well considered. Of
course, the governing law for all salaries are the
demand and supply for such services. But an agent
for a charity, even as a missionary, sometimes puts
himself voluntarily outside of such a law. He throws
himself into a great moral and religious cause, and
consumes his best powers in it, and unfits himself (it
may be) for other employments. His own field may
be too narrow to occasion much demand for his
peculiar experience and talent from other sources.
There comes then a certain moral obligation on the
managers of the charity, not to take him at the cheapest rate for which they can secure his services, but to
proportion his payment somewhat to what he would
have been worth in other fields, and thus to hold out
to him some of the inducements of ordinary life. The
salary should be large enough to allow the agent and

his family to live somewhat as those of corresponding ability and education do, and still to save something for old age or a time of need. Some benevolent associations have obtained this by a very wise arrangement—that of an "annuity insurance" of the life of their agents, which secured them a certain income at a given age.

With the consciousness thus of an appreciation of their labors, and a payment somewhat in proportion to their value, and a permanent connection with their humane enterprise, the ordinary *employés* and officials come to have somewhat of the interest in it which men take in selfish pursuits, and will exercise the inventiveness, economy, and energy that are shown in business enterprises.

Every one knows how almost impossible it is for a charity to conduct, for instance, a branch of manufacture with profit. The explanation is that the lower motives are not applied to it. Selfishness is more alert and economical than benevolence.

On the other side, however, it will not be best to let a charity become too much of a business. There must always be a certain generosity and compassion, a degree of freedom in management, which are not allowed in business undertakings. The agents must have heart as well as head. The moisture of compassion must not be dried up by too much discipline.

Organization must not swallow up the soul. Routine may be carried so far as to make the aiding of misery the mere dry working of a machine.

The thought must ever be kept in mind that each human being, however low, who is assisted, is a "power of endless life," with capacities and possibilities which cannot be measured or limited. And that one whose nature CHRIST has shared and for whom He lived and died, cannot be despised or treated as an animal or a machine.

If the directors of a benevolent institution or enterprise can arouse these great motives in their agents,—spiritual enthusiasm with a reasonable gratification of the love of honor and a hope of fair compensation,—they will undoubtedly create a body of workers capable of producing a profound impression on the evils they seek to remove.

It is always a misfortune for an agent of a charity if he be too constantly with the objects of his benevolent labors. He either becomes too much accustomed to their misfortunes, and falls into a spirit of routine with them; or, if of tender sympathies, the spring of his mind is bent by such a constant burden of misery, and he loses the best qualities for his work —elasticity and hope. Every efficient worker in the field of benevolence should have time and place for solitude, and for other pursuits or amusements.

A board of trustees for an important charity should represent, so far as is practicable, the different classes and professions of society. There is danger in a board being too wealthy or distinguished, as well as too humble. First of all, men are needed who have a deep moral interest in the work, and who will take a practical part in it. Then they must be men of such high character and integrity that the community will feel no anxiety at committing to them "trust funds." As few "figure-heads" should be taken in as possible—that is, persons of eminent names, for the mere purpose of making an impression on the public. Men of wealth are needed for a thousand emergencies; men of moderate means, also, who can appreciate practical difficulties peculiar to this class; men of brains, to guide and suggest, and of action, to impel. There should be lawyers in such a board, for many cases of legal difficulty which arise; and, if possible, physicians, as charities have so much to do with sanitary questions. Two classes only had better not be admitted: men of very large wealth, as they seldom contribute more than persons of moderate property, and discourage others by their presence in the board; and clergymen with parishes, the objection to the latter being that they have no time for such labors, and give a sectarian air to the charity.

It is exceedingly desirable that the trustees or managers of our benevolent institutions should take a more active and personal part in their management. The peculiar experience which a successful business career gives—the power both of handling details and managing large interests; the capacity of organization; the energy and the careful judgment and knowledge of men which such a life develops,—are the qualities most needed in managing moral and benevolent "causes."

A trustee of a charity will often see considerations which the workers in it do not behold, and will be able frequently to judge of its operations from a more comprehensive point of view. The great duty of trustees, of course, should be to rigidly inspect all accounts and to be responsible for the pecuniary integrity of the enterprise. The carrying-out of the especial plan of the association and all the details should be left with one executive officer. If there is too great interference in details by the board of management, much confusion ensues, and often personal jealousies and bickerings. Many of our boards of charities have almost been broken up by internal petty cabals and quarrels. The agents of benevolent institutions, especially if not mingling much with the world, are liable to small jealousies and rivalries.

The executive officer must throw the energy of a

business into his labor of benevolence. He must be allowed a large control over subordinates, and all the machinery of the organization should pass through his hands. He must especially represent the work, both to the board and to the world. If his hands be tied too much, he will soon become a mere routine-agent, and any one of original power would leave the position. Again, in his dealings with the heads of the various departments or branches of the work, he must seek to make each agent feel responsible, and to a degree independent, so that his labor may become a life-work, and his reputation and hope of means may depend on his energy and success. If on all proper occasions he seeks to do full justice to his subordinates, giving them their due credit and promoting their interests, and strives to impart to them his own enthusiasm, he will avoid all jealousies and will find that the charity is as faithfully served as any business house.

The success in "organization" is mainly due to success in selecting your men. Some persons have a faculty for this office; others always fail in it.

Then, having the proper agents, great consideration is due towards them. Some employers treat their subordinates as if they had hardly a human feeling. Respect and courtesy always make those who serve you more efficient. Too much stress, too, can hardly be laid on frank and unsuspicious dealing with em-

ployés.   Suspicion renders its objects more ignoble. A man who manages many agents must show much confidence; yet, of course, be strict and rigid in calling them to account.   It will be better for him also not to be too familiar with them.

CHAPTER XXXI.

STATE AID FOR CHARITIES.

AN important question often comes up in regard
to our charitable associations: "How shall they best
be supported?"—by endowment from the State or by
private and annual assistance? There is clearly a
right that all charities of a general nature should
expect some help from the public Legislature. The
State is the source of the charters of all corporations.
One of the main duties of a Legislature is to care for
the interests of the poor and criminal. The English
system, dating as far back as Henry VIII., has been to
leave the charge of the poor and all educational institutions, as much as possible, to counties or local bodies
or individuals. It has been, so far as the charge of
the poor is concerned, imitated here. But in neither
country has it worked well; and the last relic of it
will probably soon be removed in this State, by placing
the defective persons—the blind and dumb, and
insane and idiot, and the orphans—in the several
counties in State institutions. The charge of criminals and reformatory institutions are also largely
placed under State control and supervision.

The object of a State Legislature in all these matters is *bonum publicum*—the public weal. If they think that a private charity is accomplishing a public work of great value, which is not and perhaps cannot be accomplished by purely public institutions, they apparently have the same right to tax the whole community, or a local community, for its benefit, that they have now to tax it for the support of schools, or Almshouses, or Prisons, or Houses of Refuge. In such a case it need not be a matter of question with the Legislature whether the charity is " sectarian " or not; whether it teaches Roman Catholicism, or Protestantism, or the Jewish faith, or no faith. The only question with the governing power is, " Does it do a work of public value not done by public institutions ?" If it does; if, for instance, it is a Roman-Catholic Reformatory, or a Protestant House of Refuge, or Children's Aid Society, the Legislature, knowing that all public and private organizations together cannot fully remedy the tremendous evils arising from a class of neglected and homeless children, is perfectly right in granting aid to such institutions without reference to their " sectarian " character. It reserves to itself the right of inspection, secured in this State by our admirable Board of Inspectors of State Charities; and it can at any time repeal the charters of, or refuse the appropriations to, these private associations. But thus far its uniform practice has

been to aid, to a limited degree, private charities of
this nature.

This should by no means be considered a ground
for demanding similar assistance for "sectarian
schools." Education is secured now by public taxation for all; and all can take advantage of it. There
is no popular necessity for Church Schools, and the
public good is not promoted by them as it is by secular
schools. Where there are children too poor to attend
the Public Schools, these can be aided by private
charitable associations; and of these, only those
should be assisted by the State which have no sectarian character.

Charities which are entirely supported by State
and permanent endowment are liable, as the experience of England shows, to run into a condition of
routine and lifelessness. The old endowments of
Great Britain are nests of abuses, and many of them
are now being swept away. A State charity has the
advantage of greater solidity and more thorough and
expensive machinery, and often more careful organization. But, as compared with our private charities,
the public institutions of beneficence are dull and life-
less. They have not the individual enthusiasm working through them, with its ardor and power. They
are more like machines.

On the other hand, charities supported entirely by
individuals will always have but a small scope. The

amount of what may be called the "charity fund" of the community is comparatively limited. In years of disaster or war, or where other interests absorb the public, it will dwindle down to a very small sum. It is distributed, too, somewhat capriciously. Sometimes a "sensation" calls it forth bountifully, while more real demands are neglected. An important benevolent association, depending solely on its voluntary contributions from individuals, will always be weak and incomplete in its machinery. The best course for the permanency and efficiency of a charity seems to be, to make it depend in part on the State, that it may have a solid foundation of support, and be under official supervision, and in part on private aid, so that it may feel the enthusiasm and activity and responsibility of individual effort. The "Houses of Refuge" combine public and private assistance in a manner which has proved very beneficial. Their means come from the State, while their governing bodies are private, and independent of politics. The New York "Juvenile Asylum" enjoys both public and private contributions, but has a private board. On the other hand, the "Commissioners of Charities and Correction" are supported entirely by taxation, and, until they had the services of a Board carefully selected, were peculiarly inefficient. Many private benevolent associations in the city could be mentioned which have no solid foundation of public support and are under no public supervision, and, in consequence, are weak and slipshod in all their enterprises. The true policy of the Legislature is to encourage and supplement private activity in charities by moderate public aid, and to organize a strict supervision.

The great danger for all charities is in machinery or "plant" taking more importance in the eyes of its organizers than the work itself.

The condition of the buildings, the neat and orderly appearance of the objects of the charity, and the perfection of the means of house-keeping, become the great objects of the officials or managers, and are what most strike the eyes of the public. But all these are in reality nothing compared with the improvement in character and mind of the persons aided, and this is generally best effected by simple rooms, simple machinery, and constantly getting rid of the subjects of the charity. If they are children, the natural family is a thousand times better charity than all our machinery.

The more an Institution or Asylum can show of those drilled and machine-like children, the less real work is it doing.

Following "natural laws" makes sad work of a charity-show in an Asylum; but it leaves fruit over the land, in renovated characters and useful lives.

THE MULTIPLICATION OF CHARITIES.

One of the greatest evils connected with charities in a large city is the unreasonable tendency to multiply them. A benevolent individual meets with a peculiar case of distress or poverty, his feelings are touched, and he at once conceives the idea of an "Institution" for this class of human evils. He soon finds others whom he can interest in his philanthropic object, and they go blindly on collecting their funds, and perhaps erecting or purchasing their buildings. When the house is finally prepared, the organization perfected, and the cases of distress relieved, the founders discover, perhaps to their dismay, that there are similar or corresponding Institutions for just this class of unfortunates, which have been carrying on their quiet labors of benevolence for years, and doing much good. The new Institution, if wise, would now prefer to turn over its assets and machinery to the old; but, ten to one, the new workers have an especial pride in their bantling, and cannot bear to abandon it, or they see what they consider defects in the management of the old, and, not knowing all the difficulties of the work, they hope to do better; or their employé's have a personal interest in keeping up the new organization, and persuade them that it is needed by the people.

The result, in nineteen cases out of twenty, is that

the two agencies of charity are continued where but one is needed. Double the amount of money is used for agents and machinery which is wanted, and, to a certain degree, the charity funds of the community are wasted.

But this is not the worst effect. The poor objects of this organization soon discover that they have a double source from which to draw their supplies. They become pauperized, and their faculties are employed in deriving a support from both societies.

By and by, one organization falls behind in its charity labors, and now, in place of waiting to carefully assist the poor, it tempts the poor to come to it. If it be a peculiar kind of school, not much needed in the quarter, it bribes the poor children by presents to abandon the rival school and fill its own seats; if an Asylum, it seeks far and near for those even not legitimately its subjects. There arises a sort of competition of charity. This kind of rivalry is exceedingly bad both for the poor and the public. There are evils enough in the community which all our machinery and wealth cannot cure, and thus to increase or stimulate misfortunes in order to relieve, is the height of absurdity. One effect often is, that the public become disgusted with all organized charity, and at last fancy that societies of benefaction do as much evil as good.

This city is full of multiplied charities, which are

constantly encroaching on each other's field; and yet there are masses of evil and calamity here which they scarcely touch. The number of poor people who enjoy a comfortable living, derived from a long study and experience of these various agencies of benevolence, would be incredible to any one not familiar with the facts. They pass from one to the other; knowing exactly their conditions of assistance and meeting their requirements, and live thus by a sort of science of alms. The industry and ingenuity they employ in this pauper trade are truly remarkable. Probably not one citizen in a thousand could so well recite the long list of charitable societies and agencies in New York, as one of these busy dependents on charity. Nor do these industrious paupers confine themselves to secular and general societies. They have their churches and missions, on whose skirts they hang; and beyond them a large and influential circle of lady patronesses who support and protect them. We venture to say there are very few ladies of position in New York who do not have a numerous *clientèle* of needy women or unfortunate men that depend on them year after year, and always follow them up and discover their residence, however much they may change it. These people have almost lost their energy of character, and all power of industry (except in pursuing the different charities and patronesses), through this long and indiscriminate assistance. They are paupers, not in Poor-houses, and dependents on alms, living at home. They are often worse off than if they had never been helped.

This trade of alms and dependence on charities ought to be checked. It demoralizes the poor, and weakens public confidence in wise and good charities. It tends to keep the rich from all benefactions, and makes many doubt whether charity ever really benefits.

There are various modes in which this evil might be remedied. In the first place, no individual should subscribe to a new charity until he has satisfied his mind in some way that it is needed, and that he is not helping to do twice the same good thing.

There ought to be also in such a city as ours a sort of "Board" or "Bureau of Charities," where a person could get information about all now existing, whether Catholic, Protestant, Jewish, or secular, and where the agents of these could ascertain if they were helping the same objects twice.

Lists of names and addresses of those assisted could be kept here for examination, and frequent comparisons could be made by the agents of these societies or by individuals interested. One society, formed for a distinct object, and finding a case needing quite a distinct mode of relief or assistance, could here at once ascertain where to transfer the case, or what the conditions of help were in another associa-

17

tion.   Here, individuals having difficult, perplexing,
or doubtful cases of charity on hand would ascertain
what they should do with them, and whether they
were merely supporting a person now dependent on
an association from such an office.   Cases of poverty
and misfortune might be visited and examined by
experts in charity, and the truth ascertained, where
ordinary individuals, inquiring, would be certain to
be deceived.   Here, too, the honest and deserving
poor could learn where they should apply for relief.

Such a "Bureau" would be of immense benefit to
the city.   It would aid in keeping the poor from
pauperism; it would put honest poverty in the way
of proper assistance; simplify and direct charities,
and enable the "charity fund" of the city to be used
directly for the evils needing treatment.

Both the public and benevolent associations would
be benefited by it, and much useless expenditure and
labor saved.   Under it, each charitable association
could labor in its own field, and encroach on no
other, and the public confidence in the wise use of
charity funds be strengthened.

In such a city as ours it would probably be hardly
possible to follow the Boston plan, and put all the
offices of the great charities in one building, yet there
could easily be one office of information, or a "Bureau
of Charities," which might be sustained by general
contributions.   Perhaps the State "Board of Chari-

ties" would father and direct it, if private means supported it.

In one respect, it would be of immense advantage to have this task undertaken by the State Board, as they have the right to inspect charitable institutions, and their duty is to expose "bogus charities." Of the latter there are only too many in this city. Numerous lazy individuals make lucrative livelihoods by gathering funds for charities which only exist on paper. These swindlers could be best exposed and prosecuted by a "State Board."

CHAPTER XXXII.

HOW BEST TO GIVE ALMS?

"TAKE, NOT GIVE."

WE were much struck by a reply, recently, of a City Missionary in East London, who was asked what he gave to the poor.

"Give!" he said, "we never give now; we take!" He explained that the remedy of alms, for the terrible evils of that portion of London, had been tried *ad nauseam*, and that they were all convinced of its little permanent good, and their great object was, at present, to induce the poor to save; and for this, they were constantly urgent to get money from these people, when they had a little. They "took, not gave!"

So convinced is the writer, by twenty years' experience among the poor, that alms are mainly a bane, that the mere distribution of gifts by the great charity in which he is engaged seldom affords him much gratification. The long list of benefactions which the Reports record, would be exceedingly unsatisfactory, if they were not parts and branches of a great preventive and educational movement.

The majority of people are most moved by hearing

that so many thousand pairs of shoes, so many articles of clothing, or so many loaves of bread are
given to the needy and suffering by some benevolent
agency.

The experienced friend of the poor will only grieve
at such alms, unless they are accompanied with some
influences to lead the recipients to take care of themselves. The worst evil in the world is not poverty
or hunger, but the want of manhood or character
which alms-giving directly occasions.

The English have tried alms until the kingdom
seems a vast Poor-house, and the problem of Pauperism has assumed a gigantic and almost insoluble
form. The nation have given everything but Education, and the result is a vast multitude of wretched
persons in whom pauperism is planted like a disease
of the blood—who cannot be anything but dependents
and idlers.

In London alone, twenty-five million dollars per
annum are expended in organized charities; yet, till
the year 1871, no general system of popular education had been formed.

This country has been more fortunate and wiser.
We had room and work enough, we provided education before alms, and, especially among our native-
born population, have checked pauperism, as it never
was checked before in any civilized community.

No one can imagine, who has not been familiar

with the lowest classes, how entirely degraded a character may become, where there is an uncertain dependence on public and organized alms. The faculties of the individual are mainly bent on securing support by other means than industry. Cunning, deception, flattery, and waiting for chances, become the means of livelihood. Self-respect is lost, and with it go the best qualities of the soul. True manhood and true womanhood are eaten away. The habit of labor, and the hope and courage of a self-supporting human being, and the prudence which guards against future evils, are almost destroyed. The man becomes a dawdler and waiter on chances, and is addicted to the lowest vices; his children grow up worse than he, and make sharpness or crime a substitute for beggary. The woman is sometimes stripped of the best feelings of her sex by this dependence. Not once or twice only have we known such a woman steal the clothes from her half-starved babe, as she was delivering it over to strangers to care for. There are able-bodied men of this kind in New York who, every winter, as regularly as the snow falls, commit some petty offense, that they may be supported at public expense.

When this disease of pauperism is fairly mingled in the blood of children, their condition is almost hopeless. They will not work, or go to school, or try to learn anything useful; their faculties are all bent to the tricks of a roving, begging life; the self-respect of their sex, if girls, is lost in childhood; they are slatternly, lazy, and dissolute. If they grow up and marry, they marry men of their own kind, and breed paupers and prostitutes.

We know of an instance like this in an Alms-house in Western New York. A mother, in decent circumstances, with an infant, was driven into it by stress of poverty. Her child grew up a pauper, and both became accustomed to a life of dependence. The child—a girl—went forth when she was old enough to work, and soon returned with an illegitimate babe. She then remained with her child. This child—also a girl—grew up in like manner, and, occasionally, when old enough, also went forth to labor, but returned finally, with *her* illegitimate child, and at length became a common pauper and prostitute, so that, when the State Commissioner of Charity, Dr. Hoyt, visited, in his official tour, this Poor-house, he found *four generations* of paupers and prostitutes in one family, in this place!

The regular *habitués* of Alms-houses are bad enough; but it has sometimes seemed to me that the outside dependents on an irregular public charity are worse. They are usually better off than the inmates of Poor-houses, and, therefore, must deceive more to secure aid; the process of obtaining it continually degrades them, and they are tempted to leave regular industry for this unworthy means of support.

"Outdoor relief" is responsible for much of the abuses of the English pauper administration.

We are convinced that it ought to be, if not abandoned, at least much circumscribed by our own Commissioners of Charities.

Still, private alms, though more indiscriminately bestowed, and often on entirely unworthy objects, do not, in our judgment, leave the same evil effect as public. There is less degradation with the former, and more of human sympathy, on both sides. The influence of the giver's character may sometimes elevate the debased nature of an unworthy dependent on charity. The personal connection of a poor creature and a fine lady, is not so bad as that of a pauper to the State.

Still, private alms in our large cities are abused to an almost unlimited extent. Persons who have but little that they can afford to give, discover, after long experience, that the majority of their benefactions have been indiscreetly bestowed.

When one thinks of the thousands of cases in a city like New York, of unmitigated misfortune; of widows with large families, suddenly left sick and helpless on the world; of lonely and despairing women struggling against a sea of evils; of strong men disabled by accident or sickness; of young children abandoned or drifting uncared-for on the streets, and how many of these are never wisely assisted, it seems a real calamity that any person should bestow charity carelessly or on unworthy objects.

The individual himself ought to seek out the subjects whom he desires to relieve, and ascertain their character and habits, and help in such a way as not to impair their self-respect or weaken their independence.

The managers of the Charity I have been describing have especially sought to avoid the evils of alms-giving. While many thousands of dollars' worth is given each year in various forms of benefaction, not a penny is bestowed which does not bear in its influence on character. We do not desire so much to give alms as to prevent the demand for alms. In every branch of our work we seek to destroy the growth of pauperism.

Nothing in appearance is so touching to the feelings of the humane as a ragged and homeless boy. The first impulse is to clothe and shelter him free of cost. But experience soon shows that if you put a comfortable coat on the first idle and ragged lad who applies, you will have fifty half-clad lads, many of whom possess hidden away a comfortable outfit, leaving their business next day, "to get jackets for nothing."

You soon discover, too, that the houseless boy is not so utterly helpless as he looks. He has a thousand means of supporting himself honestly in the streets, if he will. Perhaps all that he needs is a small loan to start his street-trade with, or a shelter for a few nights, for which he can give his "promise to pay," or some counsel and instruction, or a few weeks' schooling.

Our Lodging-house-keepers soon learn that the best humanity towards the boys is "to take, not give." Each lad pays for his lodging, and then feels independent; if he is too poor to do this, he is taken in "on trust," and pays his bill when business is successful. He is not clothed at once, unless under some peculiar and unfortunate circumstances, but is induced to save some pennies every day until he have enough to buy his own clothing. If he has not enough to start a street-trade with, the superintendent loans him a small sum to begin business.

The following is the experience in this matter of Mr. O'Connor, the superintendent of the News-boys' Lodging-house :—

"The Howland Fund, noticed in previous reports as having been established by B. J. Howland, Esq., one of our Trustees, continues to be the means of doing good. We have loaned from it during the nine months one hundred and twenty-three dollars and sixty cents, on which the borrowers have realized three hundred and seven dollars and thirty-nine cents. They have thus made the handsome profit of two hundred and fifty per cent. on the amount borrowed. It has in many cases been returned in a few hours. We have loaned it in sums of five cents and upward; we have had but few defaulters. Of the seventeen dollars and fifty-five cents due last year, six dollars and fifty cents has been returned, leaving at this time standing out eleven dollars and five cents."

When large supplies of shoes and clothing are given, it is usually at Christmas, as an expression of the good-will of the season, or from some particular friend of the boys as an indication of his regard, and thus carries less of the ill effects of alms with the gift.

The very air of these Lodging-houses is that of independence, and no paupers ever graduate from them. We even discourage the street-trades as a permanent business, and have, therefore, never formed a "Boot-black Brigade," as has been done in London, on the ground that such occupations are uncertain and vagrant in habit, and lead to no settled business.

Our end and aim with every street-rover, is to get him to a farm, and put him on the land. For this reason we lavish our gifts on the lads who choose the country for their work. We feed and shelter them gratuitously, if necessary. We clothe them from top to toe; and the gifts bring no harm with them. These poor lads have sometimes repaid these gifts tenfold in later life, in money to the Society. And the community have been repaid a hundredfold, by the change of a city vagabond to an honest and industrious farmer.

Our Industrial Schools might almost be called

"Reformatories of Pauperism." Nine-tenths of the children are beggars when they enter, but they go forth self-respecting and self-supporting young girls.

Food, indeed, is given every day to those most in need; but, being connected thus with a School, it produces none of the ill effects of alms. The subject of clothes-giving to these children is, however, a very difficult one. The best plan is found to be to give the garments as rewards for good conduct, punctuality, and industry, the amount being graded by careful "marks"; yet the humane teacher will frequently discover an unfortunate child without shoes in the winter snow, or scantily clad, who has not yet attained the proper number of marks, and she will very privately perhaps relieve the want: knowing, as the teacher does, every poor family whose children attend the School, she is not often deceived, and her gifts are worthily bestowed.

The daily influence of the School-training in industry and intelligence discourages the habit of begging. The child soon becomes ashamed of it, and when she finally leaves school, she has a pride in supporting herself.

Gifts of garments, shoes, and the like, to induce children to attend, are not found wise; though now and then a family will be discovered so absolutely naked and destitute, that some proper clothing is a necessary condition to their even entering the School.

Some of the teachers very wisely induce the parents to deposit their little savings with them, and perhaps pay them interest to encourage saving. Others, by the aid of friends, have bought coal at wholesale prices, and retailed it without profit, to the parents of the children.

The principle throughout all the operations of the Children's Aid Society, is only to give assistance where it bears directly on character, to discourage pauperism, to cherish independence, to place the poorest of the city, the homeless children, as we have so often said, not in Alms-houses or Asylums, but on farms, where they support themselves and add to the wealth of the nation; to "take, rather than give;" or to give education and work rather than alms; to place all their thousands of little subjects under such influences and such training that they will never need either private or public charity.

CHAPTER XXXIII.

HOW SHALL CRIMINAL CHILDREN BE TREATED?

REFORMATORIES.

A CHILD, whether good or bad, is, above all things, an individual requiring individual treatment and care. Let any of our readers, having a little fellow given to mischief, who had at length broken his neighbor's windows, or with a propensity to stealing, or with a quick temper which continually brings him into unpleasant scrapes, imagine him suddenly put into an "Institution" for reform, henceforth designated as "D" of "Class 43," or as "No. 193," roused up to prayers in the morning with eight hundred others, put to bed at the stroke of the bell, knowing nothing of his teacher or pastor, except as one of a class of a hundred, his own little wants, weaknesses, foibles and temptations utterly unfamiliar to any one, his only friends certain lads who had been in the place longer, and, perhaps, had known much more of criminal life than he himself, treated thus altogether as a little machine, or as one of a regiment.

What could he expect in the way of reform in such a case? He might, indeed. hope that the lad would feel the penalty and disgrace of being thus imprisoned, and that the strict discipline would control careless habits, but he would soon see that the chance of a reform of character was extremely slight.

There was evidently no personal influence on the child. Whatever bad habits or traits he had, were likely to be uneradicated. The strongest agencies upon him were those of his companions; and what boys, even of the moral classes, teach one another when they are together in masses, need not be told. Were he to be there a length of time, the most power-ful forces that mould and form boys in the world outside, would be absent.

The affection of family, the confidence of respected friends, the hope of making a name, and the desire of money and position—these impulses must be banished from the Asylum or Reformatory. The lad's only hope is to escape certain penalties, or win certain marks, and get out of the place. Now and then, indeed, a chaplain of rare spiritual gifts may suc-ceed in wielding a personal influence, in such an Institution, over individual children; but this must, of necessity, be unfrequent, on account of the great numbers under his charge.

If the subject of a Reformatory be a poor boy or girl, the kind of work usually chosen is not the one best suited to a child of this class, or which he will be apt to take up afterwards. It is generally some plain and easy trade-work, like shoe-pegging, or chair-bottoming, or pocket-book manufacture. The lad is kept for years at this drudgery, and when he leaves the place, has no capital laid up of a skilled trade. He finds such employments crowded, and he seldom enters them again. Moreover, if he has been a vagrant (as in nine cases out of ten is probable), or a a little sharper and thief of the city, or a boy unwilling to labor, and unfitted for steady industry, these years at a table in a factory do not necessarily give him a taste for work; they often only disgust him.

Were such lads, on the other hand, put in gardens, or at farm-work, they would find much more pleasure in it. The watching the growth of plants, the occasional chance for fruit-gathering, the " spurts " of work peculiar to farming, the open air and sunshine, and dealing with flowers and grains, with cattle, horses, and fowls, are all attractive to children, and especially to children of this class. Moreover, when they have learned the business, they are sure in this country, of the best occupation which a laboring man can have; and when they graduate, they can easily find places on farms, where they will get good wages, and be less exposed to temptations than if engaged in city trades. There seems to me something, too, in labor in the soil, which is more medicinal to " minds diseased" than work in shops. The nameless physical and mental maladies which take possession of these children of vice and poverty are more easily cured and driven off in outdoor than indoor labor.

I am disposed to think this is peculiarly true of young girls who have begun criminal courses. They have been accustomed to such excitement and stir, that the steady toil of a kitchen and household seldom reforms them.

The remarkable success of Mr. Pease for a few years in his labors for abandoned women in the Five Points, was due mainly to the incessant stir and activity he infused into his "House of Industry," which called off the minds of these poor creatures from their sins and temptations. But, better than this, would be the idea, so often broached, of a "School in gardening" for young girls, in which they could be taught in the open air, and learn the florist's and gardener's art. This busy and pleasant labor, increasingly profitable every year, would often drive out the evil spirit, and fit the workers for paying professions after they left the School.

The true plan for a Reformatory School, as has so often been said, is the Family System; that is, breaking the Asylum up into small houses, with little "groups" of children in each, under their own immediate "director" or teacher, who knows every individual, and adapts his government to the wants of each.

The children cook meals, and do house-labor, and eat in these small family groups. Each child, whether boy or girl, learns in this way something of house-keeping, and the mode of caring for the wants of a small family. He has to draw his water, split his wood, kindle his fires, light his lamps, and take care of the Cottage, as he will, by and by, have to do in his own little "shanty" or "cottage." Around the Cottage should be a small garden, which each "family" would take a pride in cultivating; and beyond, the larger farm, which they all might work together.

In a Reformatory, after such a plan as this, the children are as near the natural condition as they ever can be in a public institution. The results, if men of humanity and wisdom be in charge, will justify the increased trouble and labor. The expense can hardly be greater, as buildings and outfit will cost so much less than with the large establishments. The only defect would, perhaps, be that the labor of the inmates would not bring in so much pecuniary return, as in the present Houses of Refuge; but the improved effects on the children would more than counter-balance to the community the smaller income of the Asylum. Nor is it certain that farm and garden labor would be less profitable to the Institution.

If we are correctly informed, the only Alms-house which supports itself in the country is one near New Haven, that relies entirely on the growth and sale of garden products. Under the Farm and Family School for children, legally committed, we should have, undoubtedly, a far larger proportion of thorough reforms and successes, than under the congregated and industrial Asylums.

The most successful Reformatories of Europe are of this kind. The "Rauhe Haus," at Hamburg, and Mr. Sydney Turner's Farm School at Tower Hill, England, show a greater proportion of reformed cases than any congregated Reformatories that we are familiar with. The Mettrai colony records ninety per cent. as reformed, which is an astonishingly large proportion. This success is probably much due to the *esprit du corps* which has become a tradition in the school, and the extent to which the love of distinction and honorable emulation—most powerful motives on the French mind—have been cultivated in the pupils.

We do not deny great services and successes to the existing congregated Reformatories of this country. But their success has been in spite of their system. From the new Family Reformatories, opened in different States, we hope for even better results.

CHAPTER XXXIV.

WHAT SHALL BE DONE WITH FOUNDLINGS?

Some of our citizens are now seeking to open in New York a Foundling Asylum to be conducted under Protestant influences. A Roman Catholic Hospital for Foundlings was recently established, and is now receiving aid from the city treasury. In view of these humane efforts, attended, as they must be, by vast expense, it becomes necessary to inquire what is the best system of management attained by experience in other countries. Of the need of some peculiar shelter or shelters for illegitimate children in this city there can be no question.

Those who have to do with the poorer classes are shocked and pained by the constant instances presented to them, of infants neglected or abandoned by their mothers, or of unmarried mothers with infants in such need and desperation, that infanticide is often the easiest escape. Something evidently should be done for both mothers and children.

THE NUMBERS.

Of the numbers of illegitimate children in New York, it is difficult to speak with any precision. In European countries, we know almost exactly the proportion of illegitimate to legitimate births. In Sardinia, it is 2.09 per cent.; in Sweden, 6.56; in England, 6.72; in France, 7.01; in Denmark, 9.35; in Austria, 11.38; in Bavaria, 20.59. Among cities, it is between 3 and 4 per cent. in English cities; in Genoa, 8; in Berlin, 14.9; in St. Petersburg, 18.8; in Vienna, 46. The general average of illegitimate to legitimate children in Europe is 12.8 per cent.

Supposing that the average in New York is the same as in Amsterdam or London, say four per cent., there were in the five years, from 1860 to 1865, out of the 144,724 children born (living or dead) in the city of New York, 5,788 illegitimate, or an average each year of 1,157 children born out of wedlock. More than a thousand illegitimate children are thus, in all probability, thrown upon this community every year.

Though this is a mere estimate, there is a strong presumptive evidence of its not being exaggerated, from the enormous proportion, in New York, of still-births, which reached in one year (1868) the sum of 2,195, or more than seven per cent. of the whole number of births. Now, it is well-known that the women who are mothers of illegitimate children are much more likely to be badly attended or neglected in their confinement than mothers in wedlock, and thus to suffer under this misfortune.

As to the relation of illegitimacy to crime, there are some striking statistics from France. Out of 5,758 persons confined in the bagnios in France, there were, according to Dr. Parry, in 1853, 391 illegitimate. Of the 18,205 inmates of the State Prisons in France during the same time, 880 were illegitimate, and 361 foundlings. "One out of every 1,300 Frenchmen," says the same authority, "becomes the subject of legal punishment, while one out of 158 foundlings finds his way to the State Prisons." In the celebrated Farm-school of Mettrai, according to recent reports, out of 3,580 young convicts since its foundation, 534 were illegitimate and 221 foundlings, or more than twenty per cent.

There can be no reasonable doubt, then, that a large number of children born out of wedlock, and therefore exposed to great hardship, temptation, and misery, are cast out every year on this community. A very large proportion of these unfortunate little ones die, or, with their mothers, are dragged down to great depths of wretchedness and crime.

What can be done for them? The first impulse is, naturally, to gather them into an Asylum. But what is the experience of Asylums?

The London Foundling Hospital, one of the most famous of these institutions, was founded in 1740. During the first twenty years of its existence, out of the 14,934 children received in it, only 4,400 lived to be apprenticed, a mortality of more than seventy per cent. The celebrated St. Petersburg Hospital for Foundlings contained, between the years 1772 and 1789, 7,709 children, of whom 6,606 died. Between the years 1783 and 1797, seventy-six per cent. died. We have not, unfortunately, its later statistics. The Foundling Hospital of Paris, another well-known institution of this class, was founded by Vincent de Paul in 1638. In the twenty years ending in 1859, out of 48,525 infants admitted, 27,119 died during the first year, or fifty-six per cent. In 1841, a change was made in the administration of this Hospital, of which we shall speak later.

In this city there is, under the enlightened management of the Commissioners of Charities and Correction, an Infant Hospital on Randall's Island, where large numbers of illegitimate and abandoned children are cared for. In former years, under careless management of this institution, the mortality of these helpless infants has reached ninety to ninety-five per cent.; but in recent years, under the new management, this has been greatly reduced. In 1867, out of

the 928 "nurse's children," or children without their
mothers, who were received, 642 died, or about
seventy per cent. In 1868, 76.77 per cent. of these
unfortunates died, and in 1869, 70.32 per cent.; while
in the same hospital, of the children admitted with
their mothers, only 20.44 per cent. died during that
year—a death-rate less than that of the city at large,
which is about twenty-six per cent.; while in Massachusetts, for children under one year, it is about
thirteen per cent.

It will be observed that the mortality of foundlings
and orphans in this institution was reduced in 1869
from 76.79 per cent. to 70.32. Again, in 1870, a still
greater reduction was made to 58.99. This most
encouraging result was brought about by the erection
of an Infants' Hospital by the Commissioners, the
employment of a skillful physician, and, above all, by
engaging paid nurses instead of pauper women, to
take care of the children. In Massachusetts the
experience is equally instructive. "In the State Alms-
house," says the able Secretary of the Board of Charities, Mr. F. B. Sanborn, "the mortality of these infants
previous to 1857, reached the large proportion of 80
out of every 100."

In the Tewksbury Alms-house the mortality in 1860
among the foundlings was forty-seven out of fifty-
four, or eighty-seven per cent.

In 1867, the most enlightened experts in charities in

Massachusetts took up the subject of founding an Infant-Asylum, and resolved to institute one which should be free from the abuses of the old system. In this new Asylum only those children should be received whose cases had been carefully investigated, and no more than thirty foundlings were ever to be collected under one roof, so that as much individual care might be exercised as is practicable. Yet even under this wise plan the mortality during the first six months at the Dorchester Asylum reached nearly fifty per cent. out of only thirty-six children; though this mortality was a great gain over that of the State Alms-houses.

The truth seems to be that each infant needs one nurse or care-taker, and that if you place these delicate young creatures in large companies together in any public building, an immense proportion are sure to die. When one remembers the difficulty of carrying any child in this climate through the first and second summers, and how a slight change in the milk, or neglect of covering, will bring on that scourge of our city, cholera infantum, and how incessant the watchfulness of our mothers is to bring up a healthy child, we can understand why from one-half to two-thirds of the foundlings, many of them fatally weakened when brought to the Asylums, die in our public institutions. Where the mothers are allowed to take care of their own children in the Asylums, as many survive as in the

18

outside world.   But to support one mother for each infant is an immense expense; so that two children are commonly put under the care of the mother.   The neglect, however, of the strange child soon becomes apparent even to the casual visitor; and these poor foundlings are often fairly starved or abused to death by the mother forced to nurse them.   The treatment of these poor helpless infants by brutal women in our public institutions is one of the saddest chapters in the history of human wickedness.

What, then, is to be done for these unfortunate foundlings?   No Asylum can afford to board and employ one wet-nurse for each infant.   How can the children be saved at a moderate expense?   The feasible and practicable course for this object is the

"PLACING-OUT SYSTEM."

This plan has been in operation in France for centuries, and is now carried out under a public department called "*Les services des Enfants Assistés*," recently under the direction of M. Husson, and known generally as the Bureau Ste. Apolline.   This bureau deals with the whole class of abandoned and outcast and destitute infants.   Instead of keeping these children in an Asylum, this office at once dispatches them to nurses already selected in the country.

The whole matter is thoroughly organized; there are agents to forward the nurses and children, inspectors to select nurses and look after the infants and take charge of the disbursements, and medical officers to investigate the condition of both children and nurses, and to visit them monthly, and give medical attendance. The nurse is obliged to bring a certificate of good character from the Commune, and of her being in proper condition to take care of a foster-child. She is not permitted to take charge of an infant unless her own is nine months old, and has been weaned. The nurse is bound to send her foster-child, as she grows up, to school, and to some place of religious instruction. The bureau has thus relieved a great number of children during ten years, from 1855 to 1864, the total number amounting to 21,944.

That it has been wonderfully successful is shown by the mortality, which is now only about thirty per cent., or nearly the same with the general death-rate among young children in New York. Under this new poor-law administration for destitute and abandoned children, the famous Hospital for Foundlings has been changed into a mere depot for children sent to places and nurses in the country, with the most happy results in point of mortality. Thus, in 1838, the hospital admitted 5,322 children, and lost 1,211; in 1868, of 5,603 admitted, only 442 died, or about eight per cent. Of 21,147 sent to the country, the deaths were only 1,783, or less than ten per cent. Of 6,009 admitted in 1869, 4,260 were abandoned children, and the deaths from the above number were 495.

The French administration does not cease with paying the board of these foundlings in their country homes; it looks carefully after their clothing, their education, their religious instruction, and even their habits of economy. The outlay by the Government for these various objects is considerable. In 1869, the traveling expenses of these little waifs reached the sum of 170,107 francs. The payments to the peasants to induce them to educate the foundlings amounted to 85,458 francs for the same year; the savings of the children, put in official savings-boxes, amounted to 394,076 francs, while 15,936 francs were given out as prizes.

The moral effects have been encouraging. In 1869, out of the 9,000 élèves from thirteen to twenty-eight years, only thirty-two had appeared before Courts of Justice for trifling offenses; thirty-two had shown symptoms of insubordination, and nearly the same number had been imprisoned.

It should be remembered that this bureau has charge of the whole class of juvenile paupers, or Alms-house children, in Paris, as well as foundlings, whom it treats by placing out in country homes. In 1869, it thus provided for and protected 25,486 children, of whom 16,845 were from one day to twelve years, and 9,001 from twelve to twenty-one years. For this pur-

pose, it employed two principal inspectors, twenty-
five sub-inspectors, and two hundred and seventy-
eight physicians.

The expense of this bureau has been wonderfully
slight, only averaging two dollars and sixty cents per
annum for each child. In an Asylum the average·
annual expenditure for each child could not have been
less than one hundred and fifty dollars. This Bureau
Ste. Apolline must be carefully distinguished from the
private bureaus in Paris for assisting foundlings,
under which the most shocking abuses have occurred,
the death-rate reaching among their subjects 70.87,
and even ninety per cent.

The "boarding-out" system has been a part of the
Alms-house system of Hamburg for years, and has
proved eminently successful and economical. In Berlin, more than half the pauper children, and all the
foundlings, are thus dealt with. In Dublin, both
Protestant and Catholic associations have pursued
this plan with destitute orphans and foundlings, with
marked success. The Protestant Society had, in 1866,
453 orphans under its charge, and had placed out, or
returned to friends, 1,256; its provincial branches had
2,208 under their care, and had placed out 5,374. All
the orphans placed out by the Society are apprenticed.
Great care is used in inspecting the homes in which
children are put, and in selecting employers. The
whole Association is well organized. The annual cost

of the children, dividing the whole expense by the
number of children placed and cared for, is only from
fifty dollars to fifty-five dollars per head. The Roman
Catholic Association, St. Brigid's, is even more economical in its work, as the labor is mainly performed
by the members of the sisterhoods. Within seven
years five hundred children were taken in charge, of
whom two hundred had been adopted or placed out.
The children thus provided for in country families are
constantly visited by the conductors of the orphanage
and by the parish priest. The expense of the whole
enterprise is very slight.

Similar experiments are being made in England
with pauper children, and, despite Prof. Fawcett's
somewhat impractical objections, they have been
found to be successful and far more economical than
the old system.

THE FAMILY PLAN.

The Massachusetts Board of State Charities, one
of the ablest Boards that have ever treated these questions, well observes in its report for 1868: "The tendency in all civilized countries is toward the family system, through (1st) the Foundling Hospital and (2d)
the Asylum or Home System; and the mortality
among infants of this class is reduced from ninety or
ninety-five per cent. under the old no-system, from
forty to sixty per cent. in well-managed Foundling

Hospitals, from thirty to fifty per cent. in good Asylums, and from twenty to thirty-five per cent. in good single families, the last being scarcely above the normal death-rate of all infants."

The "placing-out" system, is of course, liable to shocking abuse, as the experience of private offices for the care of foundlings in Paris, and recently in London, painfully shows. It must be carried on with the utmost publicity, and under careful responsibility. But under a respectable and faithful board of trustees, with careful organization and inspection, there is no reason why the one thousand illegitimate children born every year in New York city should not be placed in good country families, under the best of care and with the prospect of saving, at least, seven hundred out of the thousand, instead of losing that proportion; and all this under an expense of about one-tenth that of an Asylum. Why will our benevolent ladies and gentlemen keep up the old monastic ideas of the necessity of herding these unfortunate children in one building? Here there are thousands of homes awaiting the foundlings, without money and without price, where the child would have the best advantages the country could afford; or if it be too weak or sick to be moved, or the managers fear the experiment of placing-out, let some responsible nurse be selected in the country near by, and the foundling boarded at their expense. The experience of the Children's Aid

Society is, that no children are so eagerly and kindly received in country families as infants who are orphans. Let us not found in New York that most doubtful institution—a Foundling Asylum—but use the advantages we have in the ten thousand natural asylums of the country.

In regard to the question, how far the affording facilities for the care of illegitimate children increases the temptation to vicious indulgence, we believe, as in most similar matters, the true course for the legislator lies between extremes. His first duty is, of course, one of humanity, to preserve life. Whenever helpless or abandoned children are found, the duty of the State is to take care of them, though this care may, in certain cases, offer an inducement to crime. The danger to the child, if neglected, is certain; that to the community, of inducing other mothers to abandon their offspring, is remote and uncertain. On the other hand, the State is under no obligation to offer inducements to parents to neglect their illegitimate children; it is rather bound to throw all possible responsibility on those who have brought them into the world.

The extreme French plan of presenting "turning-tables" to those who wished to abandon their children, was found to increase the crime, and the number of such unfortunates. It has been given up even in Paris itself. The Russian Foundling Asylum in St. Petersburg found it necessary to make its conditions more strict than they were in the beginning, as laxness tended to encourage sexual vice. The universal experience is, that if a mother can be compelled to care for her infant, during a month or two, she will then never murder or abandon it. But, if she is relieved of the charge very early, she feels little affection or remorse, and often plunges into indulgence again without restraint. By requiring conditions and letting some little time pass before the mother gives the child up, she is kept in a better moral condition, and made to feel more the responsibility of her position, and is thus withheld from future vice.

On the other hand, the extreme position taken substantially by the New York legislators, whereby no mother could get rid of an illegitimate child, except by publicly entering the Alms-house, or by infanticide, undoubtedly stimulated the crimes of fœticide and child-murder. No doubt the new Catholic and Protestant Foundling Asylums contemplated in New York will steer between these two extremes, will connect the mother with the child as long as possible, and require all reasonable conditions before admitting the infant, and, at the same time, not drive a seduced or unfortunate woman with her babe out to take her chances in the streets.

CHAPTER XXXV.

RELIGIOUS INSTRUCTION FOR STREET-CHILDREN.

THE subject of applying Religion as a lever to raise up the class of neglected children whom we have been describing, is a difficult one, but vital to the Science of Reform. The objects of those engaged in laboring for this class are to raise them above temptation, to make them of more value to themselves, and to Society, and, if possible, to elevate them to the highest range of life, where the whole character is governed by Religion.

The children themselves are in a peculiar position. They have many of the traits of children, and yet are struggling in an independent and hard life, like men. They are not to be influenced as a Sunday-school audience would be, nor as an audience of adults. Their minds are acute, sharp, and practical; mere sentiment and the amiable platitudes of Sunday-school oratory are not for them. Rhetoric sets them asleep. Bombast goes by the name of " gas " among them. Sentimental and affectionate appeals only excite their contempt. The "hard fact" pleases them. They know when the speaker stands on good bottom.

If he has reached "hard pan," his audience is always with him.

No audience is so quick to respond to a sudden turn or a joke. Their faculties are far more awake than those of a company of children of the fortunate classes. And yet they are like children in many respects. Nothing interests them so much as the dramatic: the truth given by parable and illustration. Their education in the low theatres has probably cultivated this taste. The genuine and strong feeling of the heart always touches them. I have seen the quick tears drop over the dirty cheeks at the simple tone only of some warm-hearted man who had addressed them with a deep feeling of their loneliness and desolation. And yet they would have "chaffed" him in five minutes after, if they had had the opportunity. They seem to have children's receptivity; they are not by nature skeptical. They unconsciously believe in supernatural powers, or in one eternal Power. Their conscience can be reached; the imagination is, to a certain degree, lively; they are peculiarly open to Religion. And yet their "moral" position is a most perplexing one. The speaker in one of our Boys' Lodging-houses, who addresses them, knows that this may be the last and only time, for years, that many of the wild audience will listen to religious truth. To-morrow a considerable portion will be scattered, no one knows where. To-morrow, perhaps to-night, temptation will come in like a flood. In a few hours, it may be, the street-boy will stand where he must decide whether he will be a thief or an honest lad; a rogue or an industrious worker; the companion of burglars and murderers, or the friend of the virtuous. Temptations to lying, to deceit, to theft, robbery, lust, and murder will soon hunt him like a pack of wolves. His child's nature is each day under the strain of a man's temptations. Poverty, hunger, and friendlessness add to his exposed condition, while, in all probability, he inherits a tendency to indulgence or crime.

The problem is to guard such a human being, so exposed, against powerful temptations; to raise him above them; to melt his bad habits and inherited faults in some new and grand emotion; to create within him a force which is stronger than, and utterly opposed to, the selfish greed for money, or the attractions of criminal indulgence, or the rush of passion, or the fire of anger. The object is to implant in his breast such a power as Plato dreamed of—the Love of some perfect Friend, whose character by sympathy shall purify his, whose feeling is believed to go with the fortunes of the one forgotten by all others, and who has the power of cleansing from wrong and saving from sin.

The experience of twenty years' labor shows us that what are called "moral influences" are not sufficient to solve this problem, or meet this want among the children of the street. It is, of course, well at times to present the beauty of virtue and the ugliness of vice; to show that honesty brings rewards, and falsehood pains, and to sketch the course of the moral poor whom fortune has rewarded. But these considerations are not sufficiently strong to hold back the most pressing temptations. Moreover, we have often had grave doubts whether "the bread-and-butter piety" was not too much recommended in all religious meetings to children. The child is too continually reminded that righteousness brings reward in this world, though the Master calls us to "take a yoke," and "bear a cross." The essence of the religious impulse is that it is unselfish, an inspiration from above, not below, a quickening of the nobler emotions and higher aspirations. Wherever gain or worldly motive comes in, there spirituality flees away. We have, accordingly, always opposed, in our religious meetings, the employment of prizes or rewards, as is so common in Sunday Schools, to strengthen the religious influence. Experience, as well as reason, has shown us that all such motives mingled with religion simply weaken its power.

Considering the peculiar position of these children, we have never set the value on what is usually described as "Religious Instruction" which many do. Of course, there are certain foundation truths which should be taught to these audiences. But such subjects as the Jewish History and God's Providence therein, and many matters contained in the Old Testament, are not so immediately important for them as the facts and principles of Christianity. And yet there are passages in the Old Testament which seem peculiarly designed for the young. There are stories —such as those of Joseph and Moses and Samuel— which, if all others should forget, children alone would not let die. It does not seem instruction that these children need, so much as inspiration. A street-boy might be perfectly familiar with the history of the Fall of Man and the Flood; he might repeat the Commandments, and know by heart the Apostles' Creed, and yet not have one spark in his breast of the divine fire which is to save him from vice and ruin.

What the child of the streets, above all, needs to uphold him in his sea of troubles and temptations, is the knowledge and faith in Christ as his Friend and Saviour.

CHRIST can be presented and made real to these children as a perfect Being, the Son of God, who feels with all their misfortunes, who has known their temptations, who is their Friend, and only demands noble hearts and love from them, who lived and died for them when on earth, that they might love God and be saved from sin.

It is the old Faith, which has thrown the glory of Heaven over millions of death-beds, and sustained uncounted numbers of weak and hard-pressed men, true to honor, virtue, and goodness, amid all temptations and misfortunes. It has comforted and ennobled the slave under his master's tyranny. If simply presented, and with faith in God, it can redeem the outcast youth of the streets from all his vices and evil habits, keep him pure amid filth, honest among thieves, generous among those greedy for money, kind among the hard and selfish, and enable him to overcome anger, lust, the habit of lying or profanity, and to live a simple, humble, God-fearing, and loving life, merely because he believes that this Unseen Friend demands all this in his children and followers. When this Faith and this Love are implanted in the child's mind, and he is inspired by them, then his course is clear, and sure to be happy and good.

One mistake of Sunday-school oratory is frequently made in addressing these lads, and that is, a too great use of sensational illustrations, which do not aid to impress the truth desired. Attention will be secured, but no good end is gained. Where the wants of the audience are so real and terrible as they are here, and so little time is given for influencing them, it is of the utmost importance that every word should tell. There should be no rhetorical pyrotechnics at these meetings. Above all modes, however, the dramatic is the best means of conveying truth to their minds. The parable, the illustration, the allegory or story, real or fictitious, most quickly strike their mind, and leave the most permanent impression.

One of the best religious speakers that ever address our boys is a lawyer, who has been a famous sportsman, and has in his constitution a fellow-feeling for their vagrant tastes. I often fancy, when he is speaking to them, that he would not object at all to being a boy again himself, roving the streets, "turning in" on a hay-barge, and drifting over the country at "his own sweet will." But this very sympathy gives him a peculiar power over them; he understands their habits and temptations, and, while other gentlemen often shoot over their heads, his words always take a powerful hold of them. Then, though a man particularly averse to sentiment in ordinary life, his speeches to the boys seem to reveal a deep and poetic feeling for nature, and a solemn consciousness of God, which impresses children deeply. His sportsmanly habits have led him to closely observe the habits of birds and animals, and the appearances of the sky and sea, and these come in as natural illustrations, possessing a remarkable interest for these wild little vagrants, who by nature belong to the "sporting" class.

A man must have a boy's tastes to reach boys.

BIBLE IN SCHOOLS.

In treating of this subject of religious education for the youth of the dangerous classes, the question naturally arises, how far there should be religious expression or education in our Public Schools. If it were a *tabula rasa* here, and we were opening a system of National Schools, and all were of one general faith, there could be no question that every one interested in the general welfare would desire religious instruction in our Public Schools, as a means of strengthening morality, if for no other purpose. As it is, however, we have at the basis of society an immense mass of very ignorant, and, therefore, bigoted people, who suspect and hate every expression even of our form of Christianity, and regard it as a teaching of heresy and a shibboleth of oppression. Their shrewd and cunning leaders, knowing the danger to priestcraft from Free Schools, use this hostility and the pretense of our religious services to separate these classes from the Public Schools. The priests and demagogues do not, of course, care anything about the simple prayer and the reading of a few verses of Scripture, which are now our sole religious school exercises. But these furnish them with a good pretext for acting on the masses, and give them ground, among certain liberal or indifferent Protestants, for seeking a separate State support for the Catholic Schools.

Were Bible-reading and the Lord's Prayer discontinued in the Schools, we do not doubt that the priests and the popular leaders would still oppose the Free Schools just as bitterly; but they would not have as good an apparent ground, and any pretext of opposition would be taken away. The system of Free Schools is the life-blood of the nation. If it be corrupted with priestcraft, or destroyed by our dissensions, our vitality as a republican people is gone. The whole country would realize then the worst fruits of a popular government without intelligence. Demagogism and corruption, founded on ignorance, would wield an absolute tyranny, with none of the graces of monarchy, and none of the advantages of democracy. Jarring sects would each have their own schools, and the priests would enjoy an unlimited control over all the ignorant Catholics of the country.

Under no circumstance should the Protestants of the nation allow the Free Schools to be broken up. They are the foundation of the Republic, and the bulwark of Protestantism and civilization. They undermine the power of the priests, which rests on ignorance, while they leave untouched whatever spiritual force the Roman Catholic Church may truly have and deserve to have. The Protestants should sacrifice everything reasonable and not vital, to retain these blessed agencies of enlightenment.

We respect the sort of pluck of the Protestants, which looks upon the giving-up of Bible-reading in the Schools as being "false to the flag." But, in looking at the matter soberly, and without pugnacity, does spiritual religion lose anything by giving up these exercises? We think not. They are now of the coldest and most formal kind, and but little listened to. We doubt if they ever affect strongly a single mind. The religious education of each child is imparted in Sabbath Schools, in Churches, or Mission Schools, and its own home.

The Free School under our system does not need any influence from the Church. The American trusts to the separate sects to take care of the religious interests of the children. We separate utterly Church and State. There may be evils from this; but they are less than the danger of destroying our system of popular education by the contests of rival sects. We know how long every effort to secure popular education for England has been wrecked on this rock of Sectarianism.

We behold the fearful harvest of evils which she is reaping from the ignorance of the masses, especially induced by the oppositions of sects, who preferred no education for the people to education without their own dogmas.

We desire to avoid these calamities, and we can best do this by making every reasonable concession to ignorance and prejudice.

Give us the Free Schools without Religion, rather than no Free Schools at all!

CHAPTER XXXVI.

DECREASE OF JUVENILE CRIME IN NEW YORK.

THE COST OF PUNISHMENT AND PREVENTION.

VERY few people have any just appreciation of the comparative cost of punishment and prevention in the treatment of crime. The writer recalls one out of many thousand instances in his experience, which strikingly illustrates the contrast.

THE BROTHERS.

A number of years ago, three boys (brothers), the oldest perhaps seventeen, applied at the Newsboys' Lodging-house of this city for shelter. It was soon suspected that the eldest was a thief, employing the younger as assistants in his nefarious business. The younger lads finally confessed the fact, and the older brother left them to be taken care of in the Lodging-house. After a sufficient period of training, the two brothers were sent to a farmer in Illinois. They were faithful and hard-working, and soon began to earn money. When the war broke out they enlisted, and served with credit. At the close they passed through

New York, and visited the superintendent while returning to their village, having already purchased a
farm with their wages and bounty-money. They are
now well-to-do, respectable farmers.

This " prevention " for the two lads cost just thirty
dollars, for their expenses in the Lodging-house were
mainly paid by themselves.

The older brother went through a career of thieving and burglary. We have not an accurate catalogue
of his various offenses, but he undoubtedly made away
with property—wasted or destroyed it—to the amount
of two thousand dollars. [We recall three lads who,
in one night, broke into a house in Bond Street, and
destroyed or made away with property to the value
of one thousand three hundred dollars.] He was
finally arrested and tried for burglary. It would be
safe to estimate the expenses of the trial and arrest
at one hundred dollars. He was sentenced to five
years in Sing Sing. Allowing the expenses of maintenance there to be what they are on Blackwell's
Island, that is, about twelve dollars and fifty cents
per month, he cost the State while there some seven
hundred and fifty dollars, not reckoning the interest on capital and buildings; so that we have here,
in one instance, the very low estimate of two thousand eight hundred and fifty dollars as the expense
to the community of one street-boy unreclaimed.
Had the Lodging-house taken hold of him five years

earlier, he could have been saved at a cost of fifteen dollars.

His brothers have added to the wealth of the community and defended the life of the nation, and are still honest producers. He has already cost the State at least two thousand eight hundred and fifty dollars, besides much immorality and bad example, and he has only begun a career of damage and loss to the city.

PREVENTION AND PUNISHMENT COMPARED.

Our criminals last year cost this city, in the City Prisons and Penitentiaries, about one hundred and one thousand dollars for maintenance alone. Our police cost apparently over six hundred thousand dollars.

The amount of property lost or taken by thieves, burglars, and others last year, in New York city, and which came under the knowledge of the police, was one million five hundred and twenty-one thousand nine hundred and forty dollars; but how many sums are never brought to their notice!

The expenses of the arrest and trial of two criminals, Real and Van Echten, are stated, on good authority, to have been sixteen thousand dollars for the first, and twenty thousand dollars for the second.

If the expenses of a great "preventive" institution—such as the Children's Aid Society—be examined, it will be found that the two thousand and odd homeless children, boys and girls, placed in country homes, cost the public only some fifteen dollars a head; the three thousand and odd destitute little girls educated and partly fed and clothed in the "Industrial Schools," only cost some fifteen dollars for each child each year; and the street lads and girls sheltered and instructed in the "Lodging-houses," to the number of some twelve thousand different subjects, or an average of, say, four hundred each night, have been an expense of only some fifty dollars per head through the year to the public.

It may, perhaps, be urged in reply to this by the doubting, that all this may be true. "We admit the cheapness of prevention, but we do not see the diminution of crime. If you can show us that fewer young thieves, or vagabonds, or prostitutes, are breeding, we shall admit that your children's charities are doing something, and that the cost of prevention is the most paying outlay in the administration of New York city."

To this we might answer that New York is an exceptional city—a sink into which pour the crime and poverty of all countries, and that all we could expect to accomplish would be what is attempted in European cities—to keep the increase of juvenile crime down equal with the increase of population; that the laws of crime are shown in European cities to be constant, and that we must expect just about so many petty thieves each year, so many pickpockets, so many burglars, so many female vagrants or prostitutes, to so many thousand inhabitants.

We might urge that it is the duty of every friend of humanity to do his little part to alleviate the evils of the world, whether he sees a general diminution of human ills or not.

But, fortunately, we are not obliged to render these excuses.

New York is the only large city in the world where there has been a comprehensive organization to deal with the sources of crime among children; an organization which, though not reaching the whole of the destitute and homeless youth, and those most exposed to temptation, still includes a vast multitude every year of the *enfants perdus* of this metropolis.

This Association, during nearly twenty years, has removed to country homes and employment about twenty-five thousand persons, the greater part of whom have been poor and homeless children; it has founded, and still supports, five Lodging-houses for homeless and street-wandering boys and girls, five free Reading-rooms for boys and young men, and twenty Industrial Schools for children too poor, ragged, and undisciplined for the Public Schools. We have always been confident that time would show, even in the statistics of crime in our

19

prisons and police courts, the fruits of these very extended and earnest labors. It required several years to properly found and organize the Children's Aid Society, and then it must be some ten years— when the children acted upon in all its various branches have come to young manhood and woman-hood—before the true effects are to be seen. We would not, however, exclude, as causes of whatever results may be traced, all similar movements in be-half of the youthful criminal classes. We may then fairly look, in the present and the past few years, for the effects on crime and pauperism of these widely-extended charities in behalf of children.

CRIME CHECKED.

The most important field of the Children's Aid Society has been among the destitute and street-wandering and tempted little girls, its labors em-bracing many thousands annually of this unfortunate class. Has crime increased with them ? The great offense of this class, either as children or as young women, comes under the heading of "Vagrancy"—this including their arrest and punishment, either as street-walkers, or prostitutes, or homeless persons. In this there is, during the past thirteen years, a most remarkable decrease—a diminution of crime probably unexampled in any criminal records through the world. The rate in the commitments to the city prisons, as appears in the reports of the Board of Charities and Correction, runs thus :—

Of female vagrants, there were in

1857........8,449	1861..........8,172	1864..........1,342
1859..........5,778	1862..........2,248	1869.......... 785
1860..........5,880	1863..........1,756	1870.......... 671
1871.............................. ....548.		

We have omitted some of the years on account of want of space; they do not, however, change the steady rate of decrease in this offense.

Thus, in eleven years, the imprisonments of female vagrants have fallen off from 5,880 to 548. This, surely, is a good show ; and yet in that period our population increased about thirteen and a half per cent., so that, according to the usual law, the commitments should have been this year over 4,700.*

If we turn now to the reports of the Commissioners of Police, the returns are almost equally encouraging, though the classification of arrests does not exactly correspond with that of imprisonments; that

* The population of New York increased from 814,224, in 1860, to 915,520, in 1870, or only about twelve and a half per cent.

The increase in the previous decade was about fifty per cent. There can be no doubt that the falling-off is entirely in the middle classes, who have removed to the neighboring rural districts. The classes from which most of the criminals come have undoubtedly increased, as before, at least fifty per cent.

I have retained for ten years, however, the ratio of the census, twelve and a half per cent.

is, a person may be arrested for vagrancy, and sentenced for some other offense, and *vice versa*.

The reports of arrests of female vagrants run thus :—

1861 2,161	1867 1,591
1862 2,008	1869 1,078
1868 1,738	1870 701
1871............ 914	

We have not, unfortunately, statistics of arrests farther back than 1861.

Another crime of young girls is thieving or petty larceny. The rate of commitments runs thus for females :—

1859 944	1864 1,181
1860 890	1865 877
1861 880	1869 989
1868 1,188	1870 746
1871.................. .572	

The increase of this crime during the war, in the years 1863 and 1864, is very marked; but in twelve years it has fallen from 944 to 572, though, according to the increase of the population, it would have been naturally 1,076.

Another heading on the prison records is "Juvenile delinquency," which may include any form of youthful offense not embraced in the other terms. Under this, in 1860, were two hundred and forty (240) females; in 1870, fifty-nine (59).

The classification of commitments of those under fifteen years only runs back a few years. The number of little girls imprisoned the past few years is as follows:—

1863	408	1868	299
1864	295	1870	218
1865	275	1871	212

CRIME CHECKED AMONG THE BOYS.

The imprisonment, of males, for offenses which boys are likely to commit, though not so encouraging as with the girls, shows that juvenile crime is fairly under control in this city. Thus, "Vagrancy" must include many of the crimes of boys; under this head we find the following commitments of males:—

1859	2,829	1863	1,208	1865	1,350
1860	2,708	1864	1,147	1870	1,140
		1871	984		

In twelve years a reduction from 2,829 to 994, when the natural increase should have been up to 3,225.

Petty larceny is a boy's crime; the record stands thus for males:—

1857	2,450	1860	2,575	1869	2,338
1859	2,636	1865	2,847	1870	2,168
		1871	1,978		

A decrease in fourteen years of 502, when the natural increase should have brought the number to 2,861.

Of boys under fifteen imprisoned, the record stands thus since the new classification:—

1864	1,965	1865	1,984	1869	1,872
		1870	1,635	1871	1,017

Of males between fifteen and twenty, in our city prisons, the following is the record :—

1857.............2,592	1860...........2,207	1868 2,927
1859............2,636	1861...........2,408	1870 2,876
	1871... 2,986	

It often happens that youthful criminals are arrested who are not imprisoned. The reports of the Board of Police will give us other indications that, even here, juvenile crime has at length been diminished in its sources.

ARRESTS.

The arrests of pickpockets run thus since 1861, the limit of returns accessible:—

1861...... 466	1865............275	1868 848
1862.............300	1867............845	1869 808
	1870....... 274	1871.............818	

In ten years a reduction of 153 in the arrests of pickpockets.

In petty larceny the returns stand thus in brief:—

1863..........4,107	1865..........5,240	1867 5,269
	1870...........4,909	1871..............3,912	

A decrease in nine years of 195.

Arrests of girls alone, under twenty :—

1863 3,132	1867..........2,588	1870...........1,993
	1871...................................1,890	

It must be plain from this, that crime among

young girls is decidedly checked, and among boys is prevented from increasing with population.

If our readers will refer back to these dry but cheering tables of statistics, they will see what a vast sum of human misery saved is a reduction, in the imprisonment of female vagrants, of more than five thousand in 1871, as compared with 1859. How much homelessness and desperation spared! how much crime and wretchedness diminished are expressed in those simple figures! And, if we may reckon an average of punishment of two months' detention to each of those girls and women, we have one hundred and twenty-five thousand dollars saved in one year to the public by preventive agencies in this class of offenders alone.

The same considerations, both of economy and humanity, apply to each of the results that appear in these tables of crime and punishment.

No outlay of money for public purposes which any city or its inhabitants can make, repays itself half so well as its expenses for charities which prevent crime among children.

CHAPTER XXXVII.

In reviewing these long-continued efforts for the prevention of crime and the elevation of the neglected youth of this metropolis, it may aid others engaged in similar enterprises to note in summary the principles on which they have been carried out, and which account for their marked success.

In the first place, as has been so often said, though pre-eminently a Charity, this Association has always sought to encourage the principle of Self-help in its beneficiaries, and has aimed much more at promoting this than merely relieving suffering. All its branches, its Industrial Schools, Lodging-houses, and Emigration, aim to make the children of the poor better able to take care of themselves; to give them such a training that they shall be ashamed of begging, and of idle, dependent habits, and to place them where their associates are self-respecting and industrious. No institution of this Society can be considered as a shelter for the dependent and idle. All its objects of charity work, or are trained to work. The consequence is that this effort brings after it none of the bad fruits of mere alms-giving. The poor do not become poorer or less self-reliant under it; on the contrary, they are continually rising out of their condition and making their own way in the world. The laborer in this field does not feel, as in so many other philanthropic causes, doubtful, after many years of labor, whether he has not done as much injury as good. He sees constantly the wonderful effect of these efforts, and he knows that, at the worst, they can only fail of the best fruit, but certainly cannot have a bad result.

From the commencement our aim has been to put these charitable enterprises in harmony with natural and economic laws, assured that any other plan of philanthropy must eventually fail. In this view we have taken advantage of the immense demand for labor through our rural districts, which alone gives a new aspect to all economical problems in this country. Through this demand we have been enabled to accomplish our best results, with remarkable economy. We have been saved the vast expense of Asylums, and have put our destitute children in the child's natural place—with a family. Our Lodging-houses also have avoided the danger attending such places of shelter, of becoming homes for vagrant boys and girls. They have continually passed their little subjects along to the country, or to places of work, often forcing them to leave the house. In requiring the small payments for lodging and meals, they put the beneficiaries in an independent position, and check the habits and spirit of pauperism. The Evening School, the Savings-bank, and the Religious Meeting are continually acting on these children to raise them from the vagrant class. The Industrial Schools, in like manner, are seminaries of industry and teachers of order and self-help.

All the agencies of the Society act in harmony with natural laws, and touch the deepest springs of life and character. The forces underlying them are the strongest forces of society—Religion, Education, Self-respect, and love of Industry; these are constantly working upon the thousands of poor children under our charge. Thus founded on simple and natural principles, the Society has succeeded, because very earnest men and women have labored in it, and because its organization has been remarkably complete.

The *employés* have entered into its labors principally from love of its objects, and then have been retained by a just and liberal treatment on the part of the Trustees, and by each being made responsible for his department, and gaining in the community something of the honor which attends successful work.

A strict system of accountability has been maintained, step by step, from the lowest to the highest executive officer. Of many engaged in the labors of this Association, it can be truly said, that no business or commercial house was ever more faithfully and earnestly served, than this charity has been by them. Indeed, some of them have poured forth for it more vitality and energy than they would ever have done for their personal interests. They have toiled day and night, week-days and Sundays, and have been best rewarded by the fruit they have beheld. The aim of the writer, as executive officer, has been to select just the right man for his place, and to make him feel that that is his profession and life-calling. Amid many hundreds thus selected, during twenty years, he can recall but two or three mistaken choices, while many have become almost identified with their labors and position, and have accomplished good not to be measured. His principle has been to show the utmost respect and confidence, but to hold to the strictest accountability. Not a single *employé*, so far as he is aware, in all this time, during his service, has ever wronged the Society or betrayed his trust. One million of dollars has passed through the hands of the officers of this Association during this period, and it has been publicly testified* by the Treasurer, Mr. J. E. Williams, President of the Metropolitan Bank, that not a dollar, to his knowledge, has ever been misappropriated or squandered.

* See testimony before the Committee on Charities of the Senate of New York, 1871.

A most important element of the success of this Charity have been, of course, the character and influence of its Board of Trustees.

It is difficult to speak of these gentlemen without seeming to use the language of compliment; but, in making known to other cities the peculiar organization which has been so successful in this, it must always be remembered what the character of trustees should be, who bear upon their shoulders so important a trust. These men are known through the city, and indeed in distant parts of the country, as showing in their lives a profound and conscientious conviction of the responsibility which wealth and ability are under to the community. They are the best representatives of a class who are destined to give a new character to our city—men of broad and liberal views on matters of practical religion, full of humanity, sensible and judicious, educated to appreciate culture and art, as well as business, with the true gentleman's sense of self-respect and respect for others, a profound and earnest spirit of piety, and that old Puritan perseverance which causes them not "to turn their hand from the plow," however disagreeable the task before them may be. Such men, when once morally imbued with the needs of a cause, could make it succeed against any odds.

Two or three men of their position, wealth, and ability, who should take the moral interests of any

class of our population on their hands, and be in
earnest in the thing, could not fail to accomplish great
results. When they began to appear in our Board, I
felt that, under any sort of judicious management, it
was morally certain we should perfect a wide and
permanent organization, and secure most encouraging
results.

A great service, which has been accomplished by
these gentlemen, has been in tabulating our accounts,
and putting them under a most thorough system of
examination and checking, and in allotting our various branches to each trustee for inspection. Many of
the trustees, also, have their religious meetings at
the Lodging-houses, which they individually lead and
take charge of during the winter. They are thus
brought in direct contact with the necessities of the
poor children.

To no one, however, is the public so much indebted
as to our treasurer, Mr. J. E. Williams.

For nearly twenty years this charity has been the
dearest object of his public efforts, the field of his
humanity and religion. During all this time he has
managed gratuitously the financial affairs of the Society; begged money when we were straitened, and
borrowed it when temporarily embarrassed; never for
a moment doubting that, if the work were faithfully
done, the public would support it. At the end of this
period (1872), having spent over a million of dollars;

and requiring now some one hundred and seventy-five thousand dollars per annum for our various branches, we find ourselves without a dollar of debt.

THE SECTARIAN DANGER.

One rock, which the manager of such a movement must always steer clear of, is the sectarian difficulty. He must ignore sects, and rest his enterprise on the broadest and simplest principles of morality and religion. The animating force must be the religious, especially the "enthusiasm of humanity" shown in the love for Christ, and for all who bear His image. But dogmatic teachings, and disputations, and sectarian ambitions, are to be carefully eschewed and avoided in such efforts of humanity. The public must learn gradually to associate the movement, not with any particular sect or church, but with the feeling of humanity and religion—the very spirit of Christ Himself.

An essential thing, and often very disagreeable, to the earnest worker in it, is to give the utmost publicity to all its operations. The reason of this is, that such a charity depends for support and friends, not on an organized private association, but on the whole public. They need to know all its doings; this is often the only way of reminding them of their duty in this field. Moreover, the moneys spent are public trusts, and all that relates to their uses should be publicly known.

Gradually, by publicity, the general community come to have something of the same moral interest in the enterprise, that the special attendants of a church have in its welfare; and it becomes a truly public interest. To attain this, the press should be the great agency, as well as the pulpit, wherever practicable. Annual reports, designed for all classes, wherein there are figures for the statistical, facts for the doubting, incidents for the young, and principles stated for the thoughtful, should be scattered far and wide.

As the organization grows, State-aid should be secured for a portion of its expenses, that a more permanent character may be given it, and it may not be suddenly too much crippled by a business depression or disaster.

Of the modes in which money should be raised, I have already spoken. In all these matters, the general rule of wisdom is to avoid "sensation," and to trust to the settled and reasonable conviction of the public, rather than to temporary feeling or excitement.

Founded on such principles, and guided by men of this character and ability, and by those of similar purposes who shall come after them, there seems no good reason why this extended Charity should not scatter its blessings for generations to come throughout this ever-increasing metropolis.

To those now serving in it, no thought can be sweeter, when their "change of guard" comes, than that the humble organization of humanity and Christian kindness, which, amid many labors and sacrifices, they aided to found, will spread good-will and intelligence and relief and religious light to the children of the unfortunate and the needy, long years after even their names are forgotten; and for monument or record of their work, they cannot ask for more enduring than young lives redeemed from crime and misery, and young hearts purified and ennobled by CHRIST, and many orphans' tears wiped away, and wounds of the lonely and despairing "little ones" of the world healed through instrumentalities which they assisted to plant, and which shall continue when they are long gone

END.

CPSIA information can be obtained
at www.ICGtesting.com
Printed in the USA
LVHW081152100621
689701LV00019B/48